Images of America
Harlem Valley Pathways
Through Pawling, Dover, Amenia, North East, and Pine Plains

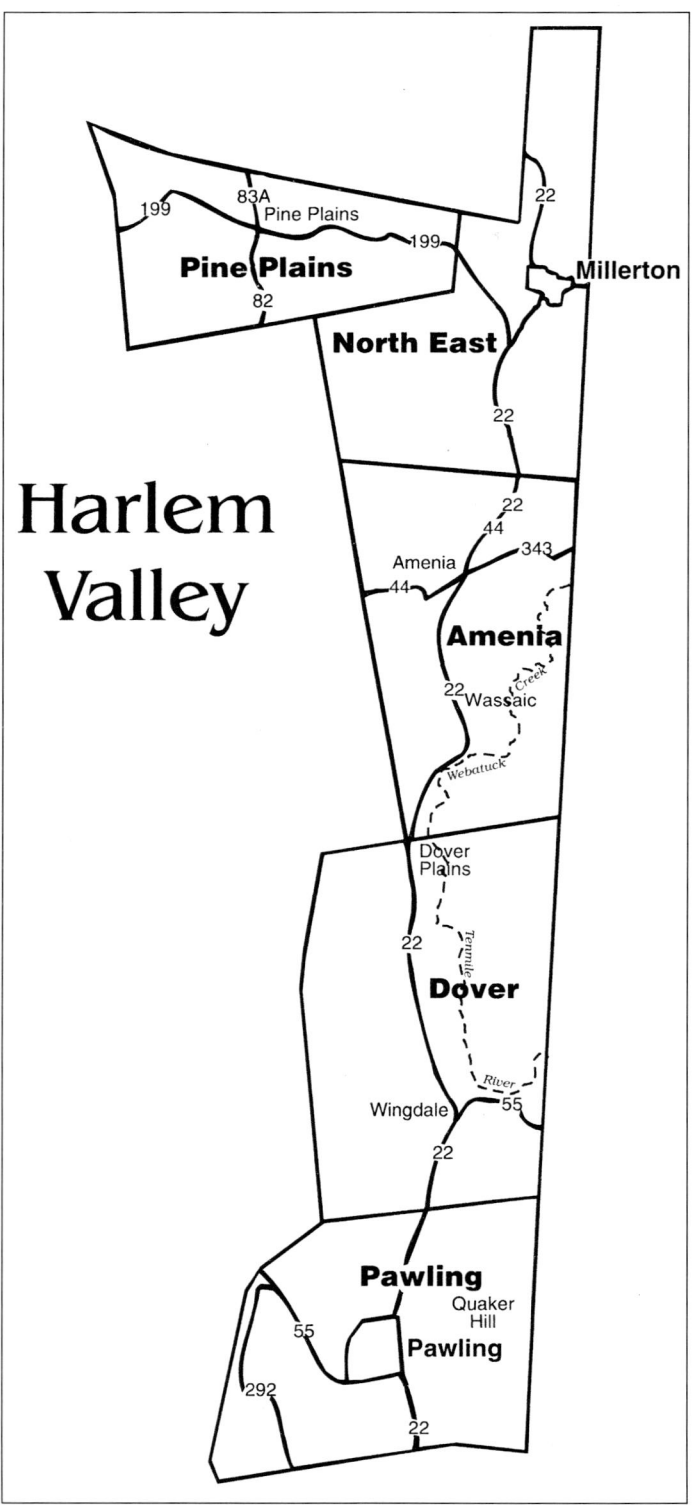

CURRENT MAP OF THE HARLEM VALLEY. This map shows the Harlem Valley as it is at the close of the 20th century, with township divisions, most important villages and hamlets, and major road systems. A comparison of historic maps to road maps of today allows researchers to see the effects of past political decisions, land subdivisions, and public works on geographic borders, natural barriers, property lines, and, ultimately, upon the future of communities. This map was created for the Dutchess County Historical Society for this book by the Dutchess County Department of Planning and Development. The Harlem Valley Partnership for Economic Development, a nonprofit agency led by Harlem Valley businessmen and government officials, was formed to encourage economic development in the five towns of Pawling, Dover, Amenia, North East, and Pine Plains. (DCDPD.)

IMAGES of America
HARLEM VALLEY PATHWAYS
Through Pawling, Dover, Amenia, North East, and Pine Plains

Joyce C. Ghee and Joan Spence

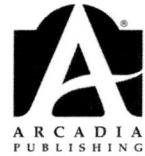

ARCADIA
PUBLISHING

Copyright © 1998 by Joyce C. Ghee and Joan Spence
ISBN 978-0-7385-8983-1

Published by Arcadia Publishing
Charleston, South Carolina

Printed in the United States of America

Library of Congress Catalog Card Number: 98-86898

For all general information contact Arcadia Publishing at:
Telephone 843-853-2070
Fax 843-853-0044
E-mail sales@arcadiapublishing.com
For customer service and orders:
Toll-Free 1-888-313-2665

Visit us on the Internet at www.arcadiapublishing.com

Contents

Introduction		7
1.	Pawling Town and Village	9
2.	Dover	31
3.	Amenia	51
4.	North East and Millerton	71
5.	Pine Plains	93
6.	Connections	113
Acknowledgments		127
Reading List		128

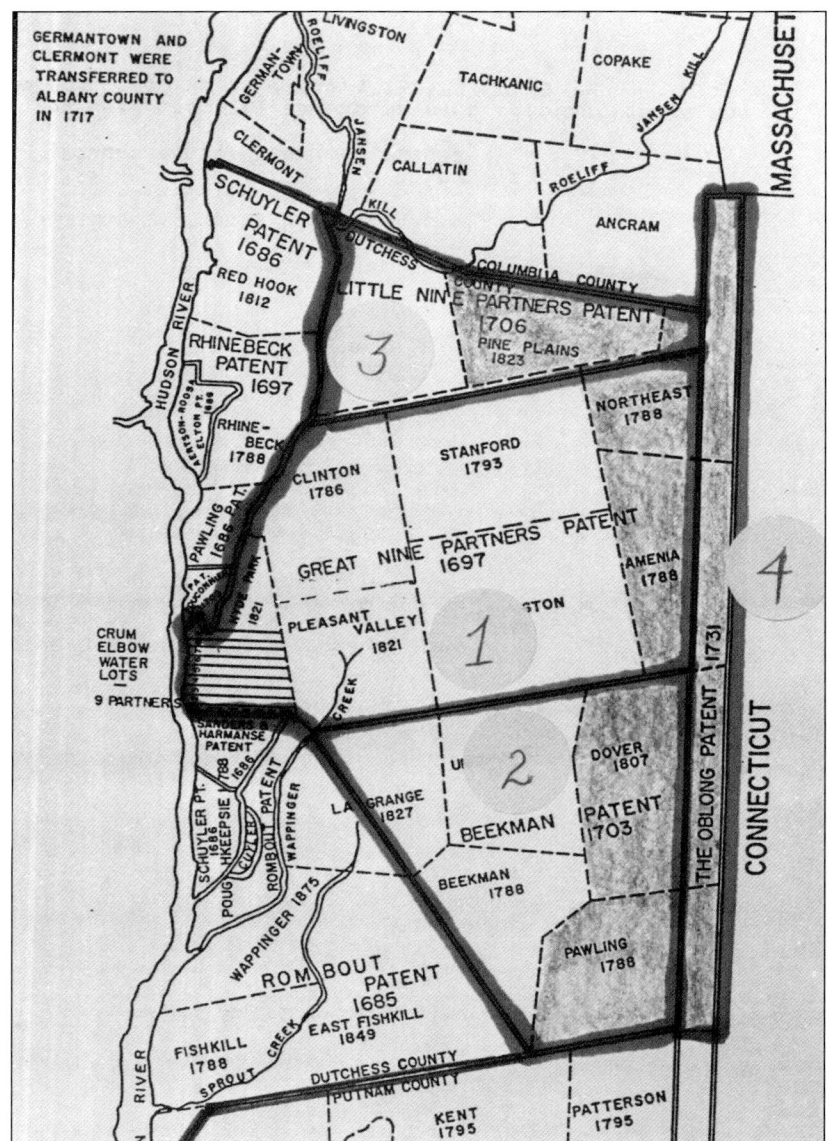

MAP OF PATENT LANDS IN THE HARLEM VALLEY. Five Dutchess towns in the Harlem Valley were carved out of the 17th/18th century patents, as shown in Dr. Henry Noble McCracken's *Old Dutchess Forever* on a map illustrating historic land divisions. Whenever the history of the Great and Little Nine Partners Patents is taught, a vision of nine dwarfs and/or giants pops into every fourth grader's head. The partners in each case were Dutch and English colonial entrepreneurs of status in New York and Albany who imitated Robert Livingston's land acquisition strategies. With Henry Beekman, they focused on Dutchess territory between 1697 and 1706 seeking Crown grants for thousands of acres of land bordering Connecticut, rightly suspecting it would be hotly sought-after by future settlers. The Treaty of Dover in 1731 answered some, but not all, long-lingering questions about land titles here, stabilizing New York/Connecticut borders along a 2-mile wide strip identified as "The Oblong," paralleling the Webatuck/Ten Mile River. (DCHS.)

INTRODUCTION

What's in a name? Probably quite a few clues about history, but little by way of accurate description when it comes to the subject of this book, *Harlem Valley Pathways: Through Pawling, Dover, Amenia, North East, and Pine Plains*. According to local tradition, the "Harlem Valley" was named after the Harlem Railroad, which gradually extended its route from downtown New York City through Harlem all the way to Columbia County. Local lore and maps assigned many names to the area over the years. The Schaghticokes knew it as Webatook/tuck. Those who followed called it Nine Partners, Beekman's, or the Oblong Valley.

Mountainous ridges separating the Harlem Valley from the rest of Dutchess County of which it is a part have protected the regional integrity and natural beauty for hundreds of years. The sole passageway available for roads and rail beds extends the length of the valley floor along Dutchess's eastern border from the northern towns of Pine Plains and North East to Pawling on the Putnam County border. Comparatively easy access to Connecticut and southern New York historically led settlers and visitors here from these areas.

The original land titles for all the present towns and villages in the Harlem Valley derive from late-17th and early 18th century Crown land grants to individuals and small groups of businessmen—the Beekman, Great, and Little Nine Partners Patents. The most easterly strip of land, part of the Oblong, was ceded in 1731 by Connecticut to New York in resolution of long ongoing boundary disputes with New England colonies. It was the site of many of the earliest settlements as the land titles were more secure there. Pre-Revolutionary civil divisions often followed some or all of such early property boundaries.

Dutchess's original towns included Pawling, Amenia, and North East, established by state law in 1788. In 1807, Dover was separated out of Pawling. In 1823, Pine Plains was divided from North East, which in turn gained a portion of Amenia. Two villages, Millerton in 1875 and Pawling in 1893, were incorporated after the coming of the railroads.

The first European settlers were of diverse backgrounds—Palatines fleeing the devastation of religious wars, Moravians seeking to convert Native Americans, Quakers, Huguenots, and farmers of English and Dutch extraction. The quest for religious liberty and land was a primary reason leading individual families to settle and build homes and farms. Small support hamlets grew around community institutions in this beautiful region, which remained relatively isolated until the coming of the railroad. Respect for individual beliefs and neighborliness continue to be valley traditions.

The Harlem Railroad, which reached Pawling and Dover in 1849 and North East (Millerton) in 1851, encouraged village and hamlet growth and presaged a flow of Irish and Italian residents and vacationers. As railway lines crisscrossed the area, it became a favorite destination for those seeking to escape the noise and sultry heat of city life.

The regional economy was based on mining and agriculture. During the second half of the 19th century, milk production in all its facets—from dairy farming to condensing and bottling factories—became a dominant industry. Over the years, small-manufacturing concerns came and went. In the 1920s and 30s, two state institutions were opened, bringing in new employees and providing additional local employment opportunities for over half a century. At the end of the 20th century, new uses for these institutions are being sought; horse farms now flourish where once there were dairy farms; a rail trail park stretches where once there were railroad tracks; and the cycle of economic change proceeds. Meanwhile, visitors, weekenders, and long- and short-term residents continue to enjoy the beauty of the Harlem Valley.

The book is divided into six chapters. The first five deal with the various townships, hamlets, and villages. Geography and transportation have shaped the contours of the settled areas within each town. Often different generations and/or branches of the same family are to be found in several towns. The last chapter re-affirms these connections and others that continue to link the communities of the region with each other and with the world.

Author's Note: We are indebted to a number of Harlem Valley residents and institutions for their assistance in preparing this book. Acknowledgments at the end of the book credit these sources. The lenders of images are identified by initials after their names. Photographs by the authors are identified (JG) or (JS). Given the richness and variety of material on the region, this book should be viewed only as an exhibit or an illustrated and selective index. In the hope that it will spur readers to seek additional information, a reading list is appended.

One

Pawling Town and Village

Both the town and village honor the Widow Pawling, Beekman heiress, who inherited some of Dutchess's richest acreage in Beekman's 1703 Patent.

Settlement from New England and Long Island began when the Treaty of Dover (1731) confirmed land titles. Quaker Nathan Birdsall c. 1728 came earlier to the high-eastern plateau defining this portion of the Oblong. A linear hamlet of farms and businesses around the Oblong Meeting House became known as "Quaker Hill." Residents prospered through hard work and lives shaped by faith. Early hamlets developed at Reynoldsville, now Holmes; Whaley Lake; and along drovers's paths in the valley and western ridges.

When the Harlem Line reached Dutchess in 1849, Hurds Corners (then the main valley hamlet) declined, and Gorestown became Pawling Station at first, and in 1893, Pawling Village. The town flourished through railroad-driven economic development and cultural amenities endowed by local boosters John Dutcher and Albert Akin.

Pawling's history mirrors the exploits of the powerful and famous—from *Monitor* commander Admiral John L. Worden and *Ben Hur* creator Lew Wallace, to Thomas E. Dewey, governor of New York and twice presidential candidate. Today's town appears to be separate communities—Quaker Hills, rural Pawling, Holmes, and the Pawling Village—but study reveals more complex and interwoven history. Quaker Hill's rolling acres reflect the interests of old wealth and influential newcomers who continue converting acreage into estates and horse-breeding stables. As residential development rapidly overtakes the rural valley and western ridges, village entrepreneurs serve natives and visitors equally. Heritage Tourism, a new force affecting all, begins to build upon Pawling's historic, scenic, and cultural assets.

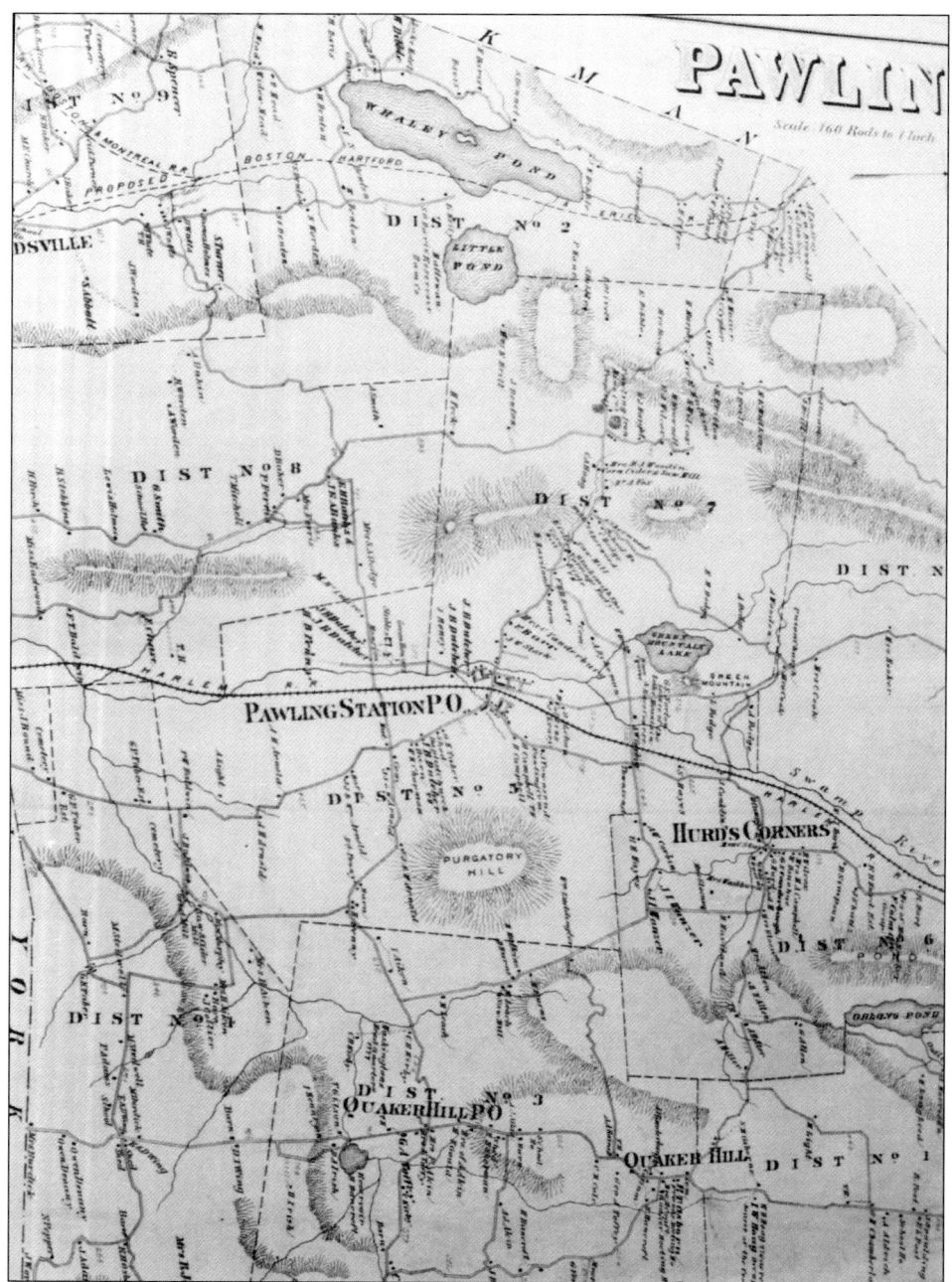

1876 Continental Insurance Map of Pawling Town. Nineteenth-century insurance companies produced maps of counties and municipalities, down to neighborhood and school district level, with all properties identified that merited protection from "conflagration," the companies' main concern. These maps are useful to latter day researchers attempting to follow developmental changes in communities such as their place names, roads, properties, and public works. This 1876 series was sponsored in part by local businesses. Continental's representative in Pawling was the firm of Holmes & Merwin. (DCHS.)

DOORS OF THE OBLONG MEETING HOUSE. These doors, one for men and another for women, have opened for generations of Quakers since 1764, when the meeting house was built, replacing an earlier one built c. 1742. The list of members—entered in meeting records in the 1740 Dutchess County landowners lists and in store owner accounts—reflects whole families in the Harlem Valley. Here, in 1767, Oblong Quakers asserted the inconsistency of slavery with Christianity. (JG.)

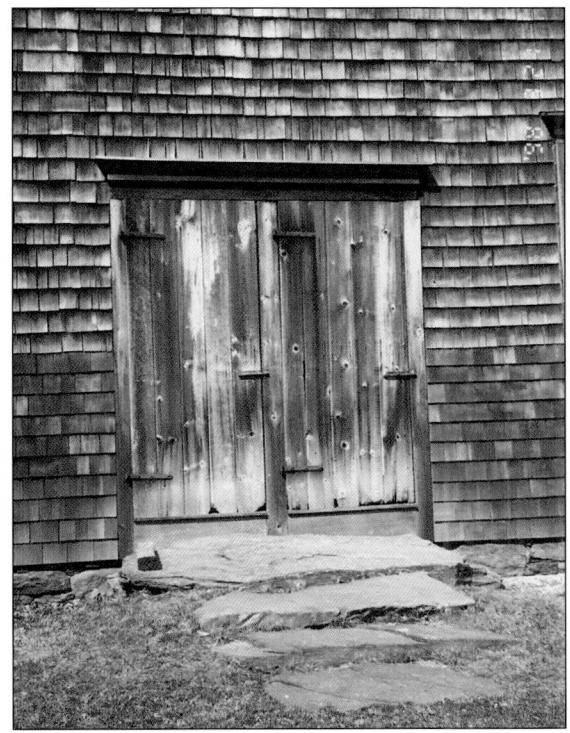

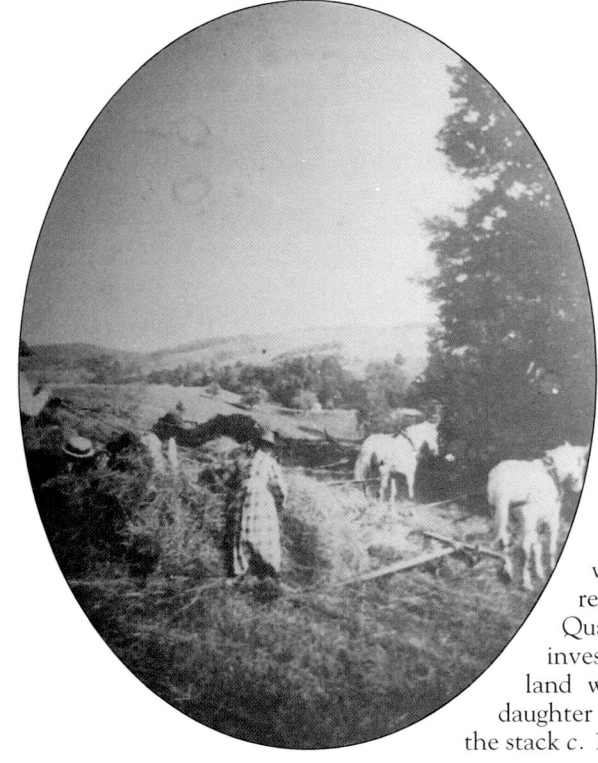

JOHN THOMAS'S GRAY TEAM HAYING ON QUAKER HILL. Abraham Thomas and Jonathan Akin were among the earliest settlers, coming before 1761. Friends established a remote community where they could live apart, practice their religion, and own a fertile piece of land. Quaker farmers, their wives, and children invested in the choice of well-watered land with hard work—without slaves. John, daughter Annie, and Helen Akin roped hay up to the stack c. 1890. (HSQHP.)

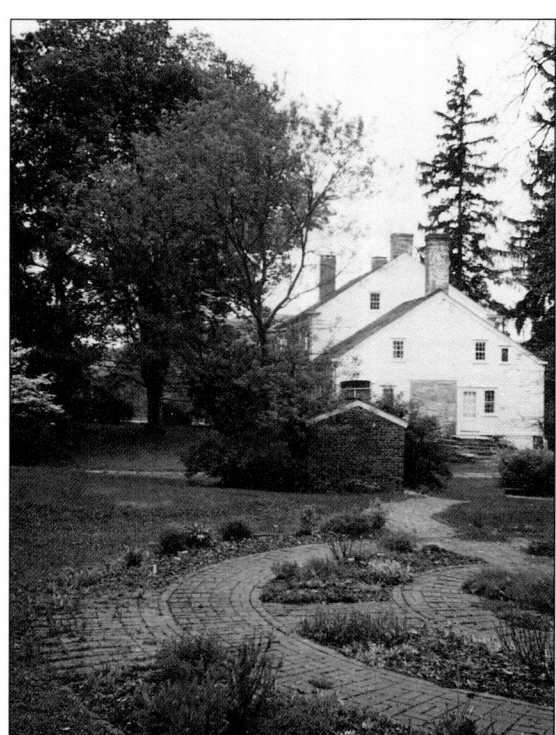

JOHN KANE HOUSE. The historical society's home tells a story of two Irishmen—John Kane and William Prendergast—caught up in revolutionary tumult. Prendergast, whose farm was across the way, led an anti-rent rebellion in 1766 that almost cost him his life. Kane, well-married and a community leader, lost all by siding with Tory interests. The house served as Washington's headquarters in 1778, and preparations were made here for the "Great Barbecue" held on Purgatory Hill hailing the anniversary of the victory at Saratoga. (JG.)

QUAKER HILL ROAD QUAKER CEMETERY. Freelove Briggs and family rest in a burial ground traditionally used by Quakers since c. 1761. In 1855, Richard T. Osborn officially deeded it to the Society of Friends. The cemetery includes a section for non-Quaker early settlers approved by the Oblong Meeting. A memorial stone located here honors Mehitabel Wing Prendergast, the indomitable Quaker wife of William Prendergast. She successfully gained the King's pardon for her errant, about-to-be-hanged husband. (JG.)

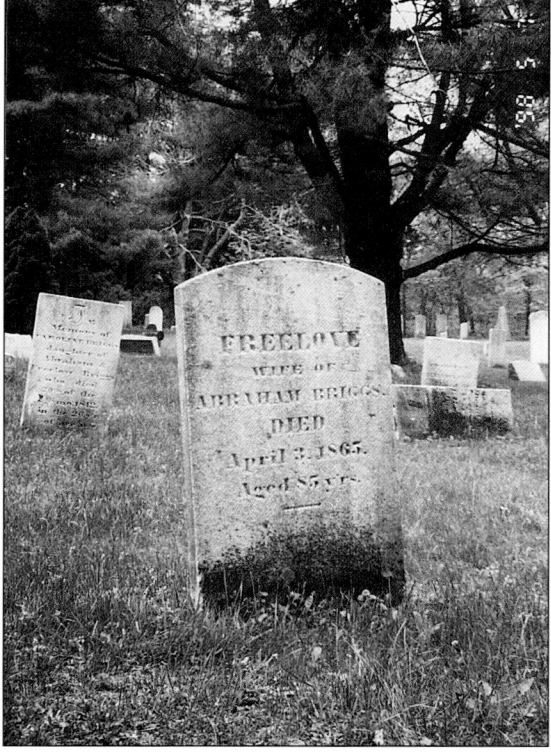

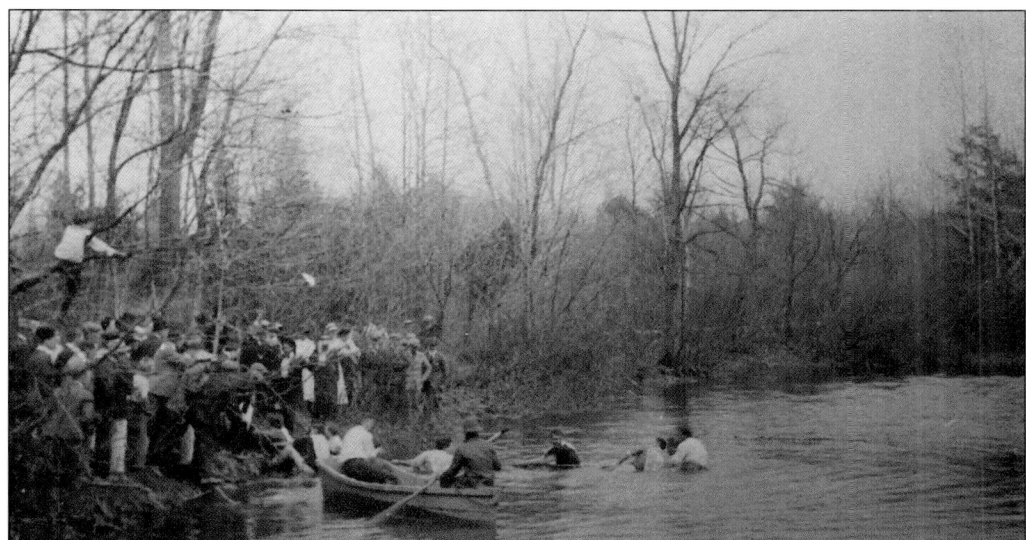

BAPTISM AT WHALEY LAKE. As reservoir and vacation destination, Whaley Lake has served many good causes. Baptist settlers c. 1755 formed a church on Whaley Lake's shores and used the lake for baptisms by immersion. The Mattewan Company dam, built in 1814, diverted the water to its Fishkill plant for textile production. By mid-century, campgrounds and the Topeco Lake Hotel were attracting vacationers. Today, many summer cottages have become year-round homes where some believe that Pawling's earliest settlement may have begun. (PH/MH.)

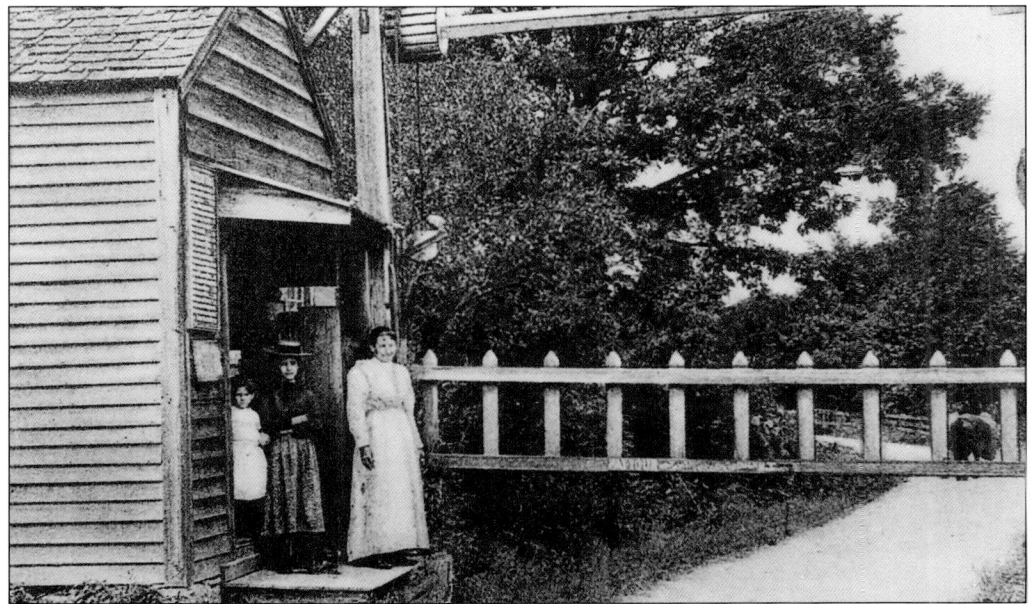

STONE HOUSE TOLLGATE. Drovers needed the log road over an earlier trail to move herds, and landowners needed to conduct business in Poughkeepsie. Market and government access pushed the extension of the Pawling-Beekman Turnpike after 1818. Stone House, now bypassed by Route 55, was a toll station. Phoebe Miller raised the gate for a fee—2¢ for pedestrians and 25¢ for pleasure carriages. An 1879 Sewell and White Blacksmiths' bill showed that horses were still big business, but rails and automobiles would do them in. (PH/MH.)

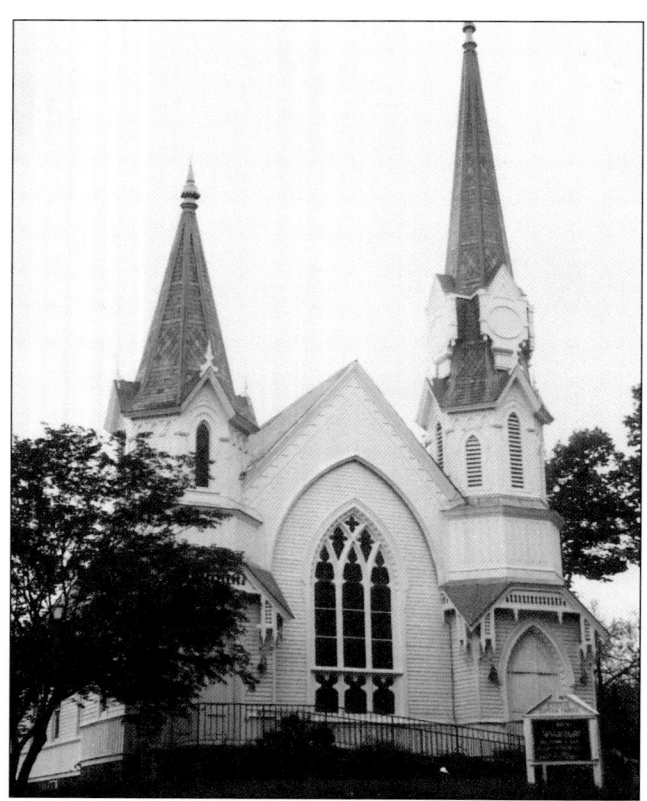

CHURCH EXPANSION. In 1853, ten members of the Whaley Lake congregation organized the Central Baptist Church in the village. The church was given a Victorian facade in 1873 by Poughkeepsie architect J.A. Wood. Pawling's growth after the railroad came in 1849, spurred church expansion. Eighteen fifty-three also saw new buildings for the Methodists in the village and in Reynoldsville. A year later, Whaley Lake had a new Baptist church, and by 1872, Methodists needed a larger house of worship in the village. (JG.)

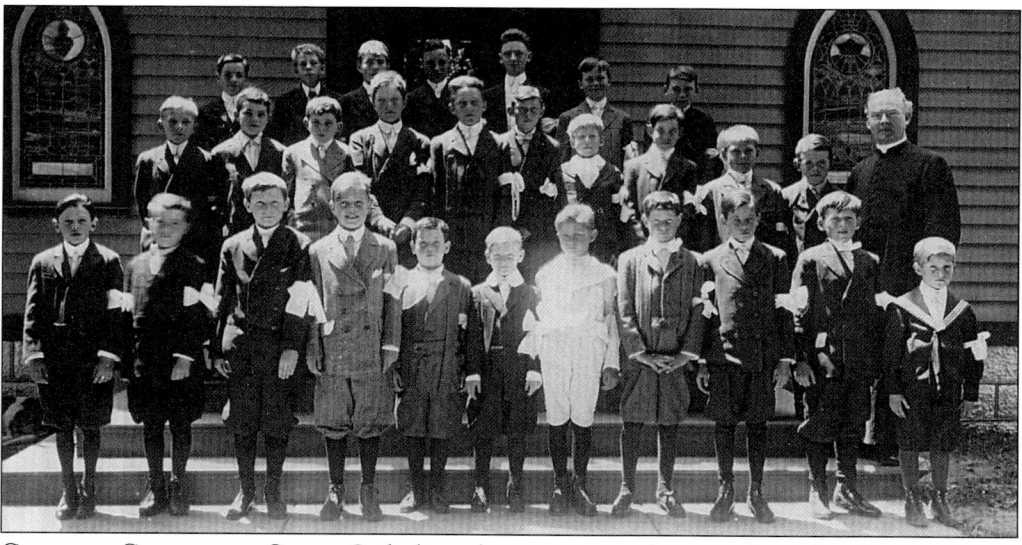

CATHOLIC COMMUNION CLASS. Catholics who came as workers on the railroad were without their own sanctuary and priest for almost 20 years. A former Methodist church, converted to a private day school, eventually housed services by visiting priests until Father Healey became the first resident priest. In 1872, when fire destroyed the old church, he led the drive to build St. John the Evangelist, completed that year. William Carey's father was a member of this all boys' First Communion class, c. 1910. (WJC.)

ALBERT J. AKIN. Akin (1803-1903) was both long-lived and highly-productive despite frail health. As a young man he went to New York City to become a successful businessman but returned to invest his wealth here. He helped raise $100,000 to bring in the Harlem Railroad, served on its board, and organized the Pawling National Bank, of which he was president until age 95. He also built Mizzentop Hotel. His wealth was spent in community building through Akin Hall Association and the Akin Library. (HSQHP/JG.)

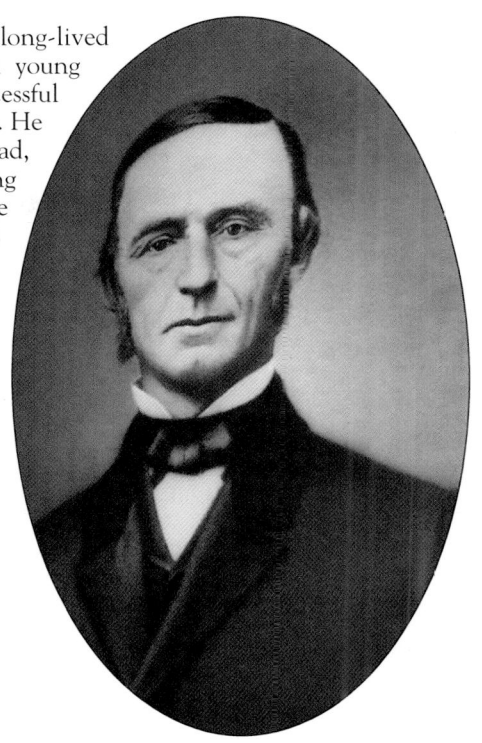

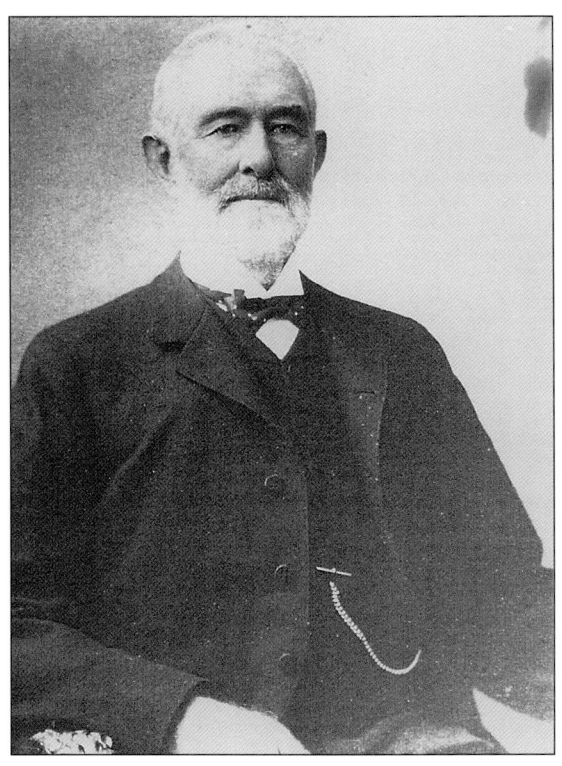

JOHN B. DUTCHER. One of Pawling's biggest boosters was born in Dover in 1830. Dutcher had started successful business and political careers there before he focused his attentions on Pawling. Foreseeing the railroad boom and its impact on Pawling Station, he invested in building local business and in railroad interests elsewhere that could feed Pawling's economy. He pressed for village incorporation and became its first president in 1893. (PH/MH.)

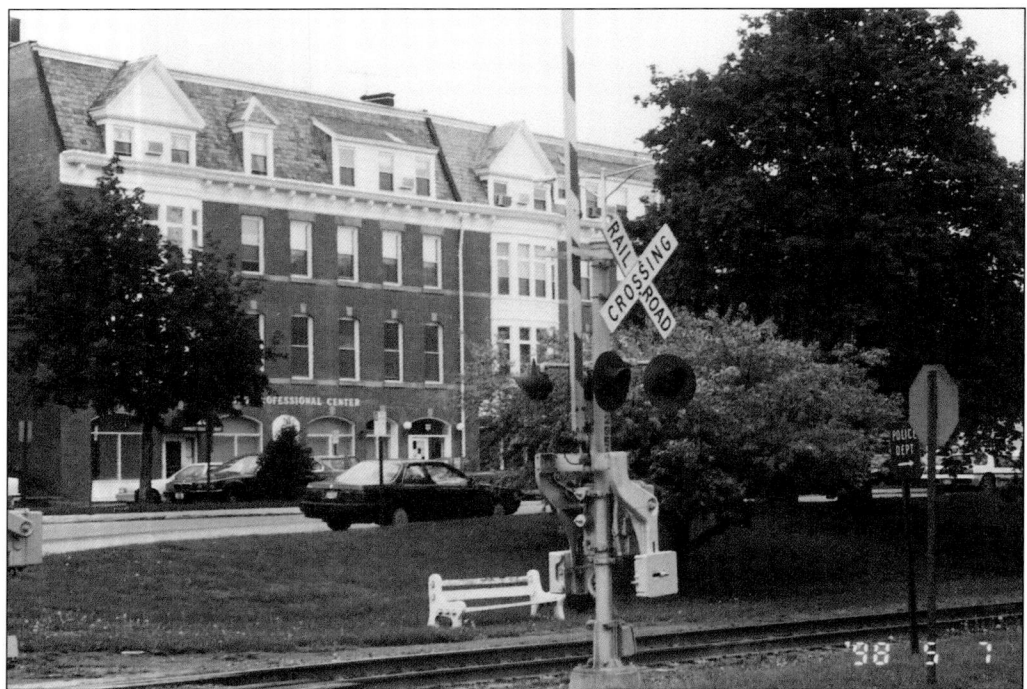

DUTCHER HOUSE AT PAWLING STATION. In 1884, Dutcher wisely built his hotel opposite the rail station, across the tracks from newsman/historian Philip Smith's *Pawling Pioneer*, and a short drive from his own Lakeside Park. The site, intended for commercial and community use, also served successfully as opera house, private school, post office, public hall, and reading room. Today, it supports stores and apartments. Residents and visitors head here and to the Ferris block to buy books, flowers, gifts, and goodies. (JG.)

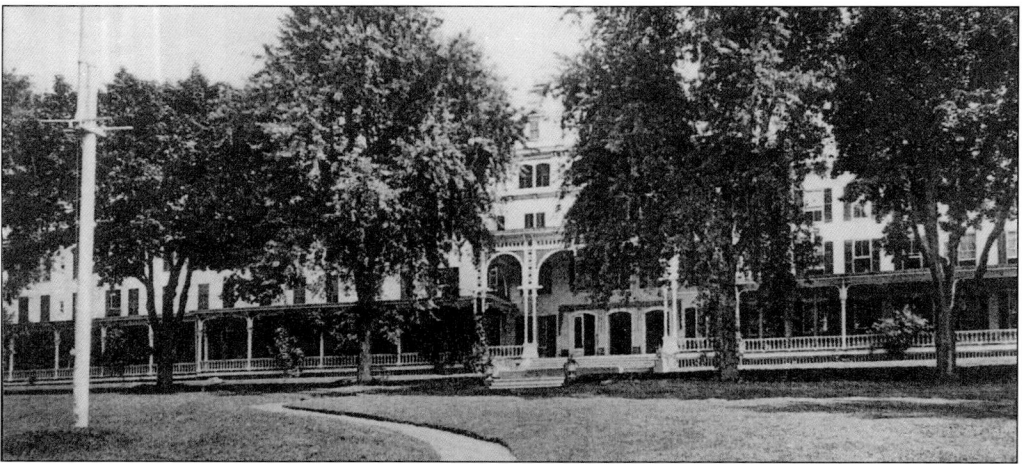

MIZZENTOP HOTEL. Pawling's success as a vacation destination was boosted by the construction of Mizzentop Hotel in 1880, named by Akin's friend Adm. John L. Worden. Sited near the old family farm atop Quaker Hill, it had every amenity desired by 19th-century tourists. Its guest register, now in the Akin Library Museum, lists the names of many wealthy New Yorkers, plus a number of relatives of local families. Changes in taste and the Depression brought the demise of the hotel. It was demolished in 1934. (LB.)

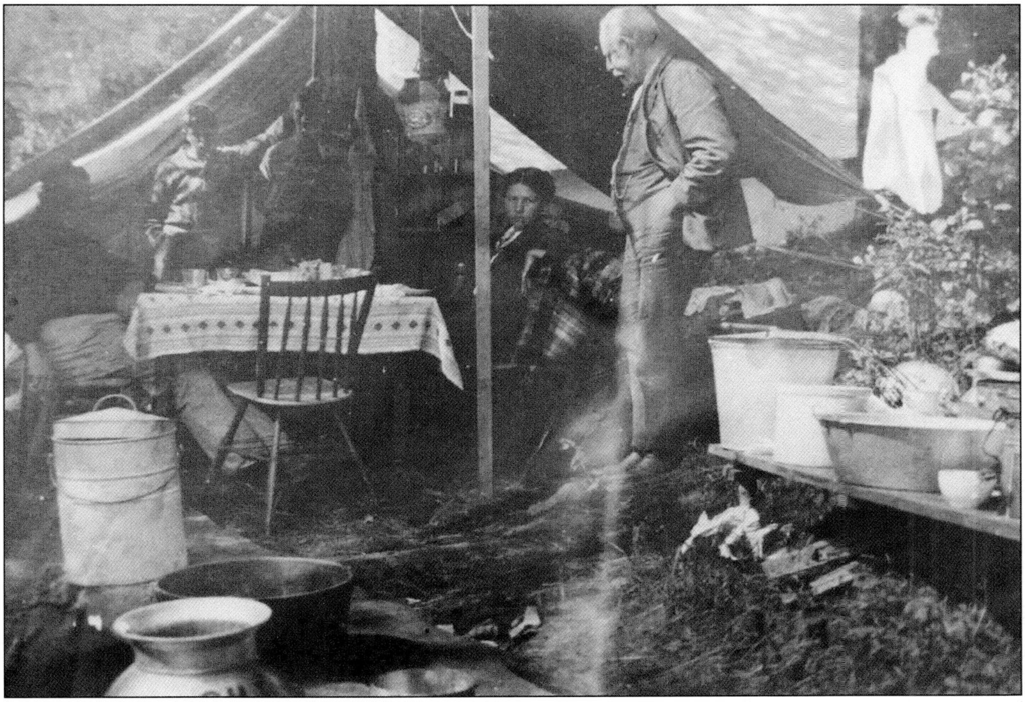

WHALEY LAKE CAMPERS. When local families took vacations at the turn of the century, they did not stray far to find a change of scenery. The Birdsall family album shows a tent encampment at Whaley Pond where the womenfolk brought along as many conveniences from home as they could manage —milk cans, tin tubs, crockery, wash lines, cots, rocking chairs, etc.—to set up housekeeping out-of-doors. The 1907 schedule included fishing, boating, and rocking. (PH/MH.)

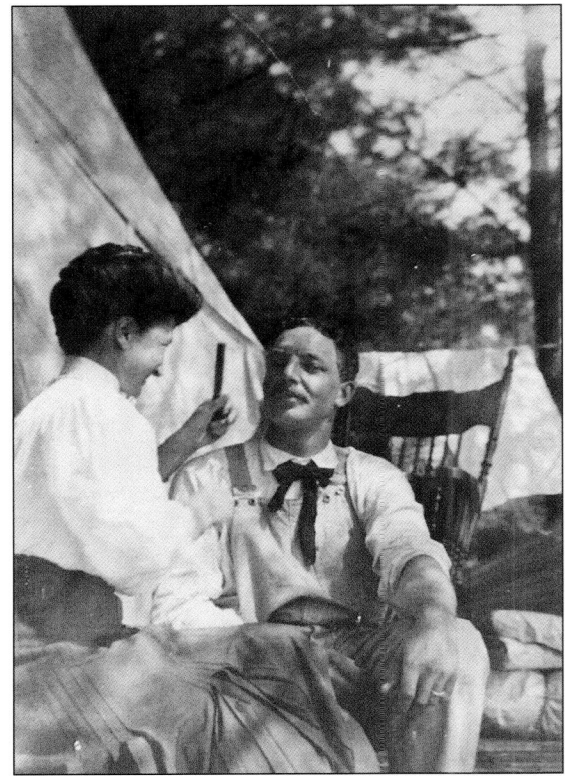

SHAVE AND A HAIRCUT, TWO BITS. Informal attire at the Birdsall encampment meant that the gentlemen could relax by removing their outer coats and were allowed to roll up their shirtsleeves. Overalls were required for fishermen. The ladies, bound to household tasks and occasional barbering duties added by Walter Birdsall, still seemed tightly corseted. (PH/MH.)

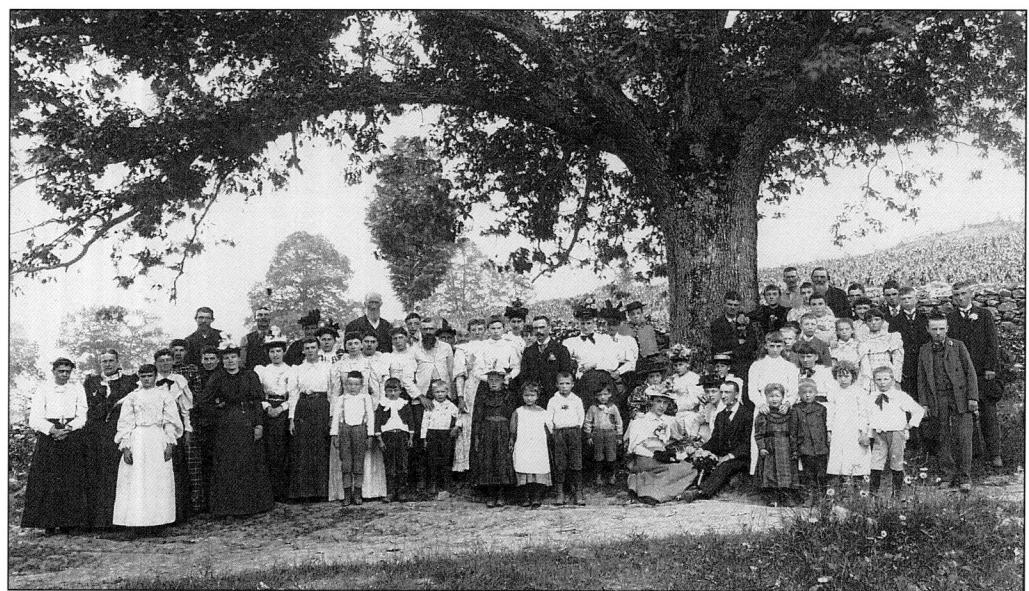

REYNOLDSVILLE/HOLMES SCHOOL PICNIC, 1895. Year-end school picnics, even near a cornfield, were community celebrations calling for Sunday best attire and behavior. Children walked miles for an education. Holmes was in School District #9, south of Whaley Lake, on the mountainous Beekman border. The "common" school near the Methodist church and Turner's Sawmill had grades one through eight. The Union Free district in Pawling Station, formed in 1890, had 143 pupils by 1895 and would eventually serve the entire town. (PH/MH.)

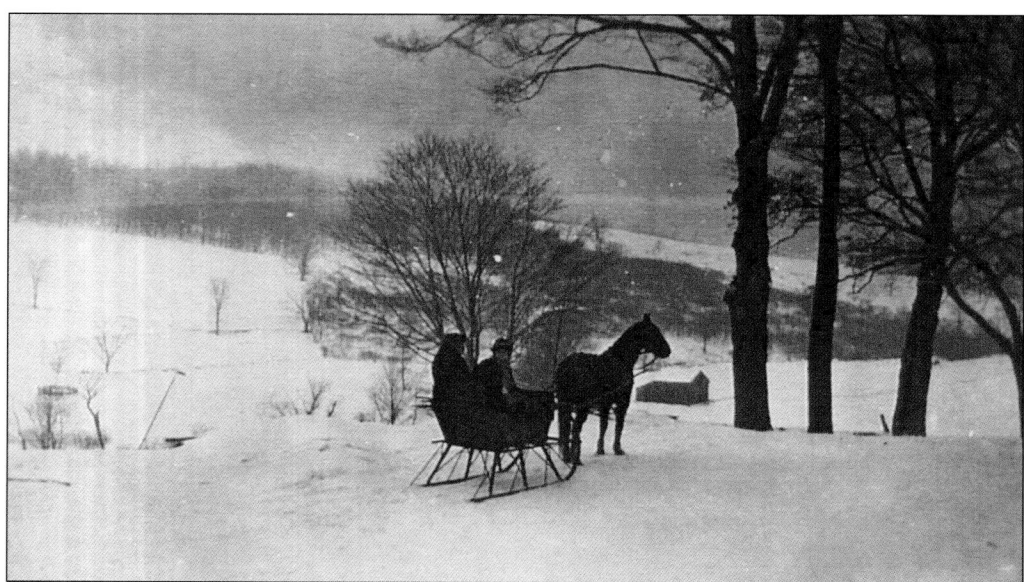

GRACE M. GOULD ON HER WAY TO SCHOOL. The Gould family of "Elmwood" are descendants of the Akin line on Quaker Hill. Public school districts in the valley or west mountains provided no transportation. Students walked or, if near the railroad, took a train. Quaker Hill families at the turn of the 19th century drove children in carriages or sleds to private or public schools, tutored them at home, or sent them to boarding schools. (PH/MH.)

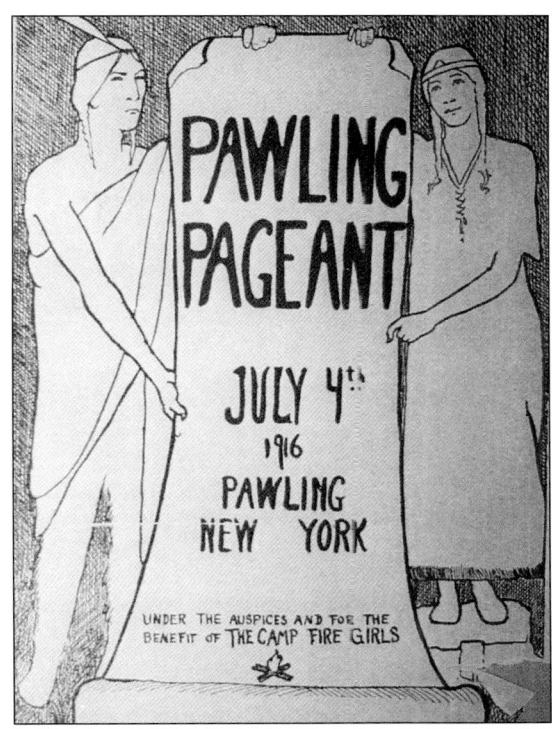

CAMPFIRE GIRLS PROGRAM. Mary F. Taber organized the Campfire Girls in Pawling in 1912, forming one of the earliest units in the country with its own camp building. On July 4, 1916, the girls and their leaders celebrated the holiday with a benefit pageant showing off Campfire Girl accomplishments. In 1986, before the historic camp building was demolished, another commemoration erected a historic marker at the site, with help from Altana Burr and Emma Clark, members of that early troupe. (AML.)

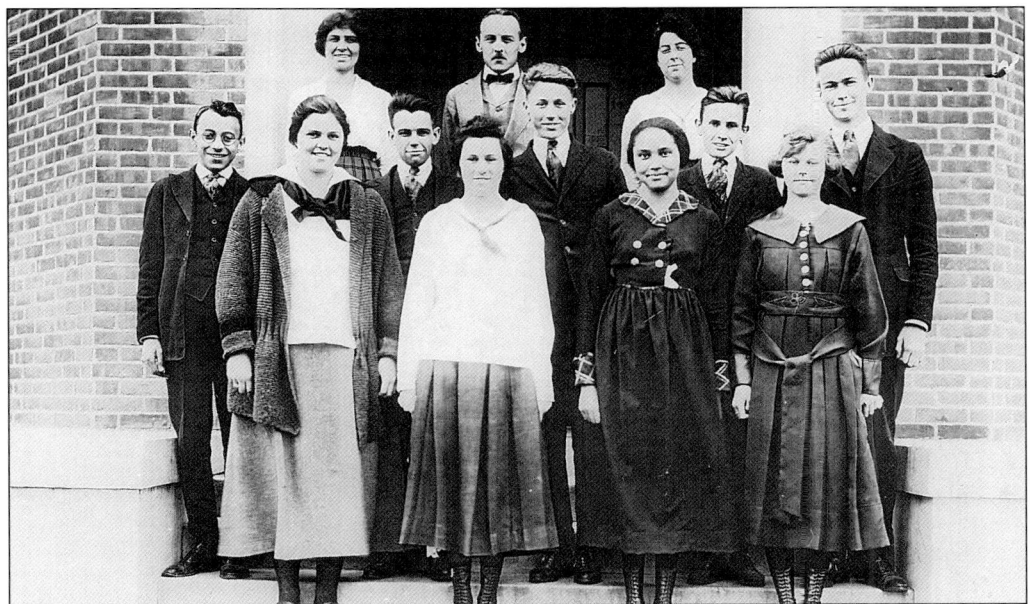

PAWLING HIGH SCHOOL CLASS. By 1914, the school built in 1890 had become too small for the student population. Voters that year approved a new facility on Haight Street, and in 1917, in the midst of World War I, they voted extra construction funds. Members of the 1920 class, whose youth saved them from service, included William Carey Sr. They posed on the front steps of the new brick building with the principal, Professor Bonowitz, and two women teachers, Ruth Green Dubocq and Marion Godfrey Loper. (WJC.)

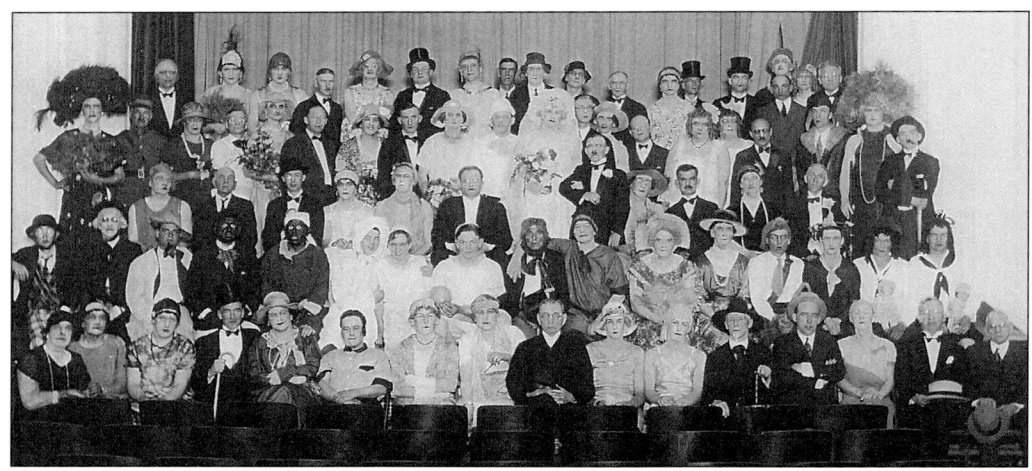

LOCAL THEATRICS, 1932. The stage of the auditorium in the Pawling Elementary School provided the setting for a homegrown production with an all-male cast. The intent was community fun, not cultural enrichment. Before the construction of a school with an auditorium, Dutcher Opera House was used for all manner of local events and productions—from concerts and lectures, to meetings, graduation ceremonies, and performances by professional troupes. (WJC.)

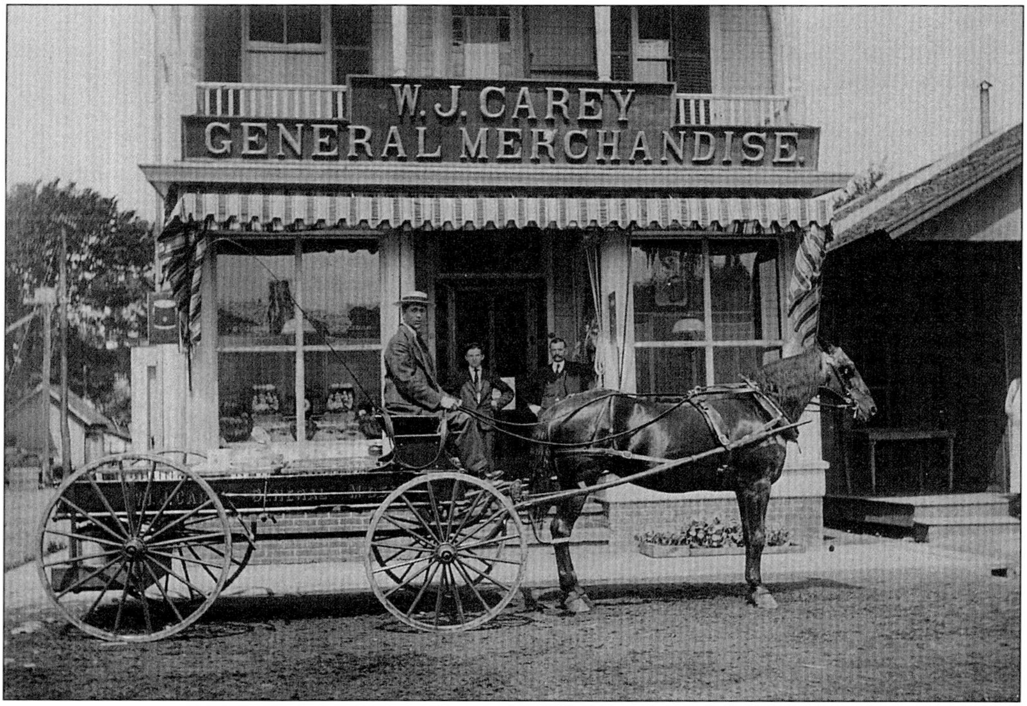

EXTERIOR CAREY STORE. The Careys did well in business for over 50 years. William Carey's first store opened on a shoestring in 1888 on Railroad Avenue. Although the store moved several times, it always stayed close to the railroad station. Carey was in a good location—a center of transportation near Dutcher House. Business increased with additions to inventory that made it a general store. After a fire in 1932, his son took over the business. (WJC.)

SOL OSBORN SERVES IN WW I. Sol Osborne honored those who died in the battles of WW I with a poppy. Veterans' groups, inspired by McCraes's poem, *In Flanders Fields*, made it a symbol of a soldier's ultimate patriotic sacrifice. After the war, Sol exchanged one uniform for another—the familiar coveralls of a mechanic. In 1928, he posed (below) with Al Short, Art Brown, and Harry Burgess, co-workers at the Valley Garage. (PH/MH.)

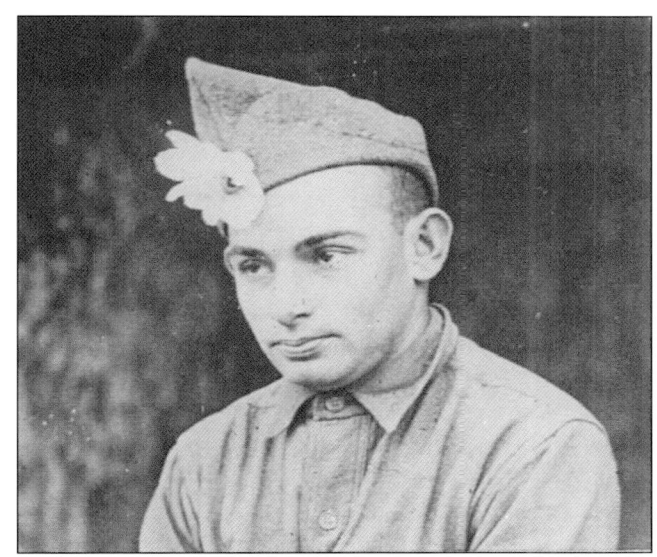

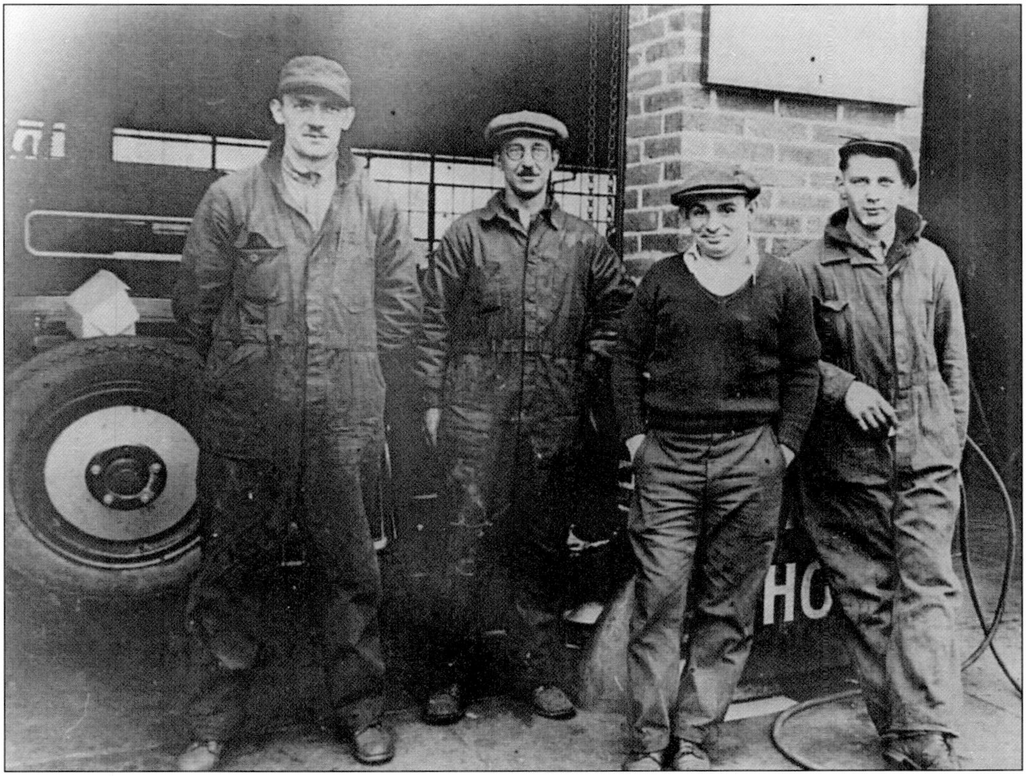

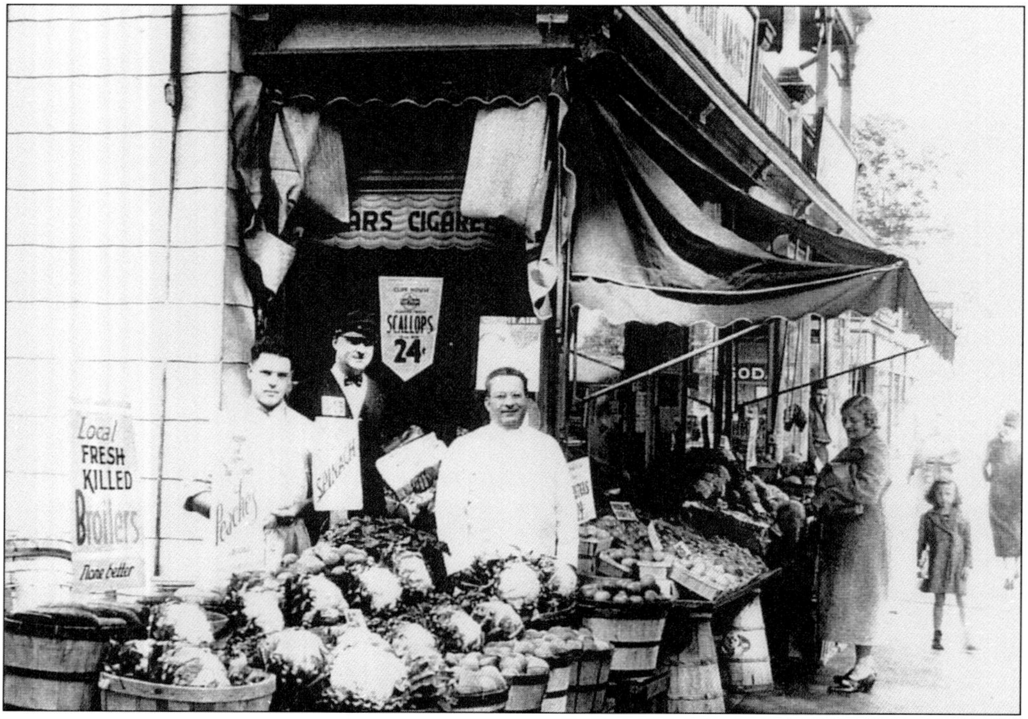

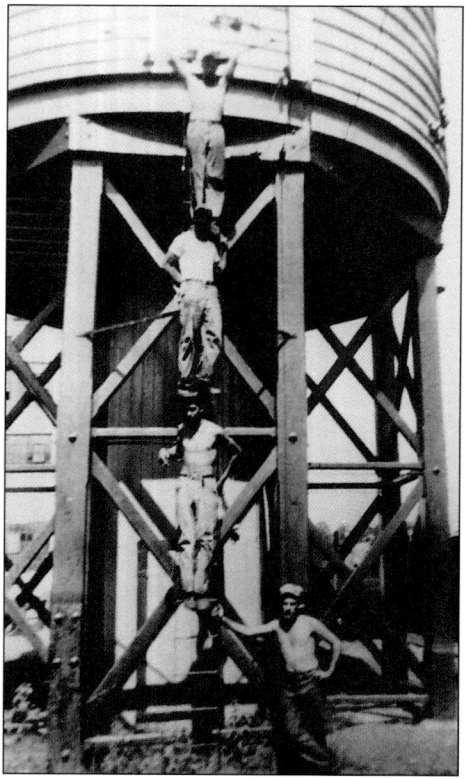

PAWLING GROCERY STORE. Before the coming of "chain stores," Valente's in the village was a popular grocery store with both village and Quaker Hill housewives. A variety of fresh fruits, produce, poultry, and seafood at fair prices survived the careful scrutiny of shoppers who chose among its interior and sidewalk offerings with pinches, sniffs, and an occasional taste offered by the owners. Groceries, loaded into bags and empty shipping cartons, were carried to customers' cars with a smile. (PH/MH.)

LOU GROGAN ON THE PAWLING WATER TOWER. When he climbed the Pawling station water tower, Lou Grogan was a railroad employee (1943-1955) paid for what boys envision as great adventure. The author of *The Coming of the New York and Harlem Railroad* grew up among railroad workers in communities bordering Harlem Line facilities. Eleven members of his family worked for the railroad. He lived a boy's fondest dream as an "insider" with a front row seat for railroading's daily maneuvers, including occasional access to the hallowed engine cab. (PH/MH.)

AKIN HALL EN ROUTE TO CHRIST CHURCH. In 1937, with Lowell Thomas's encouragement, Albert Akin's Hall—intended for community enlightenment and education—was moved from its original site near the Akin Library to a bluff overlooking the valley. This historic Quaker Hill institution received a complete architectural and institutional makeover. Paint, fenestration changes, and a steeple turned a Victorian hall into a New England neo-Greek Revival church. (LB.)

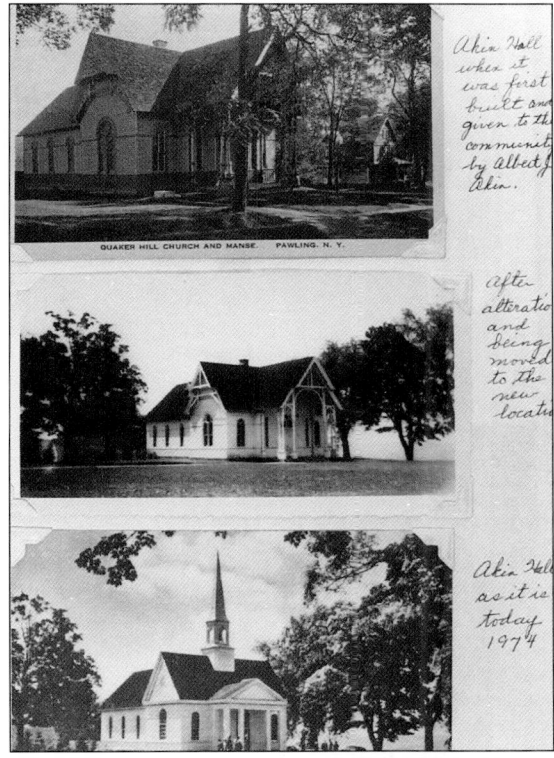

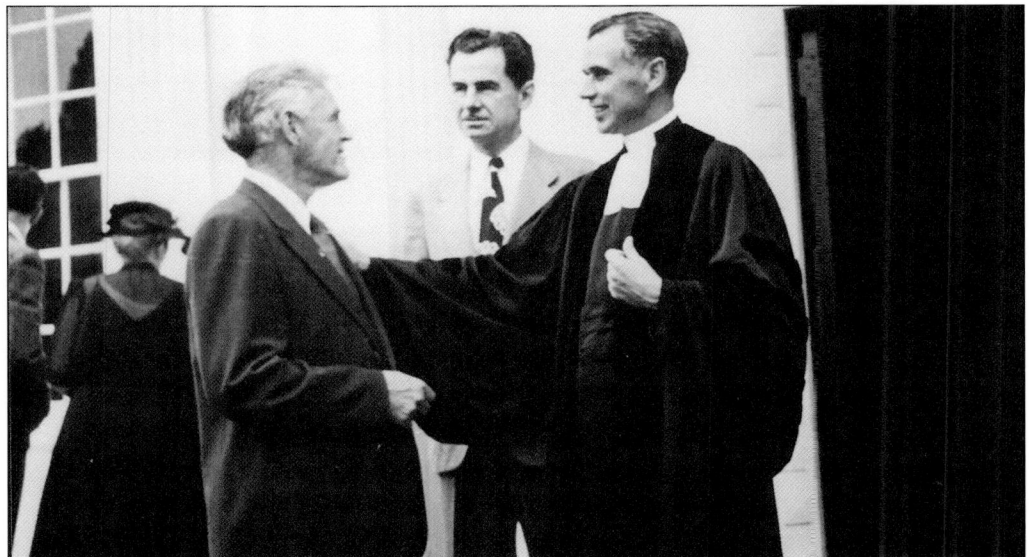

LOWELL THOMAS AND DR. LANKLER. Congressman Gwinn and Pastor Lankler chatted eagerly after Sunday services with neighbor/ world-traveler Thomas whenever he came home. The conveyance of Akin Hall to the other side of the crossroads marked a major institutional change creating Christ Church—a union church for the residents of Quaker Hill regardless of denominational affiliation. Thomas, a resident from 1926, so loved the spot that he chose it as his family burial site. (HSQHP.)

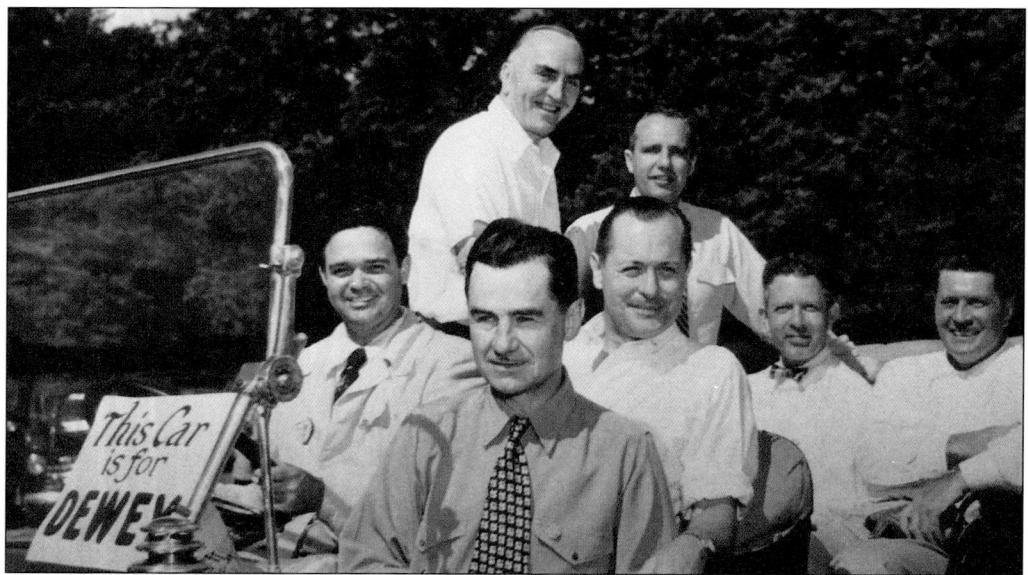

This Car for Dewey. Lowell Thomas, creator of new traditions, was as much marketer as newsman. His "Nine Old Men" team was a moveable feast of celebrities "playing" like small town boys in a pick-up game. Contests were held all over the local landscape for a variety of causes and reasons—in this case, the cause was 1948 politics. This group included tenor James Melton, Actor Robert Montgomery, Gen. Eddie Rickenbacker, Howard Morgens, Neil McElroy, and boxer Gene Tunney. (HSQHP.)

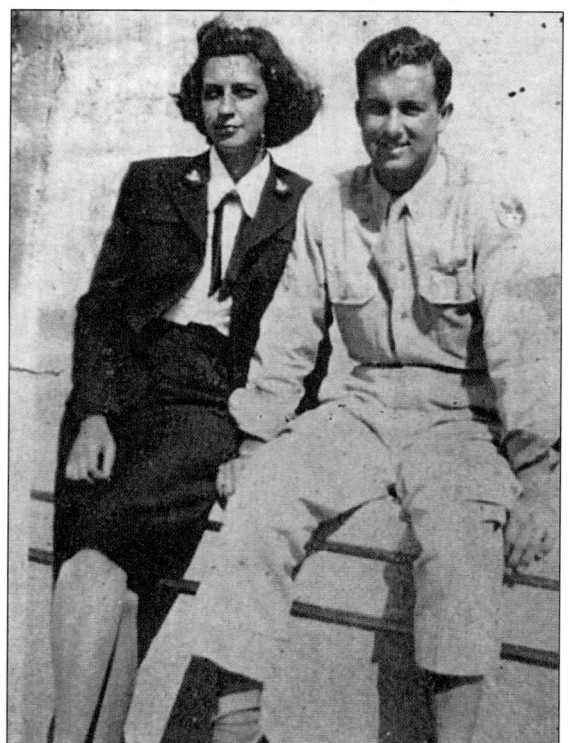

Blossom Penney and Godfrey Loper WW II. WW II took young people out of jobs or college and placed them in harm's way. A war-years' newsletter, *Elks Air Cadet Notes* written by Fred Smith, kept track of county men recruited by the Air Force. Pawling's Cpl. Godfrey Loper was a radio man/gunner on a bomber, and Blossom was a member of Women Appointed for Volunteer Emergency Service (WAVES) when love and marriage beckoned. A January 1944 article in *The Pawling Chronicle* announced their nuptials while on leave in Missouri. (PH/MH.)

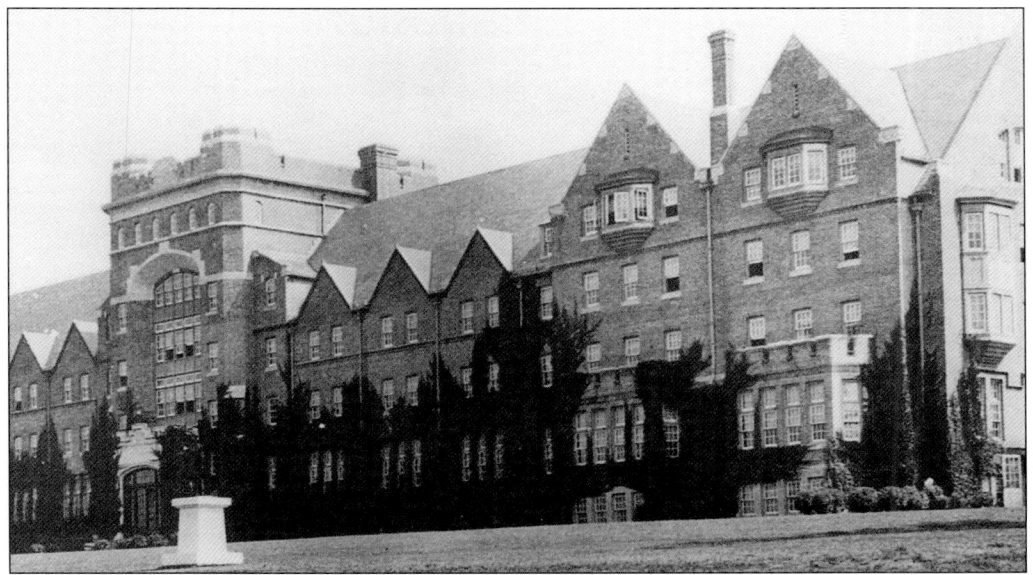

TRINITY PAWLING SCHOOL. Dr. Frederick Gamage, founder of Pawling School for Boys in 1907, held classes at Dutcher House until 1910, when the new building on Route 22 was completed. During WW II, it served two very different national needs: training school for cryptographers and convalescent center for wounded servicemen. It became Trinity-Pawling, a boarding school, in 1947 after the campus was purchased by Trinity School in New York City. (DCHS.)

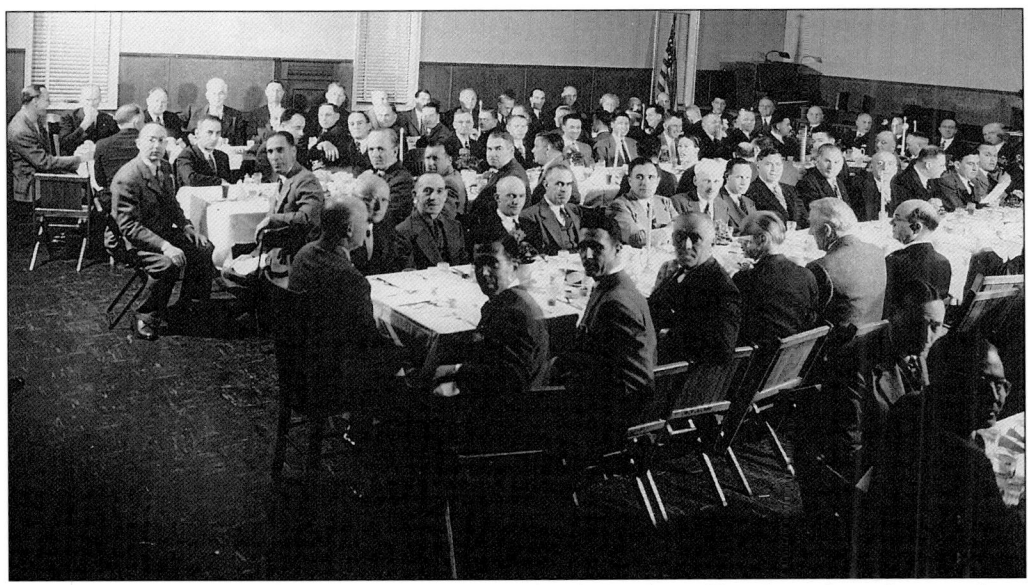

PAWLING CHAMBER OF COMMERCE, 1947. In 1945, Pawling Chamber planted trees along Memorial Avenue in memory of servicemen killed in the war. Members saw servicemen's sacrifices as being linked to planning a different kind of peacetime economy. The energy of the workforce, mobilized and tested by the demands of war, needed a new focus. Postwar chambers found new members in returning servicemen who, with help from federal programs, sought to find jobs, begin families, build homes, and start businesses. (PH/MH.)

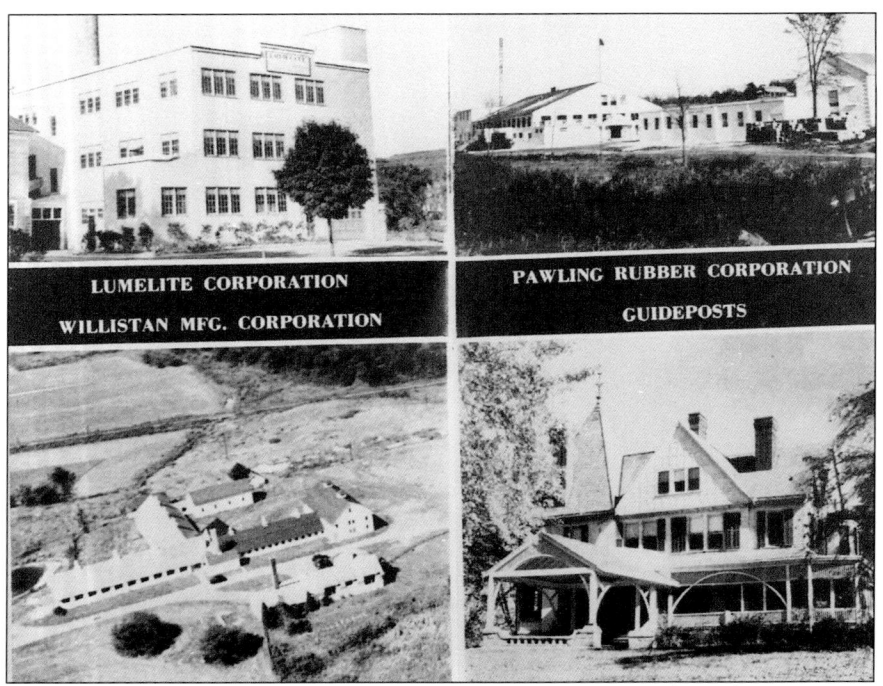

PAWLING VILLAGE INDUSTRY. A 1950s Chamber brochure presented Pawling's economic and cultural resources, inviting all to a "typical American village." Lumelite plastics replaced Sheffield milk. Pawling Rubber manufacturing gaskets and Willistan Mfg. Corporation making drapery goods, were among Pawling's most important industries. Norman Vincent Peale's Center for Christian Living began as Guideposts, an inspirational publications firm, in a Quaker Hill house. (LB.)

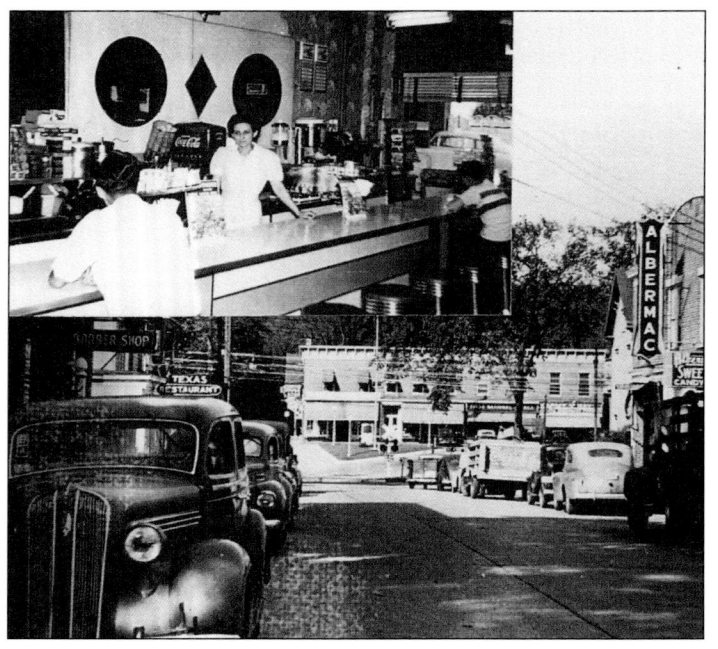

ALBERMAC'S THEATRE AND SWEET SHOP, 1940s. According to *Life* magazine, the hottest spot in town for Pawling's teen population, from the late 1940s through the 50s, was the Albermac Sweet Shop. Marguerite Ruberg dispensed sodas while the jukebox bounced between Dorsey's swing and Sinatra's crooning. The theater next door with a weekly change of films did away with the need for a weekend social calendar, completely supplying the cultural demands of local youth. (PH/MH.)

HOLIDAY HILLS LIFEGUARDS. The YMCA staff posing for 1950s PR shots is part of a recreational history extending into the 19th century when Holiday Hills was Lakeside Park. It was a short drive for Dutcher House guests wishing to enjoy its waterside and park pathways. It was also the site of the Harlem Valley Agricultural Fair. Then, boating on Green Mountain Lake and fair attractions competed for attention with racehorses, not bathing beauties. (YMCA.)

YMCA CAMPERS. Teaching children to swim and enjoy the out-of-doors is part of the Y's mission. Before the Metropolitan YMCA of Greater New York turned it into a camp and conference center in 1947, Holiday Hills serviced as a community park and vacation/convalescent center for employees of Con Ed. The Y has been a good neighbor to the village, offering residents access to park and recreational facilities, including summer camp. It is also an economic asset attracting visitors and employing residents. (YMCA.)

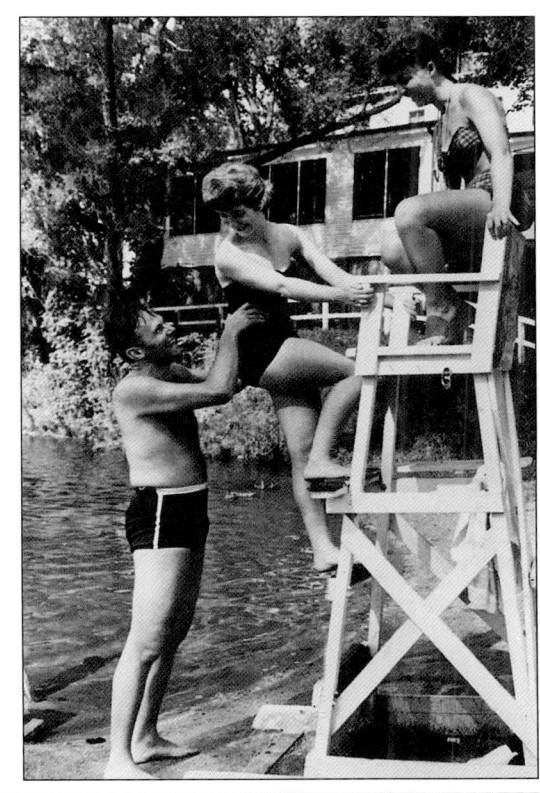

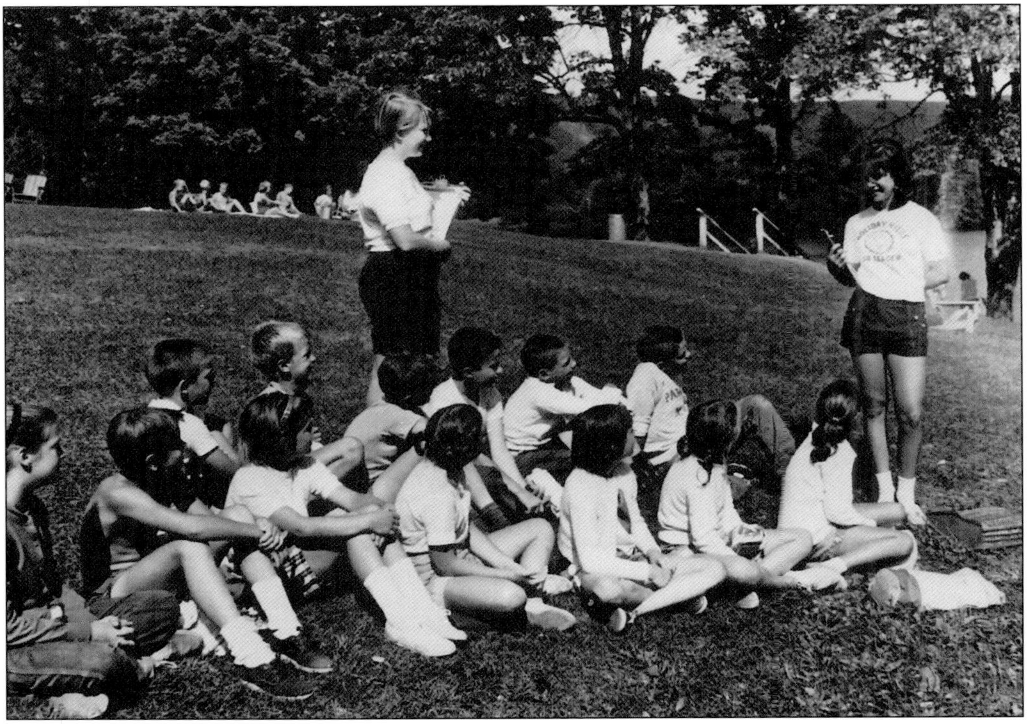

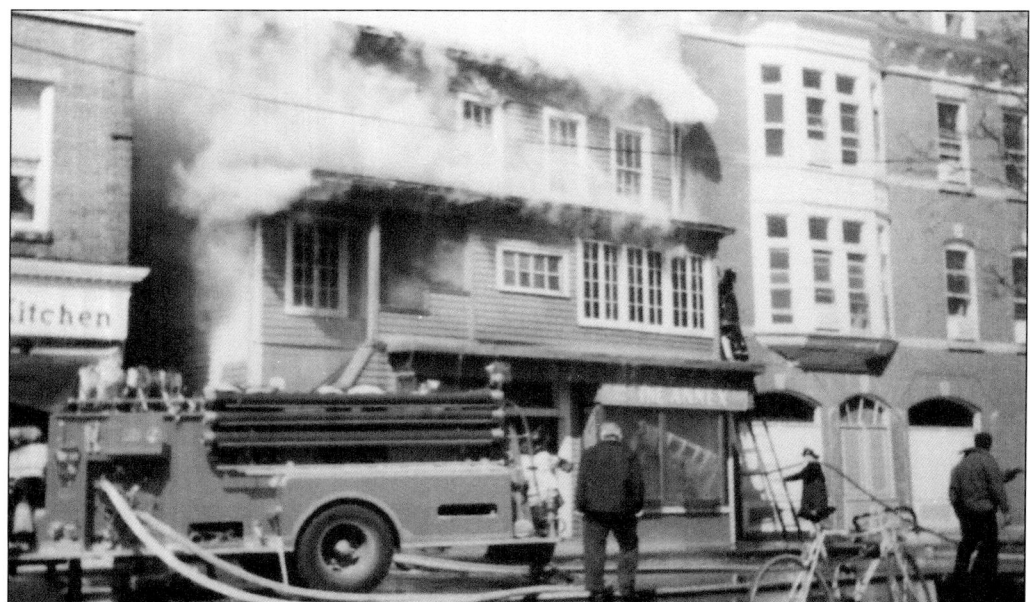

ANNEX FIRE, 1976. Pawling Village has suffered several devastating fires in and near its center, including one at the Trinity-Pawling School in 1969, when lives were lost. Dutcher House and the Ferris block symbolize the village for most residents, so the 1976 fire in Mahaffey's Annex Gallery in the former Merwin and Holmes General Store brought out many concerned villagers and businessmen. The volunteers of the fire department, which was formed in 1895, were out in force and saved the day. (EMM.)

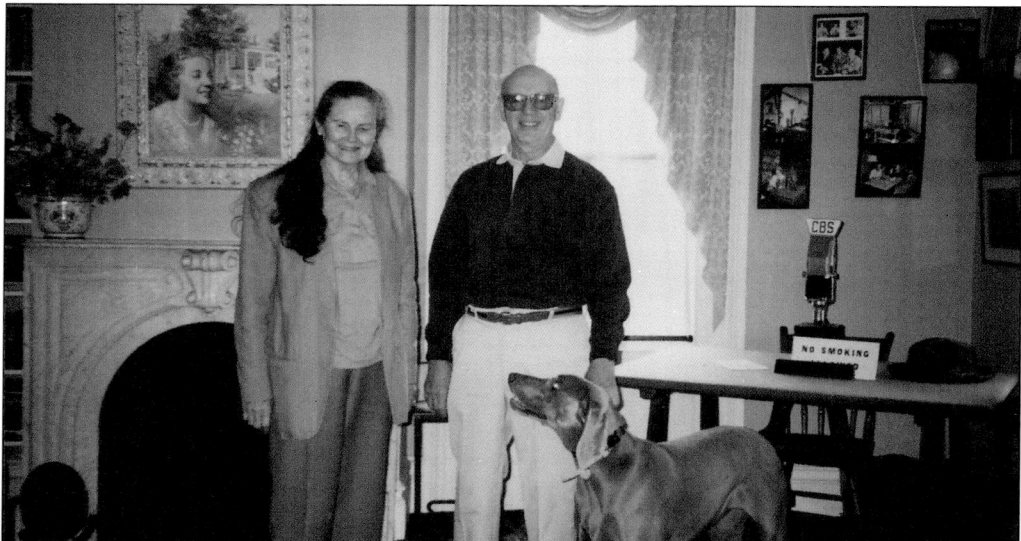

JOHN KANE HOUSE LOWELL THOMAS EXHIBIT. In 1982, spurred by the energy of national history celebrations, the Historical Society of Quaker Hill and Pawling took on the challenge of saving the John Kane House. Their efforts to raise funds were assisted by Thomas's family. Director of Docents Molly McLean and Treasurer John Daniels with friend Heidi, show off the exhibit of Thomas's "at home" broadcasting center, in the room set aside for one of Pawling's favorite adopted sons. (JG.)

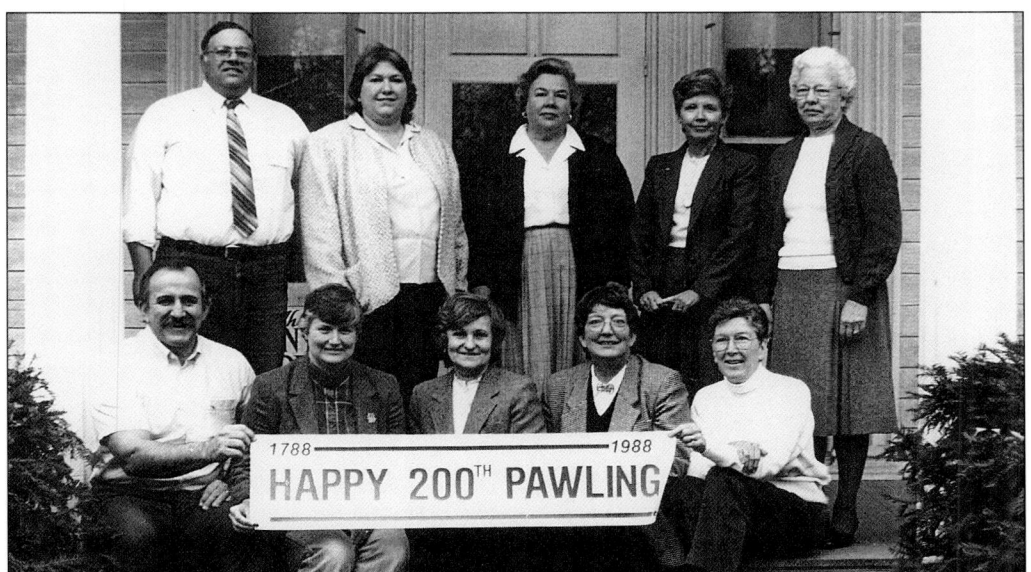

200TH ANNIVERSARY COMMITTEE. From 1976 until 1993, Pawling was in the midst of planning or carrying forth historic celebrations. As one of Dutchess's and New York's original 1788 towns, Pawling was part of a state-wide effort to bring history alive. Parades, dinners, retrospective publications, quilts, balls, oratory, monuments, and marker development were the products of much hard work. The committee, under Town Historian Myrna Hubert, took a well-deserved bow. (PH/MH.)

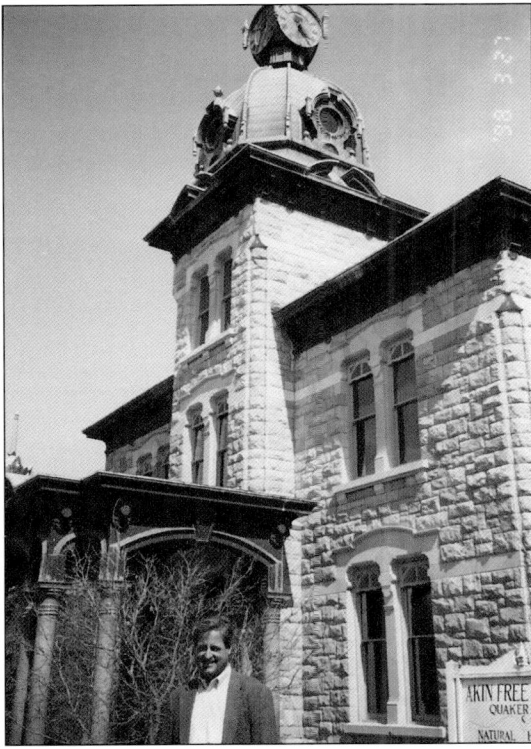

AKIN FREE LIBRARY AND CLOCK. In 1998, Quaker Hill's Akin Hall Association in partnership with the Historical Society of Quaker Hill and Pawling celebrated one hundred years of service to Hill residents and the public. The association administers its founder's endowment, caring for The Akin Library and Museum and its bibliographic, archival, and Gunnison Natural History collections, while the society manages the History Museum. Volunteer Tom Schroth took on fixing the tower clock as his birthday present. (JG.)

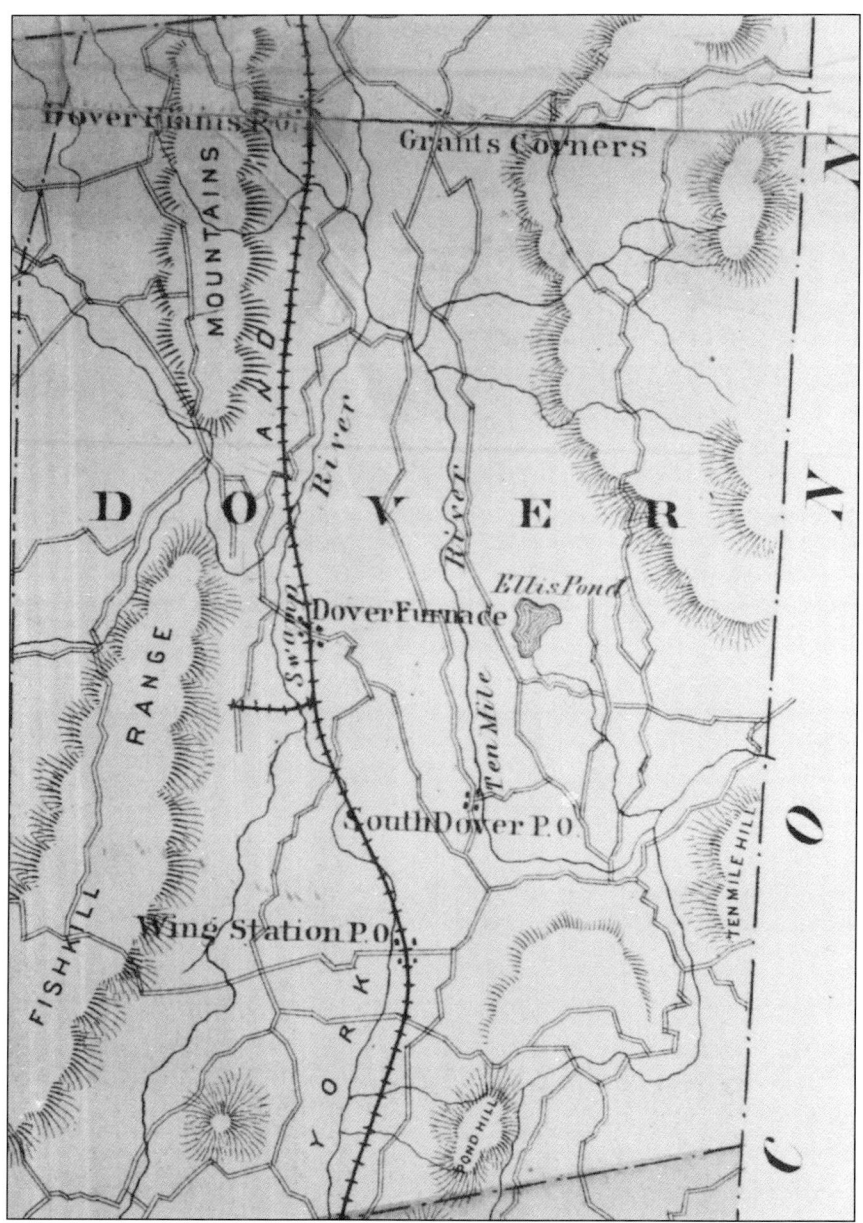

MAP OF THE TOWN OF DOVER. The 1876 Continental Insurance Map series outlined geographic and demographic features of the Town of Dover—the mountain chains rising on either side of the Webatuck/Ten Mile River and the Swamp River valley. The map identifies only five hamlets as being of any size. Small settlements of the past, like Grants Corners, have either disappeared or become part of a neighborhood in the surviving communities. Those that survived to the present also have post offices and railroad stations , for these designations brought businesses, residents, and visitors. Dover Plains, the largest hamlet, is at the terminus of the Dover Turnpike (now NYS 343). This public highway began as a trail/dirt path from Poughkeepsie to "Nine Partners" or "Beekman's" (patent lands), then became a toll road to Dover early in the 19th century and eventually became a state road. (DCHS.)

Two

Dover

Until the early 18th century, this was western Schaghticoke territory, watered by the Ten Mile River and protected by rocky ridges revered as holy places. Dover Stone Church, a natural cavern near Dover Plains, holds a special place in Pequod lore as Chief Sassacus's shelter as he fled King Philip's War (1676). Early Crown patents, using soil quality as criterion, identified the ridges as "poor" land. Nonetheless, pre-Revolution Dutch and English settlers from western Dutchess and Connecticut joined with Quaker families from Pawling to farm and develop mills and mines. Dover shares early civic history with Pawling, from which it was separated in 1807.

According to tradition, Dover's name was inspired by the English Channel's white chalk cliffs. Rocky outcroppings, reminiscent of chalk, are marble—part of the mineral resources of this stretch of the Harlem Valley—where a northerly wall of rock in glacial eras checked soil movement. Farther south, sub-surface stone and mineral wealth spawned 18th and 19th century quarries, mines, furnaces, and mills powered by the town's swift streams. Cattle drovers followed the valley and streams south directly to city markets or west to the Hudson through a mountain pass (NYS 343) near Dover Plains. Other hamlets grew at Chestnut Ridge, Wingdale, South Dover, Webatuck, and Dover Furnace. Around 1850, rail line communities became "stations"—entry points for visitors drawn by the area's scenic beauty, and new settlers, Irish and Italians, seeking employment.

In the 1930s, the construction of the "State Hospital" brought employment opportunities and new residents. Recent improvements to the Harlem Line and Heritage Tourism forecast another wave of visitors and citizens.

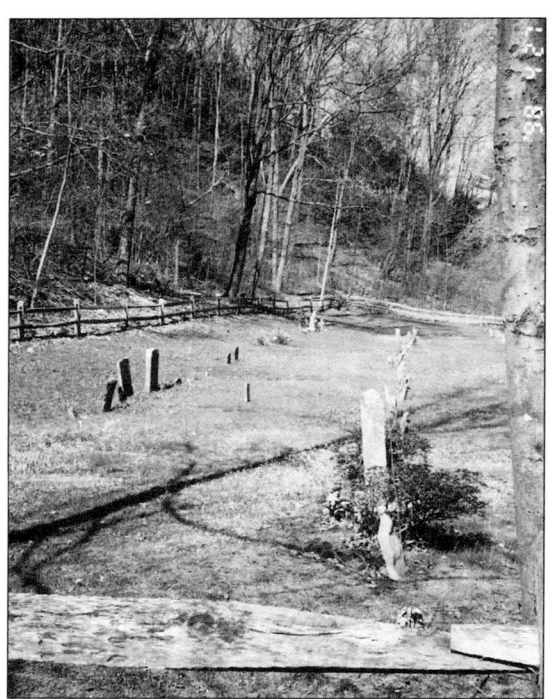

SCHAGHTICOKE BURIAL GROUND, KENT CONNECTICUT. According to Paulette Crone-Morange, Tribal Administrator, Schaghticoke historical and familial roots are found in Pequod, Mahican, and Pootatuck peoples. Aboriginal tribal lands stretched along the Oblong in eastern New York to the Housatonic River. European settlement pressed Christianized Schaghticokes farther east to the present reservation beyond the Webatuck/Ten Mile River over the Connecticut line. Tribal members rest here in the reservation burial grounds on the banks of the Housatonic. (JG.)

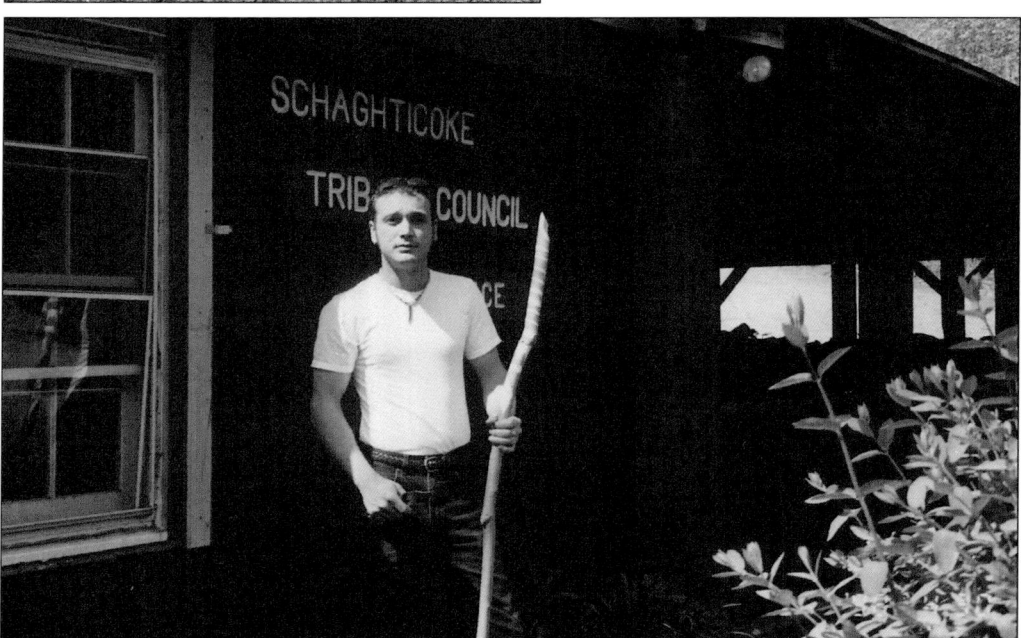

TERRY MANNING AND "TALKING STICK." Since 1752, the State of Connecticut has recognized this ground between the Housatonic and the Webatuck as Schaghticoke land. Today, many young Native Americans study their history and lore, proudly recapturing unique traditions, crafts, and skills to pass on to their children. Terry Manning, a Schaghticoke tribal-member responsible for the grounds of the 400-acre reservation beyond Bulls' Bridge, near Kent, is in the process of carving a "Talking Stick." (ST/JG.)

DOVER STONE CHURCH. Movements of earth and water over eons formed a cavern where light and the sound of moving water cast a spell. Magnetite in the rock fools compasses and ancient petroglyphs confound archaeologists. Schaghticoke adventurers, Paulette Crone-Morange, Luciann Lavin, and Donna Hearn, recently conquered the overgrown, boulder-strewn path along a dangerous gorge near Dover Plains to view the natural stone arch leading into a mystical place where time stands still. This revered place continues to mystify. (ST.)

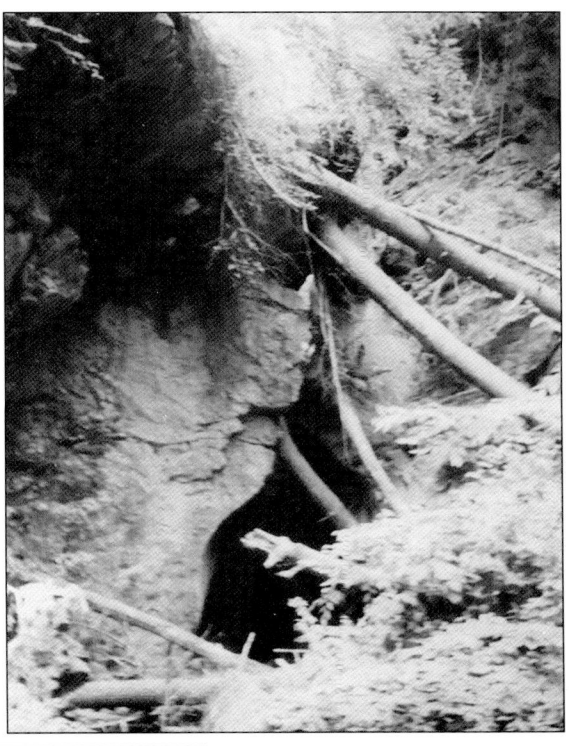

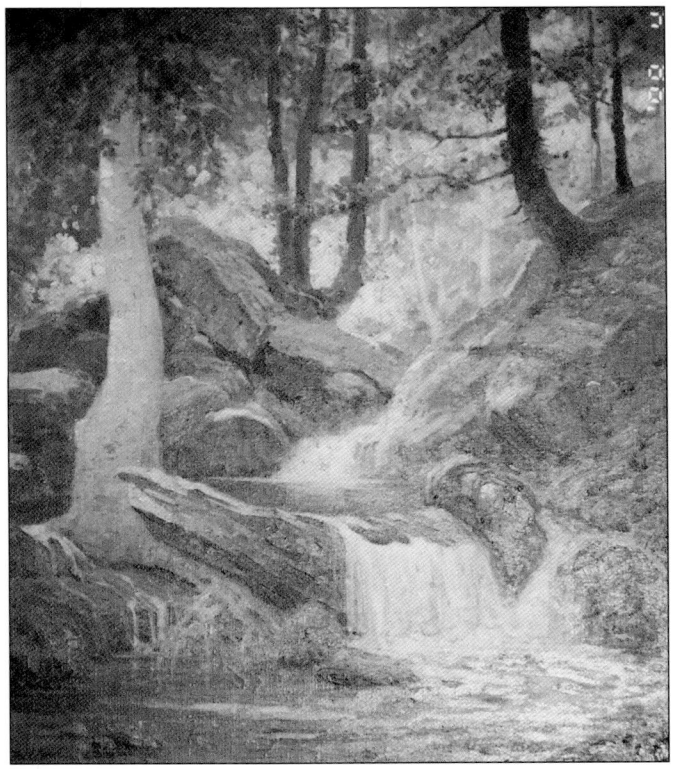

POWELL PAINTING OF "THE WELLS." Near "Stone Church" is a series of pools formed by the flow of Seven Wells Brook. Beautiful, but surrounded by slippery rocks, they are deep and dangerous. *The Wells* by Arthur Powell hangs on the walls of the J.H. Ketcham Fire Company with other paintings done by "The Dover Four," expatriate New York City artists who set up studios here during the WPA era and stayed to record the rural beauty of Dover. (JHKFC/JG.)

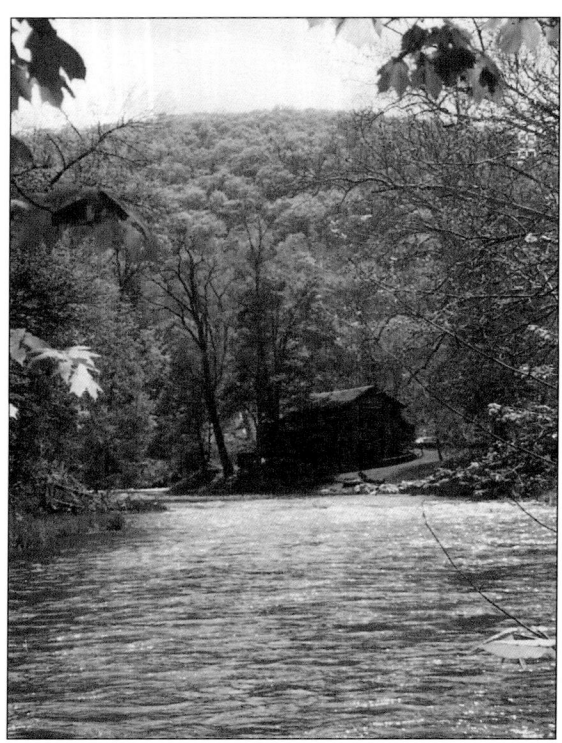

PRESTON MARBLE MILL SITE. Ebenezer Preston's family, among Dover's earliest settlers, came c. 1727 to the banks of the Webatuck/Ten Mile River. Their holdings included farms, mills, and quarry sites. Webatuck Craft Village in South Dover sits on a former Preston farm where three mills were powered by the current at a marble dam. An "s" turn in the river carried its flow into Connecticut. The river, source of potable water, fish, power, and recreation, is as important today as it was then. (JG.)

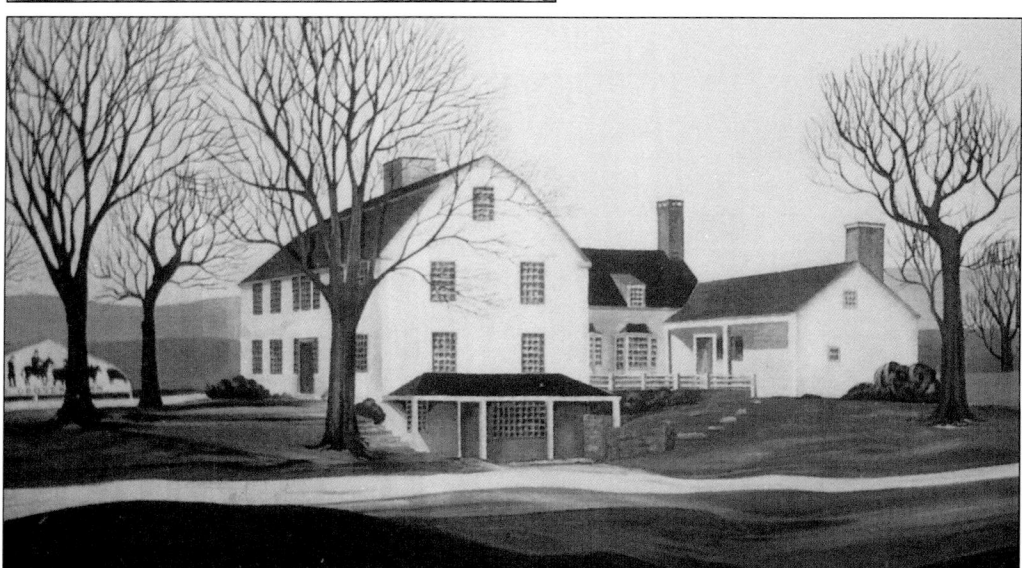

OLD DROVERS INN. Farmers accommodating travelers was a historic practice to attract cash. John Preston's 1750 farmstead on the Great Road from New York to Albany and Vermont became Clear Water Tavern. An 1840s barn-wall sign inviting drovers still beckons. Later owners imprinted personal touches on this National Register Inn. Historic site murals by Edward Paine were added to a careful restoration by Olin Chester Potter after 1937. Innkeepers Alice Pitcher and Kemper Peacock are pleased by the inn's inclusion in the world-renowned guide *Relais & Chateaux*. (AP.)

OLD DROVERS INN EARLY KITCHEN. Amid innovations, a reputation for fine food has remained constant—even when "cook" roasted the meat on an open spit and kept butter in the cooling well. In its early years, accommodations in the house were reserved for administrative drovers ("cowboys"), while those who actually worked the cattle ("anklebeaters") slept in the barn. Both house and barn dwellers enjoyed the tavern board, as do today's guests who are served by a "chef" from a modern well-appointed kitchen. (AP.)

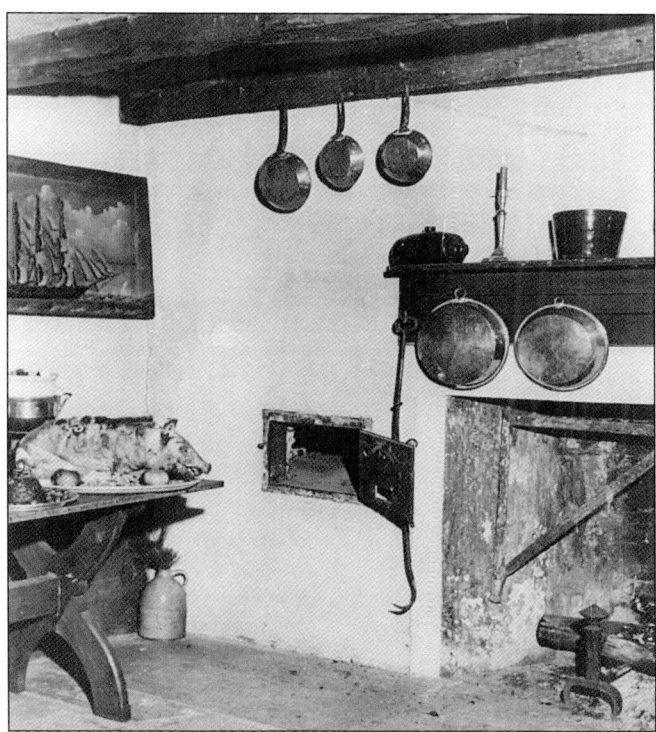

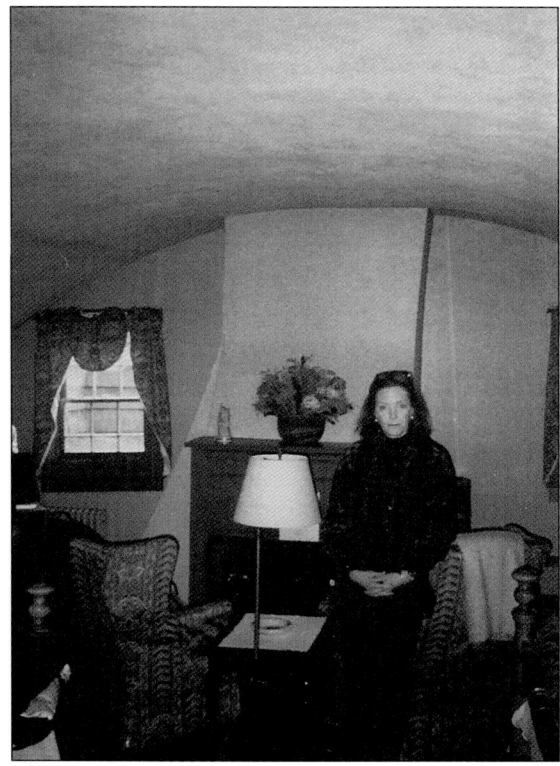

THE "MEETING ROOM." Alice Pitcher, the innkeeper, takes pleasure in the lively history of the house, including clientele like Richard and Elizabeth Burton. Guests vie for the "Meeting Room," Preston's barrel-vaulted upstairs room with its window benches, one of few spaces large enough for early public meetings. Here Dover Township was separated from Pawling in 1807. The imagined sounds of raucous debates and drovers' noisy partying echo through the dreams of those who now rest snugly in its quilt-covered beds. (JG.)

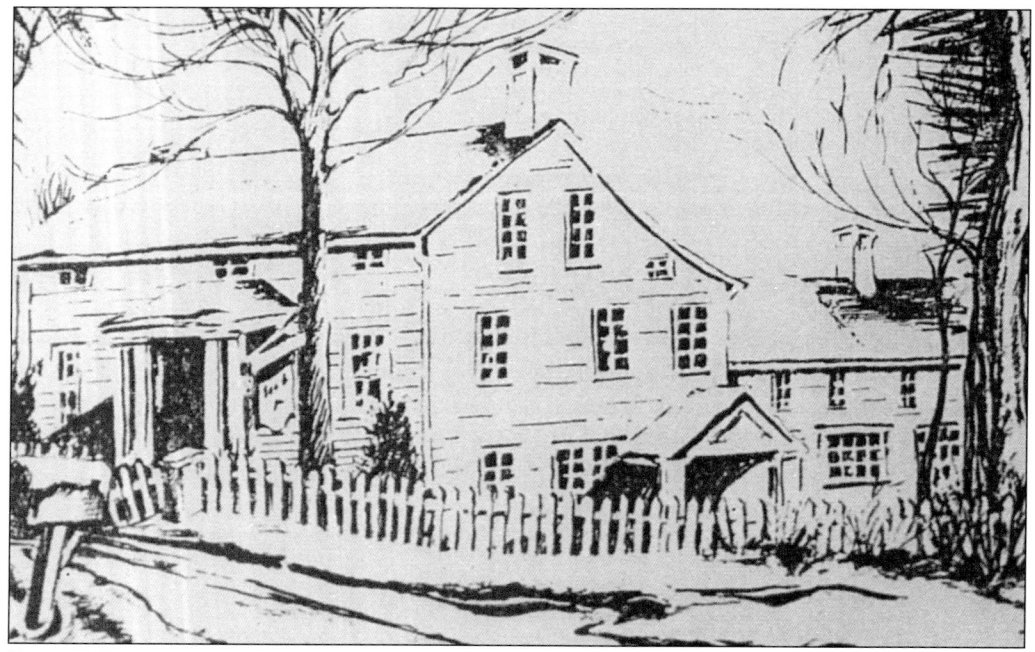

PALMER FARM AT DOVER FURNACE. The home of John and Hope Thomas Palmer, still a working farm today on Dover Furnace Road, was built before the American Revolution. According to local lore, this was the scene of a dramatic confrontation between British soldiers who came to arrest Palmer for revolutionary activities. They were held at bay by Palmer's daughter Mary who suffered a bayonet stab wound while her father escaped through a back door. (LB.)

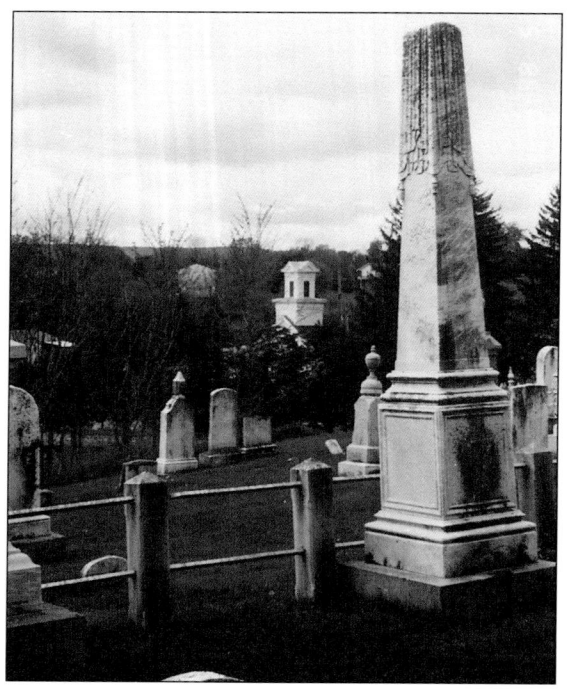

SOUTH DOVER CEMETERY. This peaceful burial ground rises on a hill beyond the home of Dover's earliest congregation; the First Baptist Church organized in 1757. The next year founders built a small structure east of the property known as "Red Meeting House." In *Old Gravestones*, Poucher states that the cemetery was probably intended by the congregation to be used as a community burial ground. It overlooks the Methodist church formed in 1852. (JG.)

DOVER PLAINS SECOND BAPTIST CHURCH. Preacher Samuel Waldo, who served the First Baptist Church in Wingdale, should get some credit for the Greek Revival style Second Baptist Church on Mill Street in Dover Plains. Waldo's First Baptist Church of Pawlingstown in South Dover, miles from Dover Plains, served congregants from all over Dover. A year after the good preacher's death in 1793, members who lived in Dover Plains were inspired to petition Waldo's church for their own congregation—the Second Baptist Church. (JG.)

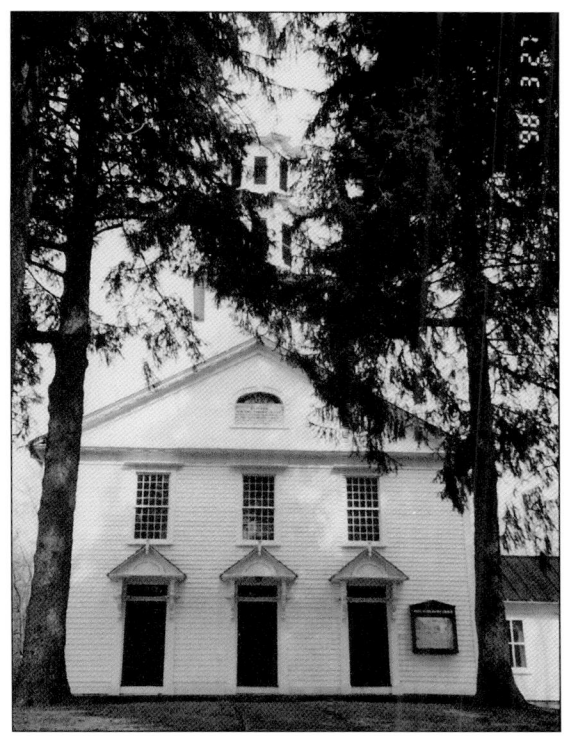

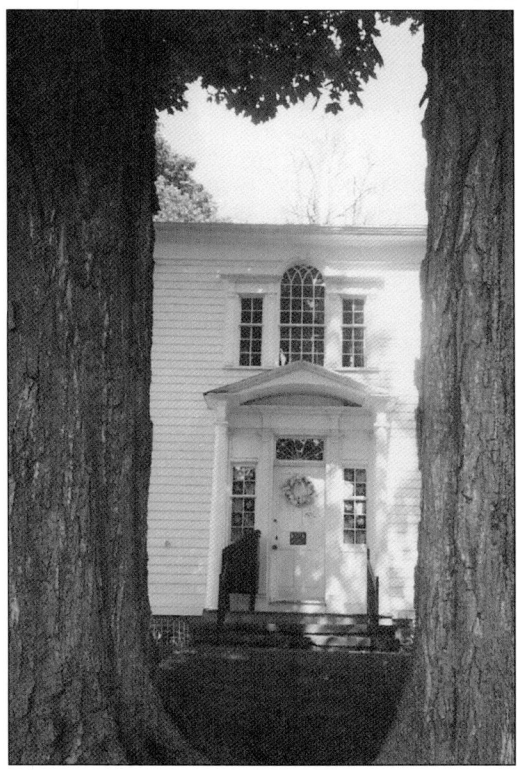

TABOR-WING HOUSE DOVER PLAINS. According to Town Clerk Caroline Reichenberg, Mahlon Wing's home was built c. 1813 by members of two families with roots deep in Harlem Valley history. The Wings, among the earliest Quaker families to emigrate here, married into other local families, in Mahlon's case, to a Tabor. Many a Baptist, or Methodist, has Quaker forebears. Jackson Wing's Tavern in Wingdale hosted the meeting that gave Dover its name, and Mahlon's home serves as town library. (JG.)

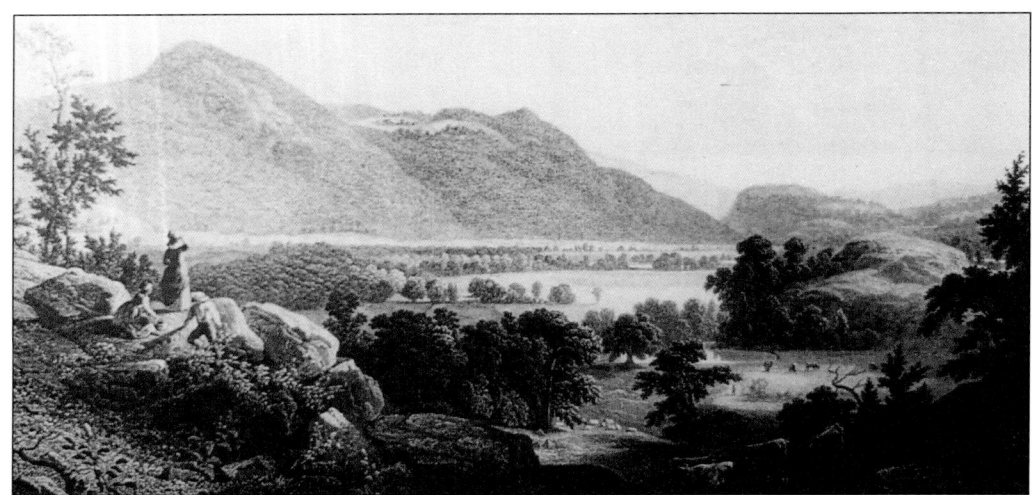

ASHER DURAND VIEW OF DOVER PLAINS. Asher Brown Durand (1796-1886) is among the respected painters of the Hudson River School of landscape art. The beauty of the Harlem Valley is apparent in an etching of his epic *Dover Plains, Dutchess County, New York* 1848 painting, now in the Smithsonian collection. Even before the railroad came, the valley attracted intellectuals and artists seeking inspiration, and visitors in search of recreation. (DCHS.)

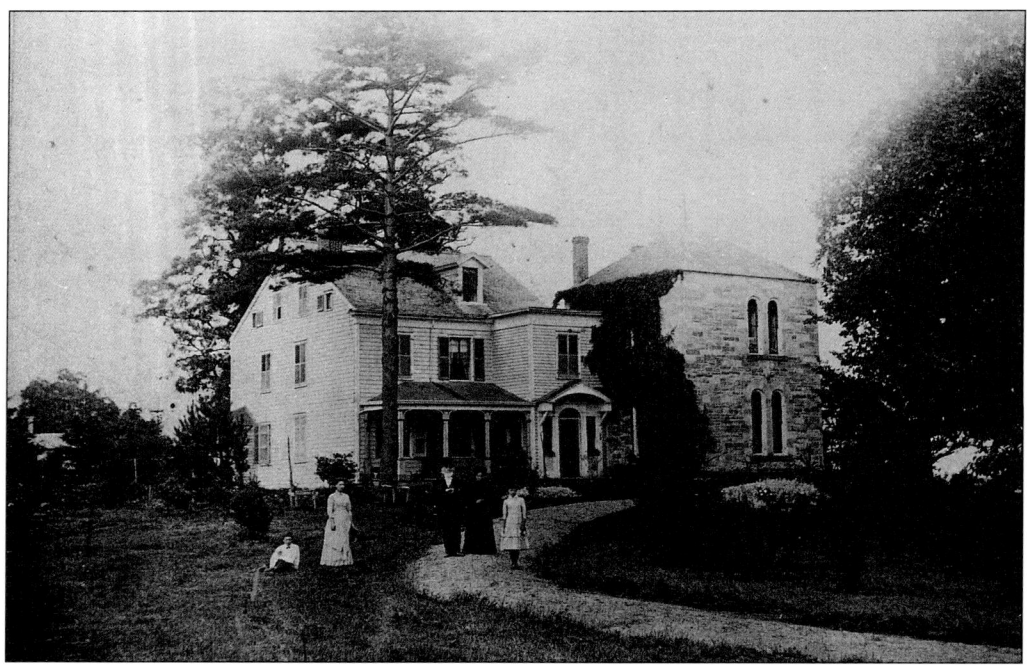

BENSON J. LOSSING HOME ON CHESTNUT RIDGE. Lossing (1813-1891) combined careers as he was a journalist, historian, and artist. Carefully researched, his still important works on American history were illustrated by meticulous engravings of sites along the east coast that he visited and, like Durand, sketched. Lossing worked in the stone tower of a farmstead built in 1801 by Nehemiah Sweet, his father-in-law. A c. 1880 photograph of the family at home shows the tower and house, still intact today on Holsapple Road. (DCHS.)

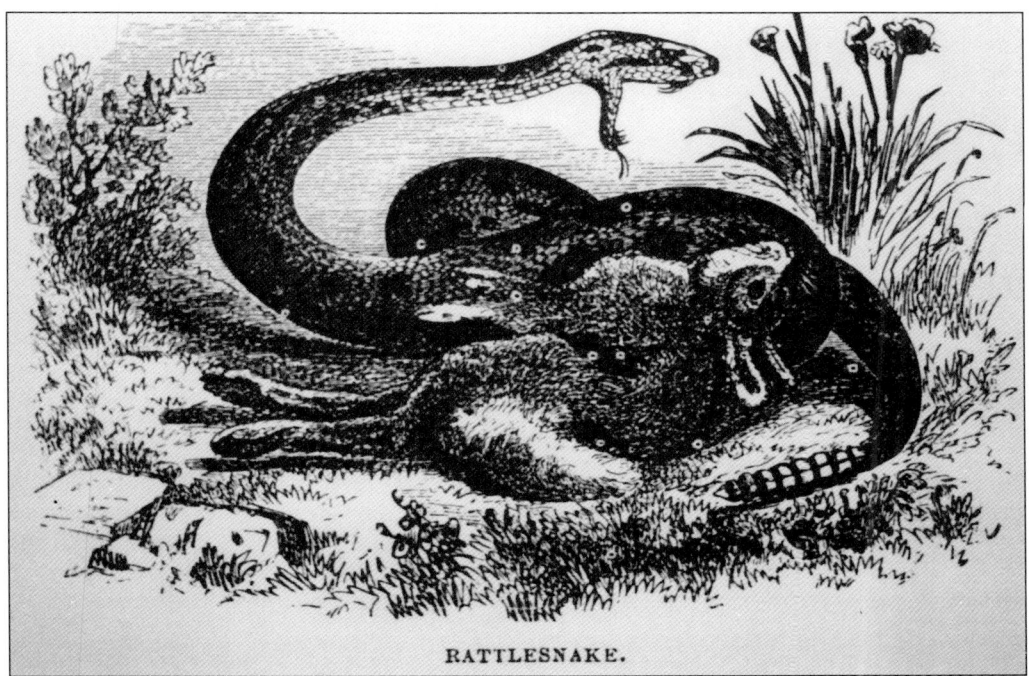

BENSON LOSSING DRAWING FROM THE HUDSON. Lossing learned about rattlers as a valley farm boy. Formal self-education began with apprenticeship to a watchmaker who eventually became his partner. By 22, he was partner/editor of *The Poughkeepsie Telegraph* where he learned wood engraving from J.A. Adams, illustrator of *The Casket,* the paper's literary journal. It was the beginning of a lifelong career in writing and illustrating that earned him recognition for his scholarship. (DCHS.)

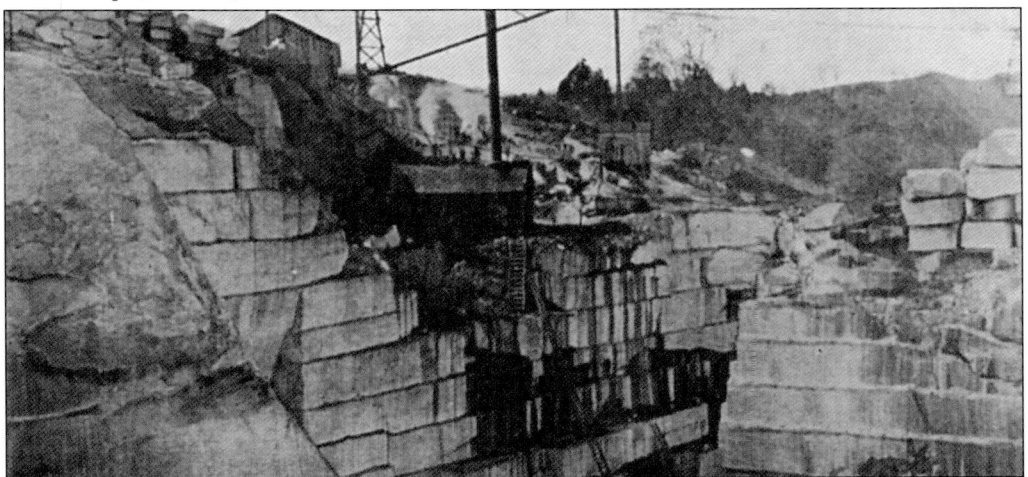

SOUTH DOVER MARBLE QUARRY. Quarries have been operating in the Harlem Valley since the 18th century. The coming of the Harlem Line in the mid-19th century improved access to markets and offered employment for Italian immigrants, many with skills learned in their original homeland. Stone bridge abutments rising out of the Ten Mile River south of Reagan's Mills Bridge testify to an electric work trolley that once connected quarry and finishing plant near the railroad in Wingdale. (HC.)

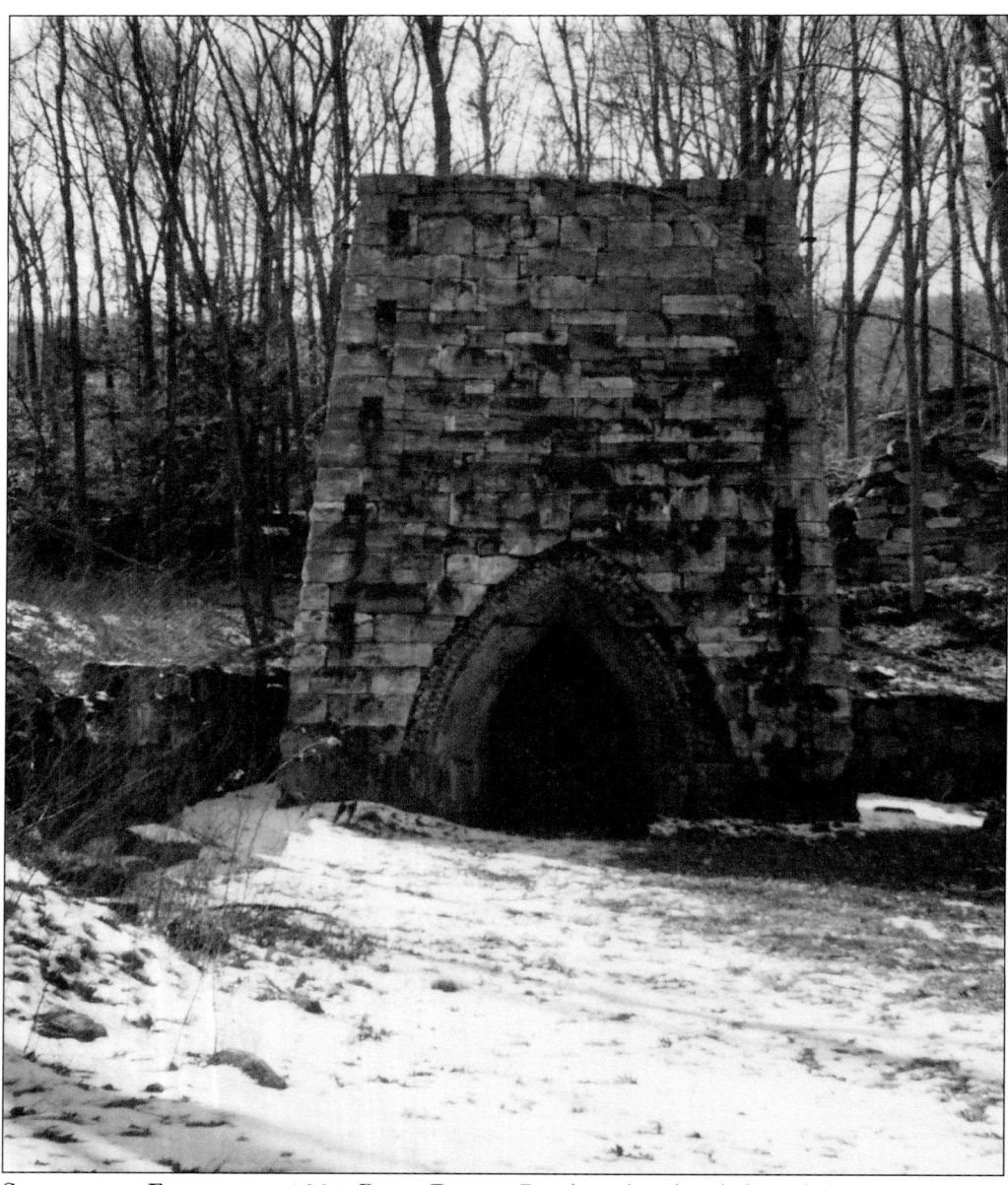

SHARPAROON FURNACE, C. 1881. Dover Furnace Road was lined with farms belonging to either Cutlers or Vincents whose land adjoined the works of the Dutchess County Iron Works or the South Boston Iron Company. For a generation, farmers and furnace owners negotiated, trading soil for mineral rights beneath the ground. Land transactions from 1864 to 1884 point to a former quarry, Sharparoon Pond, as the main interest. Since the late 1920s, city youngsters at New York City Mission Society's Camp—known now as Camp Minisink—have trekked its grounds to view the shell of South Boston Iron Company's Sharparoon Furnace. Huge marble-faced furnaces attest to an industry that thrived in Dover from the 18th century. Fueled by charcoal and belching fire, the furnaces smelted ore to be formed into "pigs" i.e. iron bars. These were shipped out and made into useful products. Campers delight in collecting beautifully colored slag still remaining from the smelting process a century ago. (JG.)

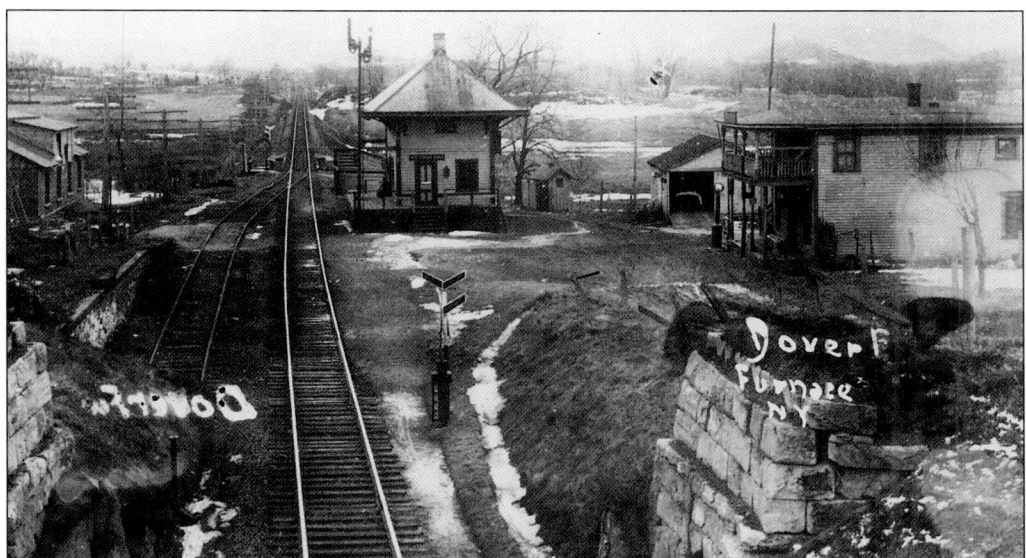

DOVER FURNACE STATION. The railroad enlivened "the Furnace." The overpass and original station were replaced c. 1910 by the Harlem Line. The two-story station housed a waiting room with station master's quarters upstairs. A hotel, store, cattle pen, storage barns for farm products awaiting shipping, the W.S. Sterling Co. making dry goods, and a spur to the South Boston Iron Co. furnace were here. Regular daily stops were made for freight, mail, and passengers, including students going to classes. (LB.)

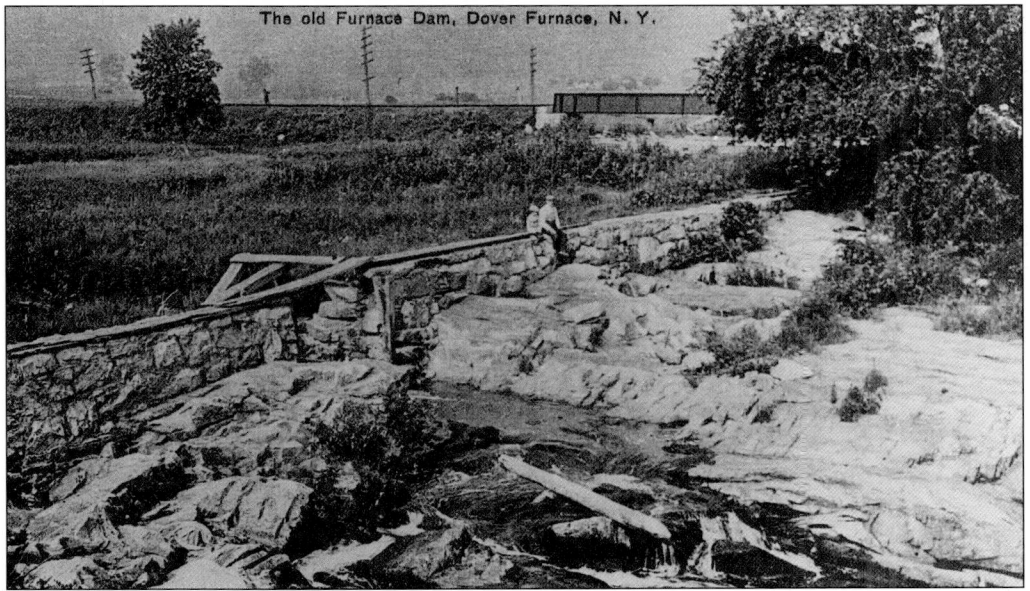

DAM ON THE SWAMP RIVER. Dover streams powered everything from gristmills to generators. Upriver, a dam over the Swamp River west of Dover Furnace provided waterpower for the South Boston Iron Company. The 1938 hurricane destroyed much of their equipment, still visible from the road. Down river, in the 1920s, the owner of the W.S. Sterling Co. planned to use waterpower to generate electricity for both his factory and employees' homes but did not complete the plant. (LB.)

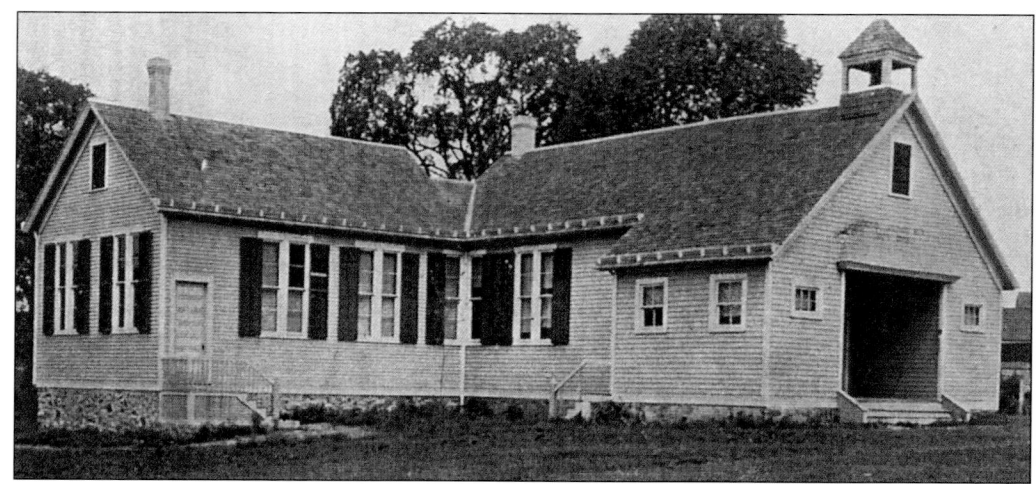

WINGDALE SCHOOL. New York mandated public schools in 1795, but most rural communities supported only eight grades of education linked to farm season work. A 19th-century map outlines 12 neighborhood school districts in Dover accommodating those within walking distance or near a rail line. Lou Grogan tells of a teacher in the 1920s commuting from Wingdale to a one-room school in Dover Furnace by train. Young female teachers were boarded locally, paid a pittance, and directed not to marry. (LB.)

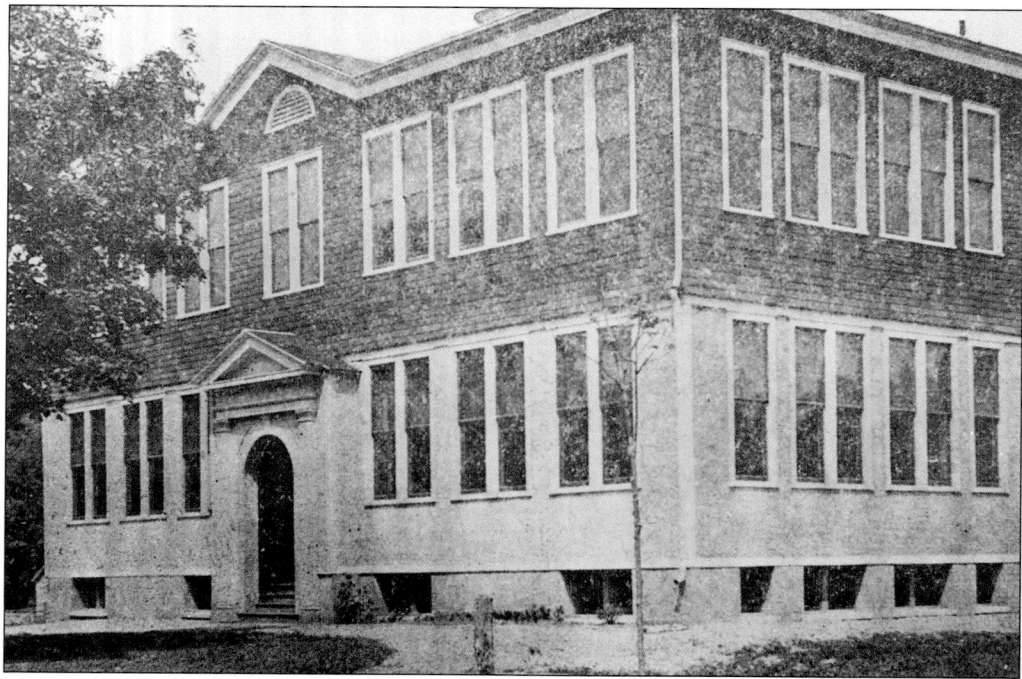

UNION FREE SCHOOL, DOVER PLAINS. Lenora Buck also recalls train rides to school from Dover Furnace to Dover Plains in the 1940s. Until the mid-20th century, when central school districts brought busing, transportation options were still limited to trains, horses, or feet. The Dover Plains Union Free School, established in 1908, was the first in town to house 12 grades. By the 1940s, the building was showing its age. Older students upstairs found joy in annoying elementary teachers downstairs by purposely bouncing on the squeaky floorboards. (LB.)

JENNIE MOREY'S REPORT CARD, 1890. In 1850, Arthur E. Bangs applied to the state for "guns and accouterments" for a military academy/select school. It was immediately fully subscribed. Long before Virginia Military Institute gave over to co-education, Norman Benson's grandmother proved an excellent student, making all 9s and 10s at Dover Plains Military Academy which admitted girls. A spring examination for the same school in 1892 calls it "Dover Plains Academy," suggesting less emphasis on military aspects. (NB.)

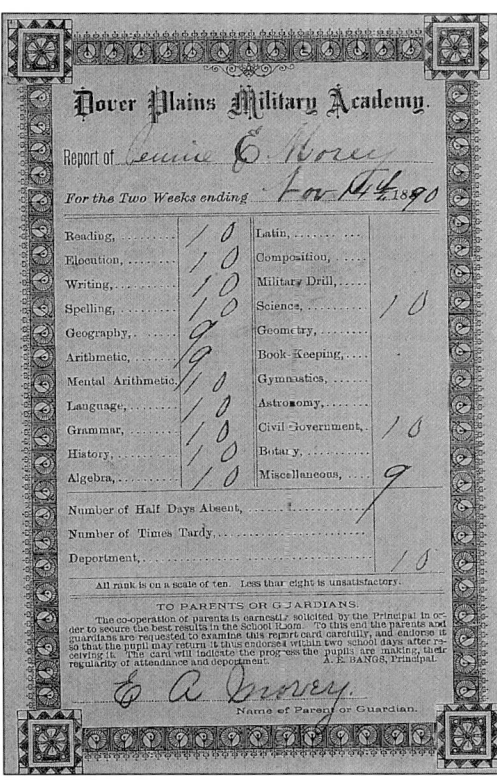

SCHOOL TAX BILL, 1897. Most of us would willingly trade school tax bills with Emmanuel Benson, Norman Benson's grandfather, who is on record in 1897 as paying $13.08 to James S. Brant, the local tax collector. By using his own business, stationery Brant may have saved the district a few dollars, but in exchange he got free advertising for his contracting and building business: " Estimates Cheerfully Given." (NB.)

J.H. KETCHAM. John Henry Ketcham (1832-1906) proves the adage that heroes are made, not born. He earned his stripes on a local farm and marble business before election as town supervisor, going on to serve in both State Assembly and Senate. The Civil War was a watershed for Ketcham when he was appointed by Governor Morgan to the War Committee and later commissioned to raise the 150th N.Y. Infantry. The war took a heavy toll, leaving him with a severe hearing loss. (LB.)

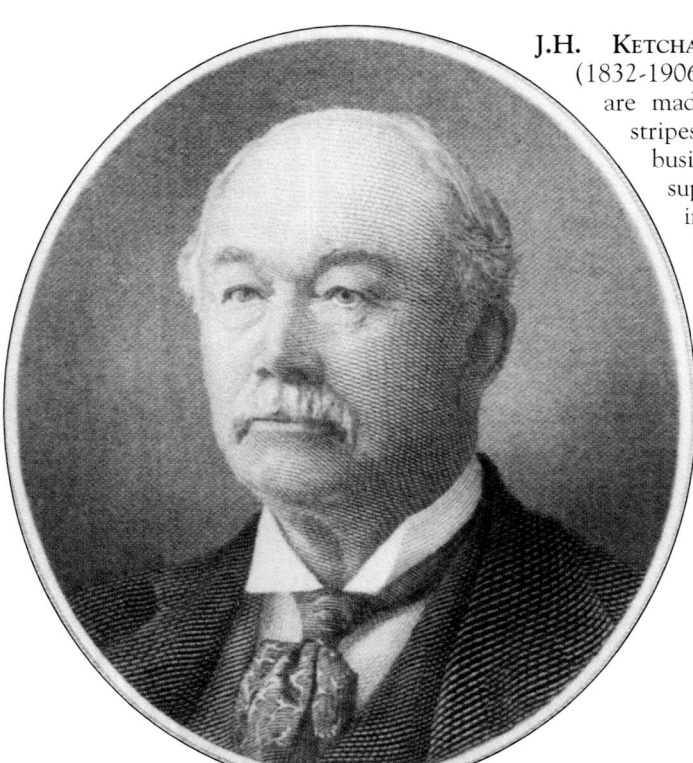

DR. WELLMAN'S BILL FOR SERVICES. Not all town heroes become famous, but communities remote from modern health services during the last century were dependent upon the skills and patience of those like Dr. George Marvin Wellman, who made house calls. His Civil War service as a Washington D.C. hospital ward master led him to Georgetown Medical College where he completed his studies in 1868. In 1869, Dover was his next and last stop. (AM.)

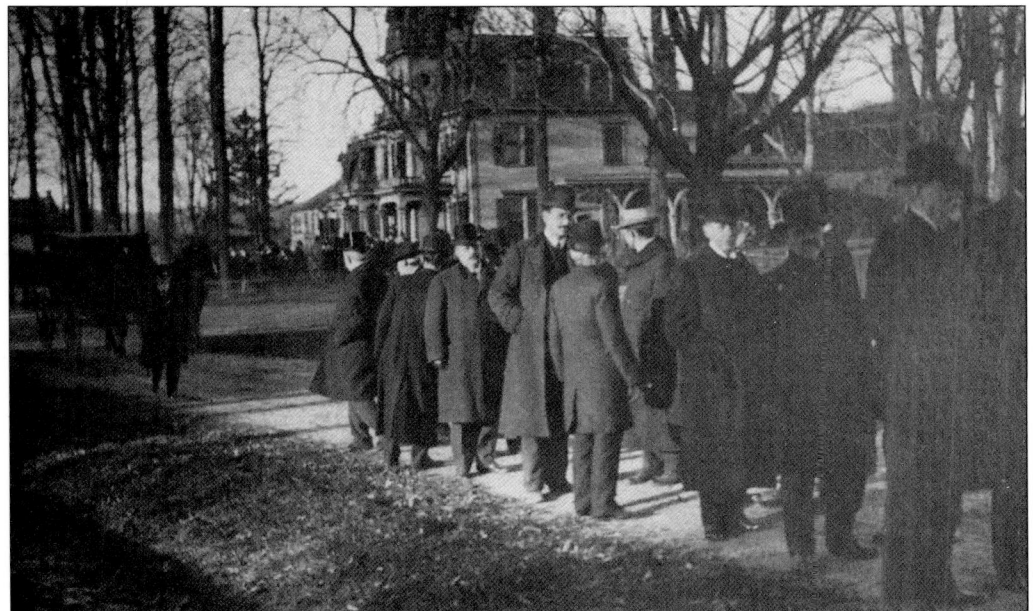

CONGRESSMAN KETCHAM'S FUNERAL, 1906. After the Civil War General Ketcham ran for Congress, where he served for 34 years despite war-related deafness, which he made an asset. This old-fashioned practical politician believed, according to many congressmen and senators who eulogized his passing, that "to the victors belong the spoils." His family's handsome Victorian residence on the corner of Route 22 and Mill Street, now the site of a popular delicatessen, was the setting for a state funeral of epic proportions. (LB.)

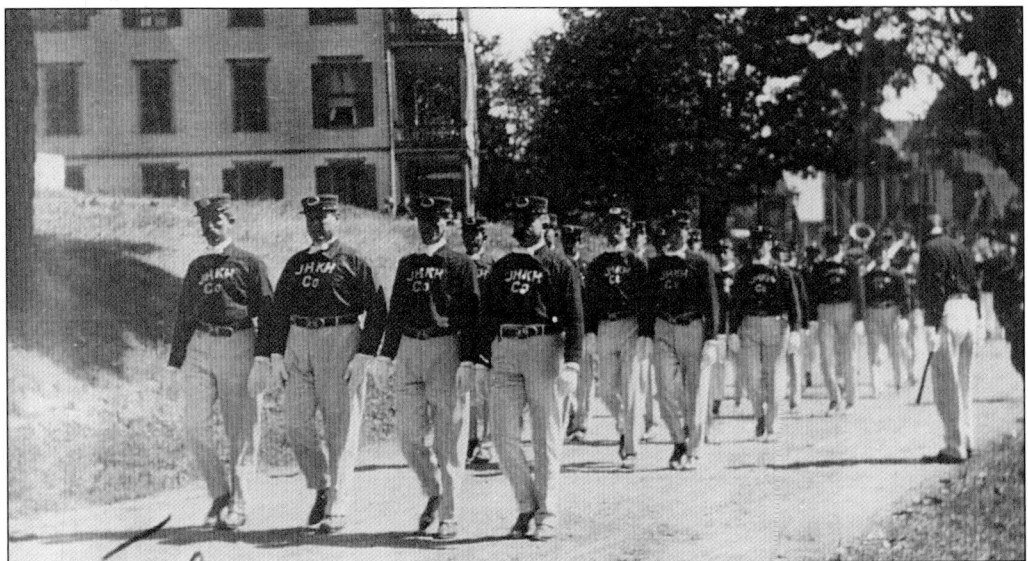

FIRE COMPANY ON PARADE. In 1903, three years before Congressman Ketcham died, he was honored by the new fire company that took his name. Richard Polhemus' great-grandfather John Hanna, shown here with baton in hand, was a proud member of the John H. Ketcham Fire Company, serving as chief from 1903 to 1936. Countywide firemen's parades gave hard-working volunteers an opportunity to show off their military demeanor and fire-fighting skills. (RP.)

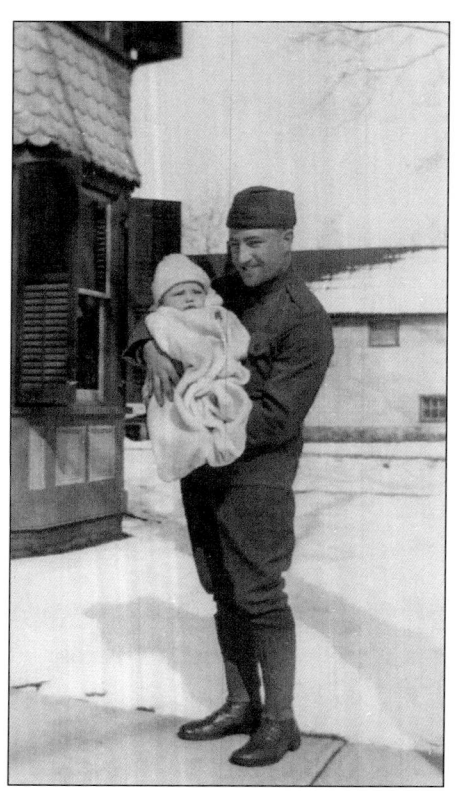

WYMAN WW I SERVICEMAN. Several generations of Richard Wyman's family have been doing business in Dover Plains selling feed and coal, fixing cars, and brokering insurance. Infant Harold Wyman was proudly held by his father, a WW I soldier on leave c. 1917. Like many other young family men, Harold's father set aside his own interests to join in the effort to end aggression in the "War to End All Wars," but sadly lost his life the next year. (RW.)

FIRST MOTORIZED FIRE ENGINE. According to Frank Kelly, a 50-year member of the J.H. Ketcham Hose Company, this Wyman photograph from the 1930s shows members proudly seated atop the 1927 motorized Seagraves fire engine. Chief Creque (at the wheel) is seated between James Benson (with mustache) and Dover banker Thomas Boyce. Kellys have served as chiefs through three generations. Wymans, in the garage business with an interest in motor vehicles, have been active volunteers from the company's early years. (RW.)

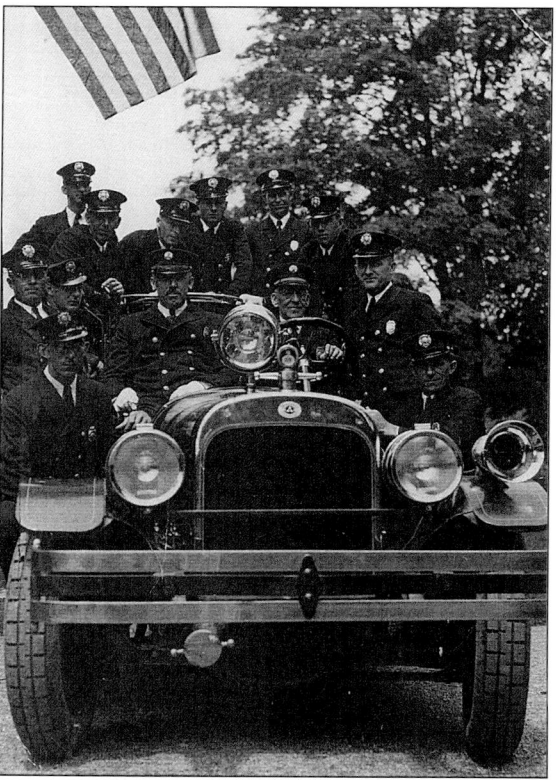

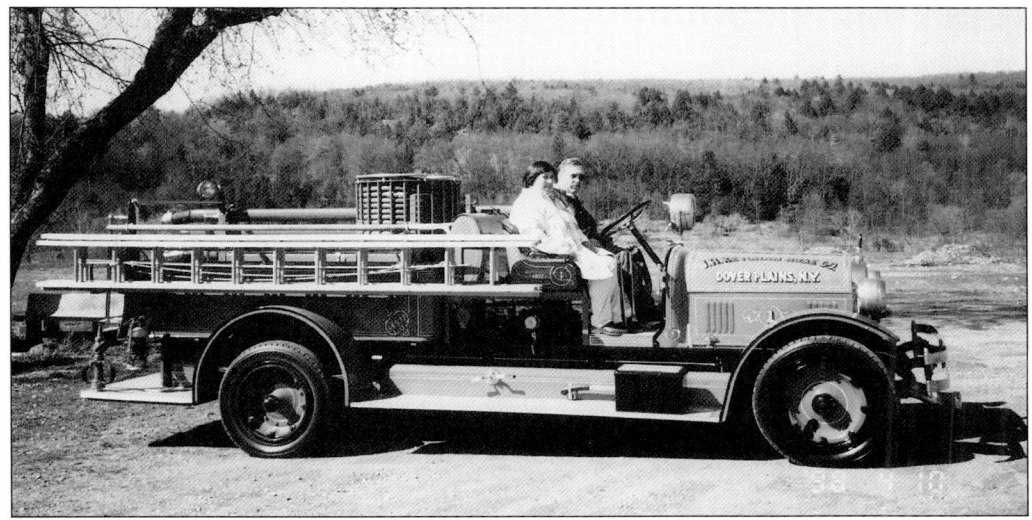

THE RESTORED ENGINE. When that vintage fire engine had outlived its usefulness as a working vehicle, it was sold to Union Vale Fire Company. In recent years, the new generation of volunteers bought it back and raised funds for its restoration. Bob Sartori, current fire chief, and his wife, Bridget, president, are actively involved in the company. They took part in the restoration effort and enjoy showing off the engine, which is brought out frequently for parades and demonstrations. (JHKFC/JG.)

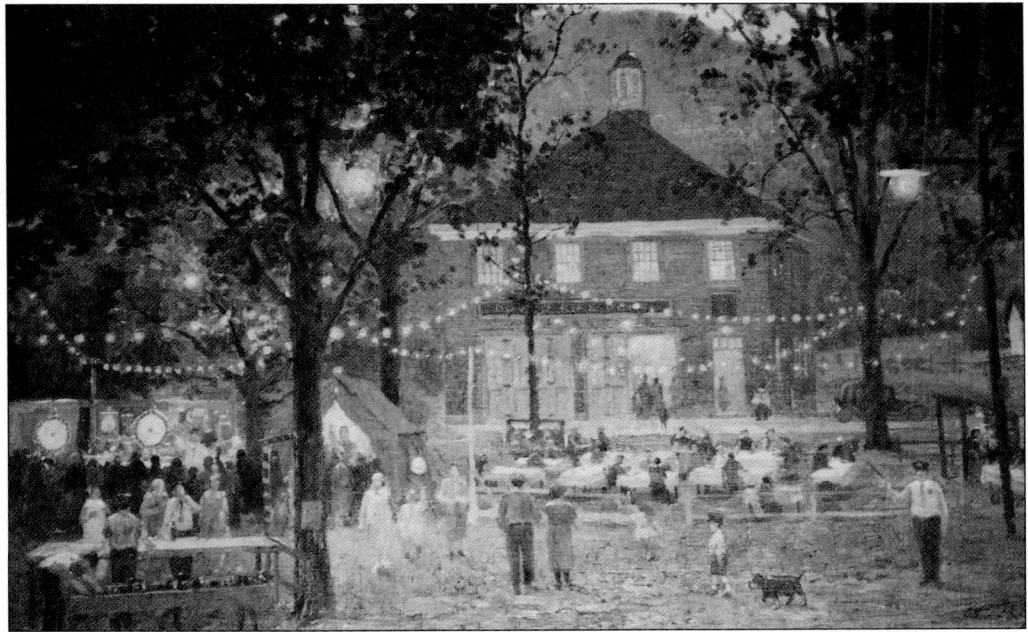

FIREMAN'S CARNIVAL AT THE FIRE COMPANY. Arthur Powell's painting of a J.H.K. Firehouse Carnival in Dover Plains hangs in the chief's office today. It captures the spirit of a small rural town at play. The firehouse built in 1932 had become the center of local events and activities—dinners, fund-raisers, training exercises—and a gallery for a number of the paintings of "The Dover Plains Four" WPA era artists. Some of their other works are found in the junior high school. (JHKFC/JG.)

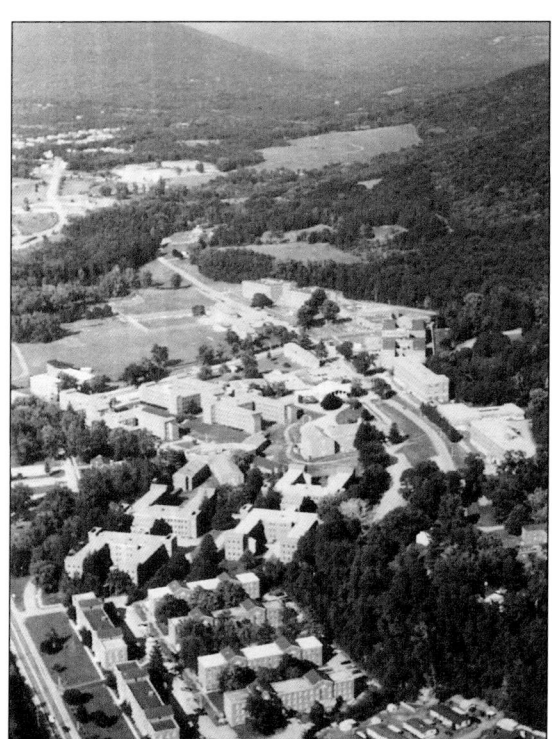

HARLEM VALLEY PSYCHIATRIC CENTER AIR PHOTOGRAPH. The 20th-century decline of farming and mining led to government endeavor to stimulate the local economy. Construction of the "State Hospital," as it was known in the 1930s, brought jobs to the area. Efforts by former County Executive Pattison and State Senator Rolison in the 1980s located the Division for Youth there. In February 1994, the Psychiatric Center was closed. Today, the Harlem Valley Partnership for Economic Development, citizens, and planners seek new economic strategies to recycle the facility. (HVP.)

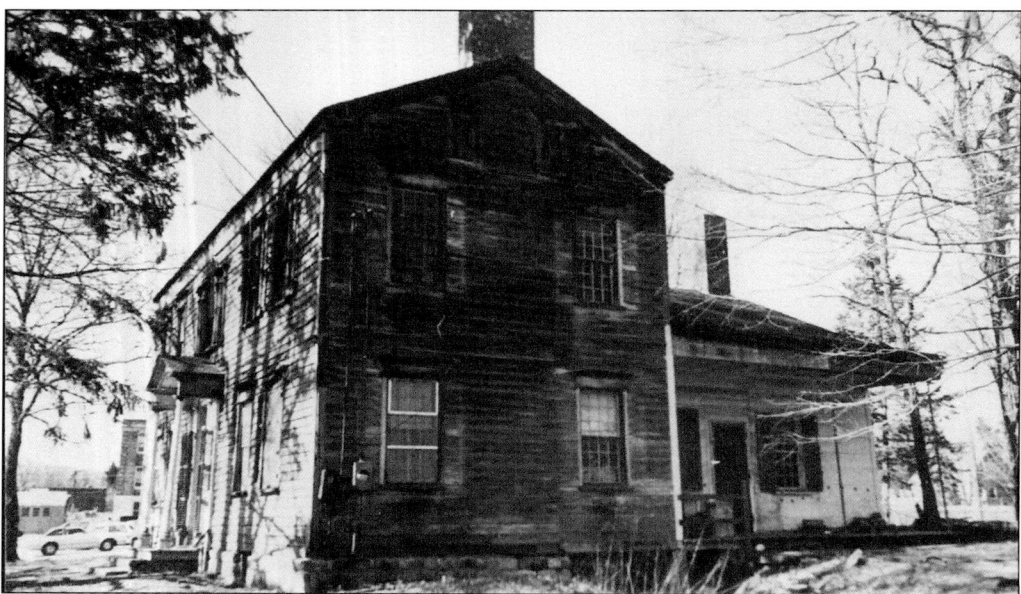

TABOR WING HOUSE BEFORE RESTORATION. The Bicentennial of the American Revolution in the 1970s lit a fire under many communities, encouraging renewed interest in their past. The work of local citizens like Caroline Reichenberg and Doris Diedrick brought the founding of the Dover Plains Historical Society, which in turn purchased and restored the deteriorated Tabor-Wing House. Their successful effort improved the town center while providing an important history lesson. (CR.)

THE GREAT CHAIR AT WEBATUCK. Historic Preston properties gained new life and identity in the 20th century as a result of the work of the Hunt family who moved here in the 1920s and turned outbuildings into craftsmen's workshops. Shelley M. Hunt followed his father, Lockwood, and Uncle Julian into the furniture building business and introduced other crafts to the complex as a marketing idea in 1969. The Great Chair, an eye-grabber, lures customers to Webatuck Craft Village. (JG.)

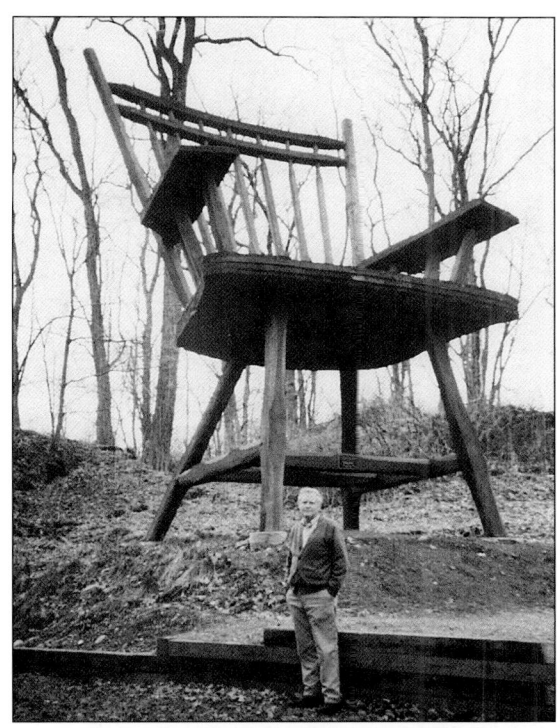

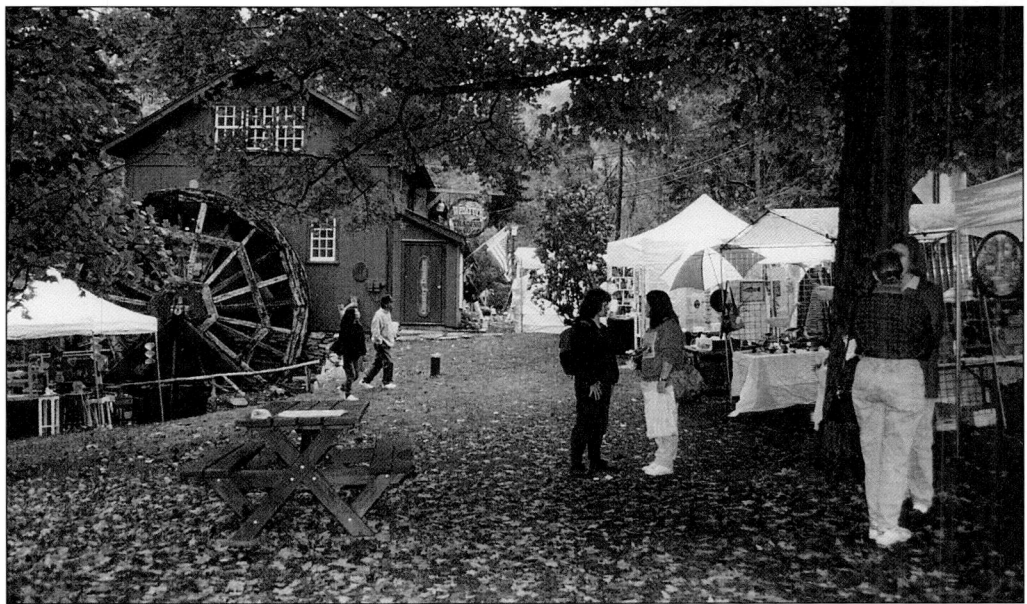

WEBATUCK CRAFT VILLAGE CRAFT FAIR. Today's Webatuck residents foresee Heritage Tourism as a strong economic focus in the future. Seasonal fairs like the Strawberry Moon and Harvest Festivals build upon the area's artistic, historic, and scenic resources to attract craft exhibitors and shoppers. The shores of the Ten Mile River at Dog Tail Road, where Schaghticokes once crafted household items and tools, now shelter furniture builders and a host of artisans in many media. (WR.)

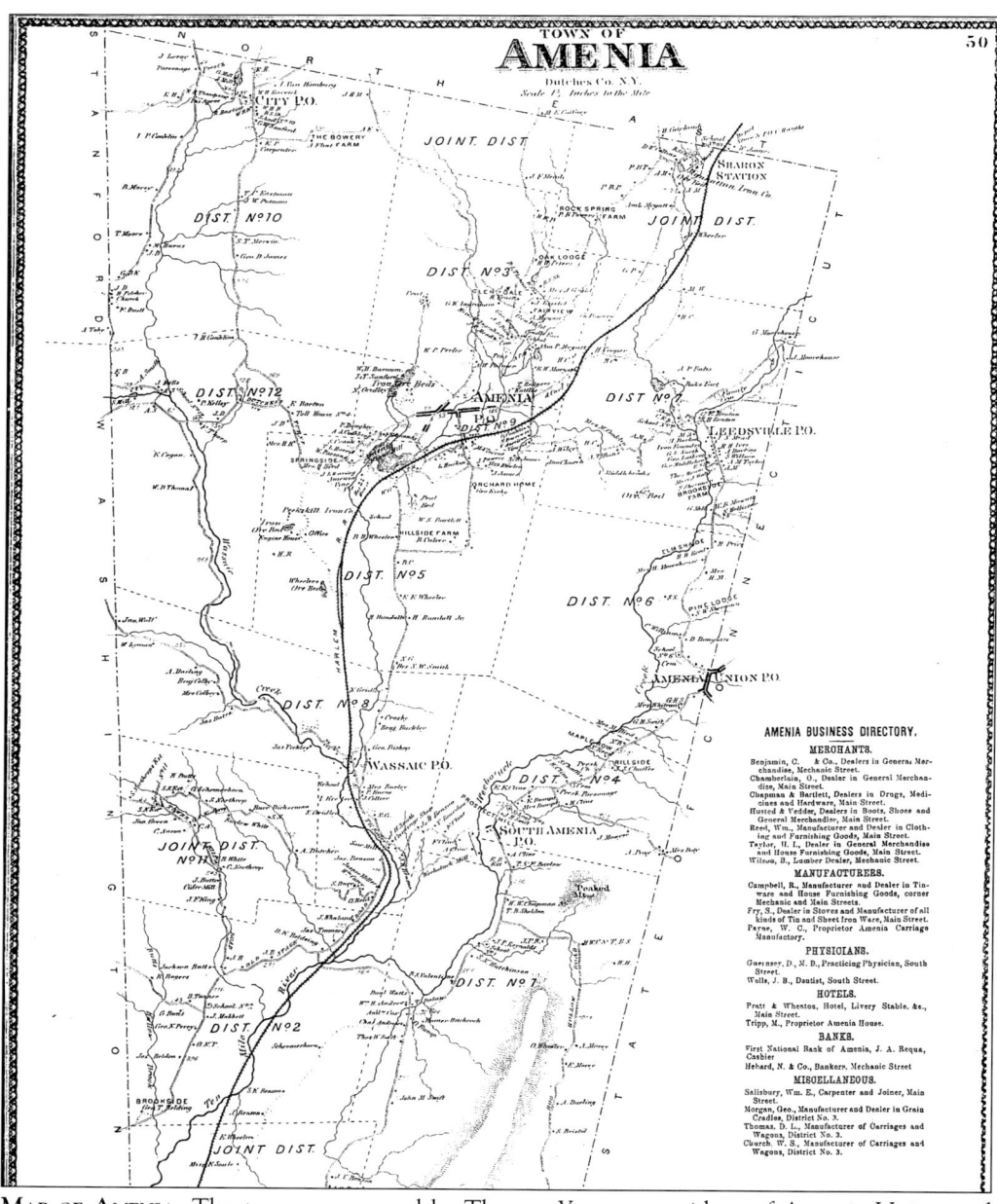

MAP OF AMENIA. The town was named by Thomas Young, a resident of Amenia Union and a poet who derived "Amenia" from the Latin word "amoena" meaning "pleasant to the eye." This 19th-century map shows the town and its hamlets: Leedsville, Amenia Union, and South Amenia in the Oblong; Wassaic and Amenia along the Harlem Railroad; and in the northwest, "The City," which at the end of the 19th century became known as Smithfield. The present-day borders of Amenia, one of the original towns in the county, date from 1823 when what was known as North Amenia, which also included Federal Square to the west and Coleman's Station to the east, was ceded to North East and the name of the post office changed to North East Center. The relative importance of the various hamlets has changed through the centuries. (MQ.)

Three

AMENIA

Sometime before 1711, Richard Sackett, one of the Little Nine Partners who was never able to clarify his title to land in the Oblong, is credited as starting the first white settlement at "Washiack." The settlement was near the "Steel Works" where a furnace and foundry were built during the Revolutionary War. It is probable that Sackett encouraged the Palatines, victims of religious persecution and economic exploitation, to settle in Amenia. Around 1740, families also began to come from New England, hoping to enjoy religious liberty and to better their futures by the purchase of cheap farms.

Until the coming of the railroad in the mid-19th century, most families relied on varied farming and the iron mining industry for their livelihoods. However, after Gail Borden located his first condensed milk factory in Wassaic with the financial support of Noah Gridley, owner of the Gridley Iron Works, dairy farming became dominant. After Gridley's death in 1887, his business came to an end.

In the late 1920s and early 1930s, New York State sited the "State School" in Wassaic; a self-sufficient community, the school became the largest employer. In the second half of this century, dairy farming gradually declined, sometimes replaced by horse breeding, and the future of the State School has become uncertain. Train service, which had been ended north of Dover, is being restored as far as Wassaic. To the north, the Harlem Valley Rail Trail on the former railroad bed has become a popular destination for residents and visitors alike.

The natural beauty and tranquillity of Amenia have always attracted renowned thinkers such as John Burroughs, Joel Spingarn, and Lewis Mumford. New England farmers pursuing religious liberty and cheap land, Irish and Italian emigrants looking for employment, Jewish families seeking better educational opportunities, and city dwellers desiring a respite from urban life have all been drawn to Amenia.

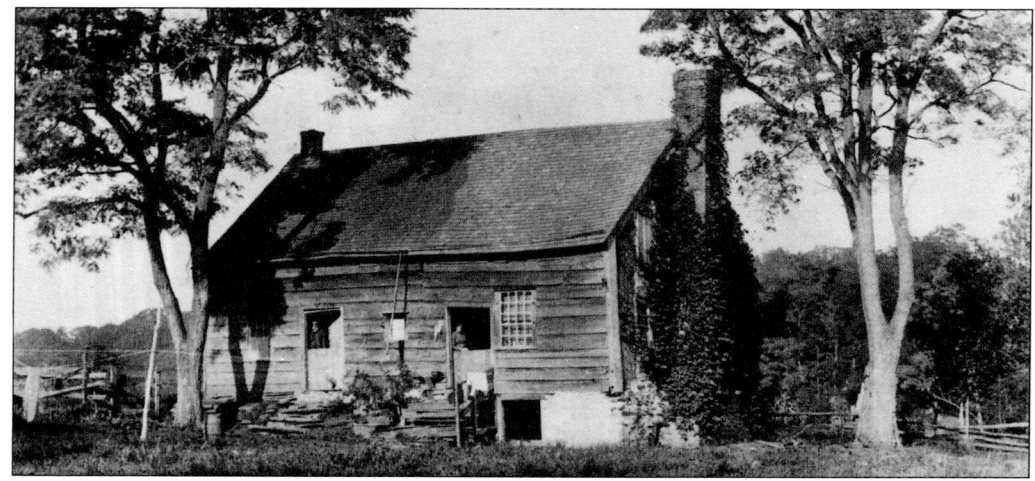

DELAMETER HOUSE. Capt. Isaac Delameter of Huguenot ancestry came from Kingston, New York, in 1740; his son John, who married Maria Kip, built the house in 1761. Black bricks inlaid among the red bricks of the east gable wall record the initials J, M, and D. Caleb Benton from Connecticut acquired the homestead in 1794. His grandson Myron, a friend of Burroughs, Thoreau, and Emerson, named the property Troutbeck after the almost pet trout that frolicked in the brook. (Benton Collection, DCHS.)

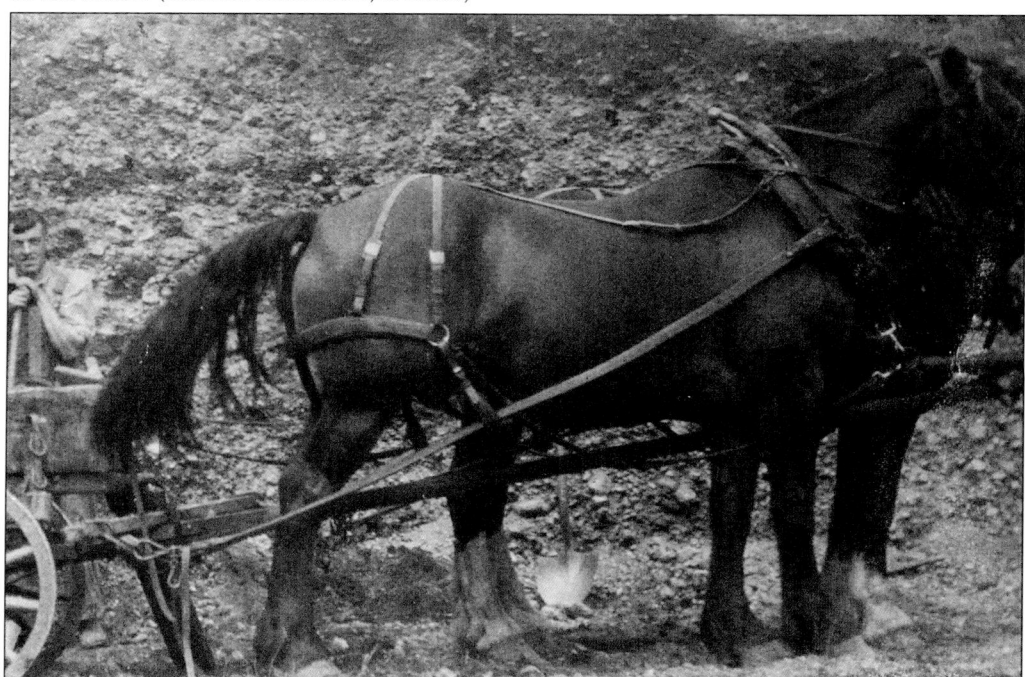

HENRY DUFFY AND HORSES. Henry Duffy, who emigrated from Ireland c. 1909, was the superintendent of Troutbeck for the Spingarn family, who had acquired it after the turn of the century. He is shown here getting gravel from the river for the roads in and around Troutbeck, which is on Leedsville Road. Leedsville, reputedly named after Leeds in England, home of one of the workers in an early 19th-century woolen mill owned by the Bentons, was a commercial center and the "chief point" of the township until 1835. (MQ.)

AMENIA FIELD DAY. Joel Spingarn, a retired professor from Columbia University who was interested in the well-being of rural Amenia, founded Amenia Field Day: a "countryside day of free and wholesome recreation managed by the whole community." Held at Troutbeck, it attracted not only neighbors and friends, but also those from the entire Harlem Valley and beyond, more than ten thousand in 1913. It gained national prominence, but the outbreak of WW I in 1914 signaled its end. (MQ.)

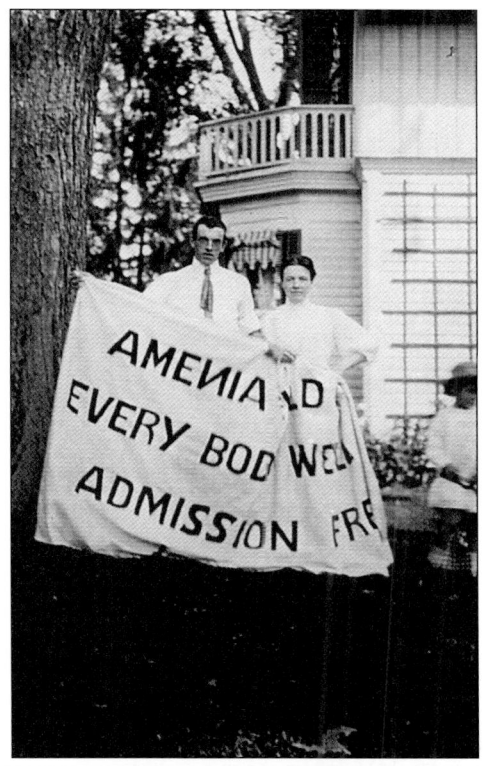

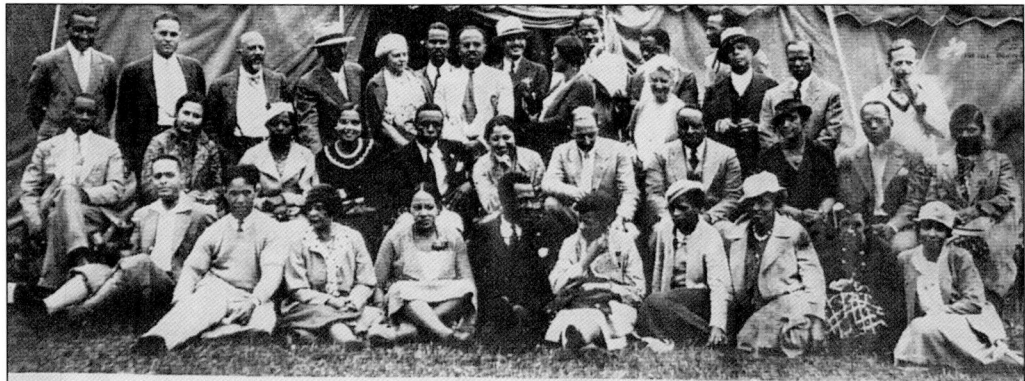

ont Row—*Seated (Left to Right):* **Dr. Ernest Alexander; Edward P. Lovett; Ruth McGee; Dr. Virginia Alexan ward Shaw; Anna Arnold Hedgemen; Sara E. Reid; Pauline Young; Frances Williams; Unidentified.** *Sec w—Seated:* **Harry Green; Hope Spingarn; Hazel Brown; Juanita Jackson Mitchell; M. Moran Wes enona Bond Logan; Joel E. Spingarn; Elmer A. Carter; Mabel J. Byrde; Frank Wilson; Marion Cuthbert.** *T w—Standing:* **Roy A. Ellis; Ralph J. Bunche; Dr. W. E. B. DuBois; Abram Harris; Mrs. James Weldon Johns y Wilkins; E. Franklin Frazier; Sterling Brown; Lillian Alexander; Emmett Dorsey; William Pickens; Mary W ington; Ira DeA. Reid; James Weldon Johnson; Max Yergan; Walter White.** (*Photo by Amy Spingarn*)

THE AMENIA CONFERENCE OF 1916. A wide spectrum of participants came to the "Amenia Conference" held at Troutbeck to discuss ways for African Americans to achieve basic human rights. The natural beauty of Troutbeck, the excellent food, and the involvement of Joel Spingarn himself contributed to the emergence of the NAACP as a multi-dimensional organization. Spingarn served as chair of its board and his brother Arthur served as counsel and later president. The family established the Spingarn medal to honor black leaders. (NAACP.)

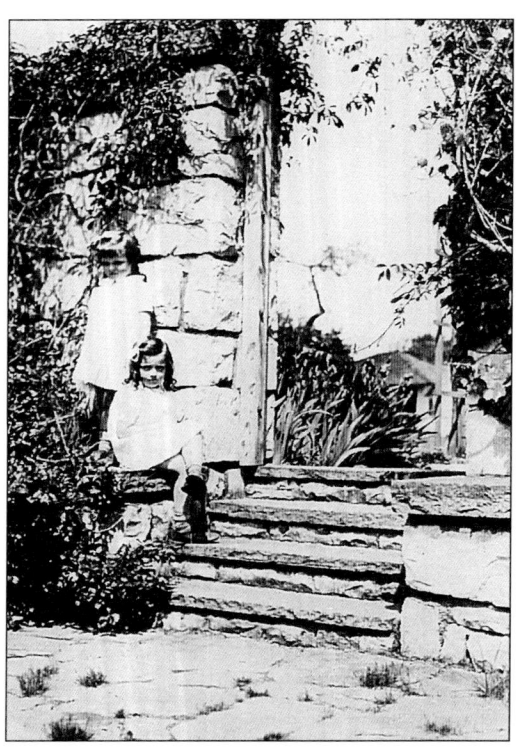

DUFFY TWINS AT TROUTBECK, MID-1930S. Alice and Margaret Duffy are shown in the formal gardens at Troutbeck, which Joel Spingarn, continuing the Benton tradition, had made a "Mecca for horticulturists." In addition to his involvement in politics and social issues, Spingarn researched and developed clematis. Today, the beautiful grounds and buildings serve as a conference center. (MQ.)

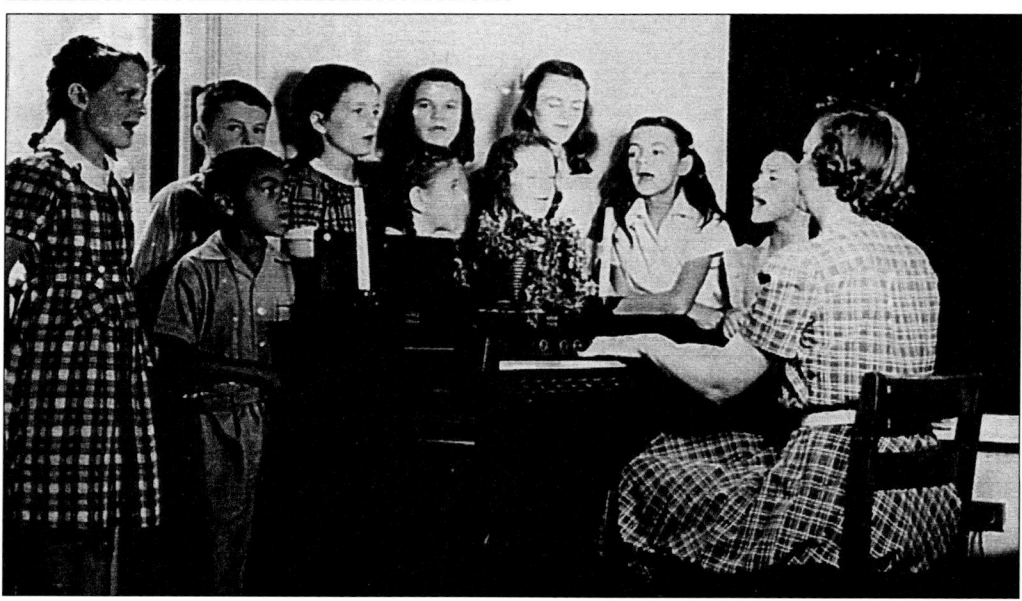

LEEDSVILLE SCHOOLHOUSE MUSIC CLASS. The building, once a one-room schoolhouse and now a residence, still stands near Leedsville Road. Among its pupils were the Duffy twins and Alison Mumford, daughter of Lewis Mumford, the world-renowned thinker, who praised the school and the "capable, indeed inspired, young teacher, Kathryn Kane . . . " The children grouped around the piano enjoyed giving concerts in neighboring communities. The school was closed in the early 1940s. (MQ.)

AMENIA UNION SCHOOL. Amenia Union, to the south of Leedsville, also had its own one-room schoolhouse. According to the *Harlem Valley Times*, this picture is of the Fourth District Sharon School class at Amenia Union. The area was first settled by Palatines Capt. Garret Winegar and his father, Uldrick, in 1724. Also known as "Hitchcock's Corners," Amenia Union has many ties to its New England neighbors, and in fact, some properties lie in both New York and Connecticut. (KH/AHS.)

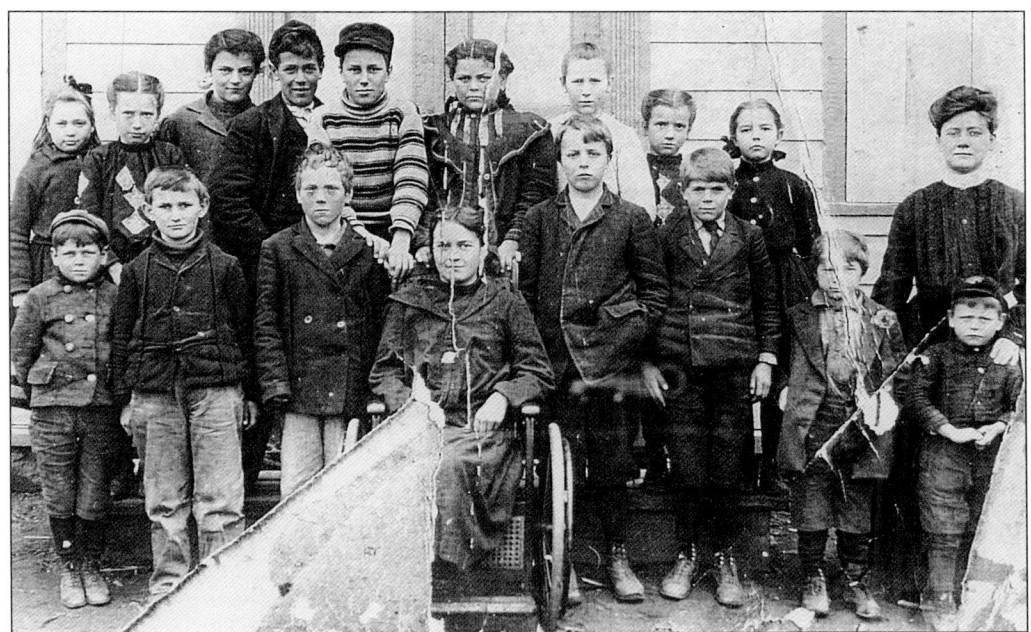

ST. THOMAS EPISCOPAL CHURCH. The church in Amenia Union was designed by Richard Upjohn, architect of Trinity Church in New York City. The Gothic-style edifice was built mid-19th century and seats only about one hundred people. It shows on a small scale various European Gothic elements such as the buttresses and pointed windows. (KH/AHS.)

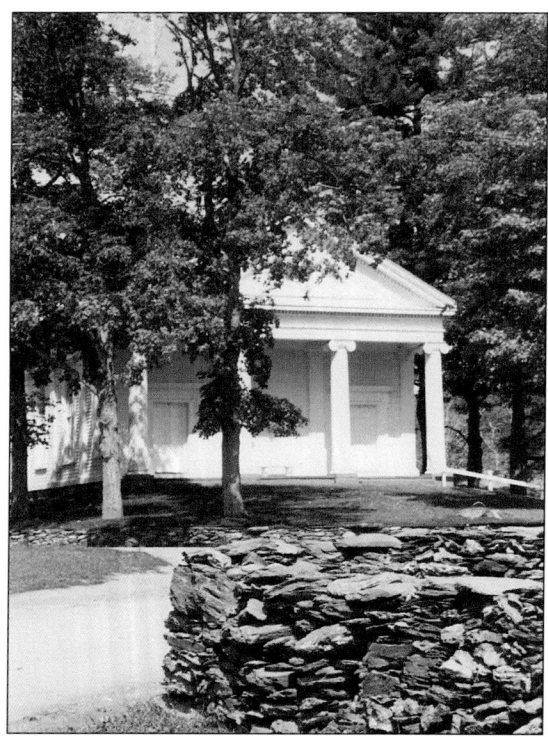

SMITHFIELD CHURCH. The Smithfield Presbyterian Church traces its roots back to 1742. In the summer of 1770, the revivalist preacher George Whitefield spoke under the great oak opposite the site in the area then known as "The City." In the early 19th century, one of the town's six post offices was located there. Shown in this photograph is the third Presbyterian church, a Greek revival building erected in 1847. In 1889, the post office changed the name to Smithfield. (DCTPA/JG.)

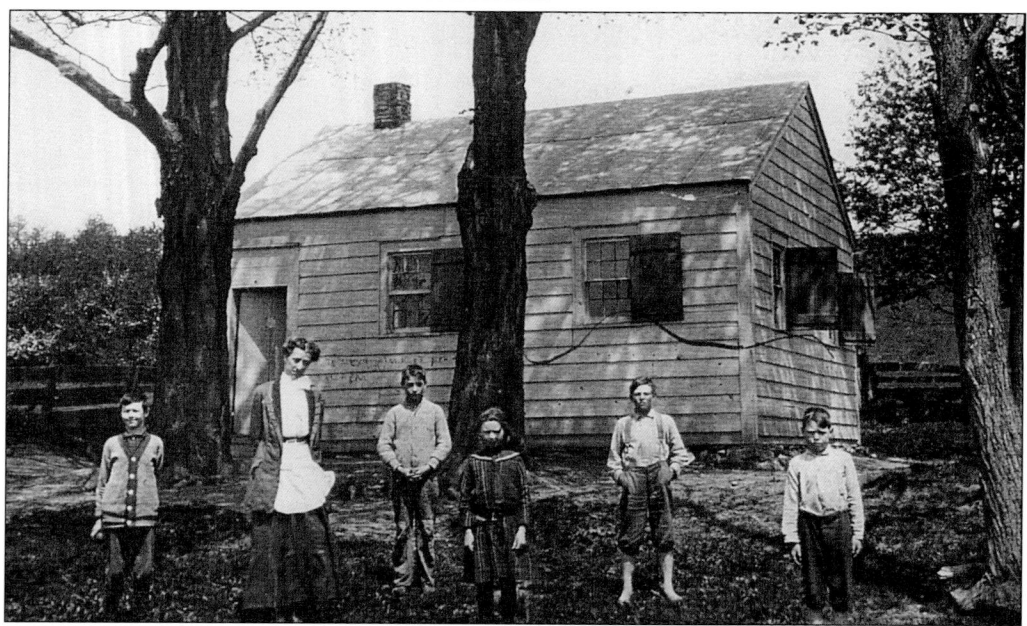

SMITHFIELD SCHOOL. This photograph, which dates from c. 1889, shows the building that served as a one-room school from the early 1800s to c. 1950. It was built by the great great- grandfather of Catherine Flint Leigh. Mrs. Leigh was the Amenia town historian from 1965 to 1989, and she attended Smithfield School, as did her daughter in the early 1940s. Mrs. Leigh noted on the picture the apple trees on the left. Today the school is a residence. (KH/AHS.)

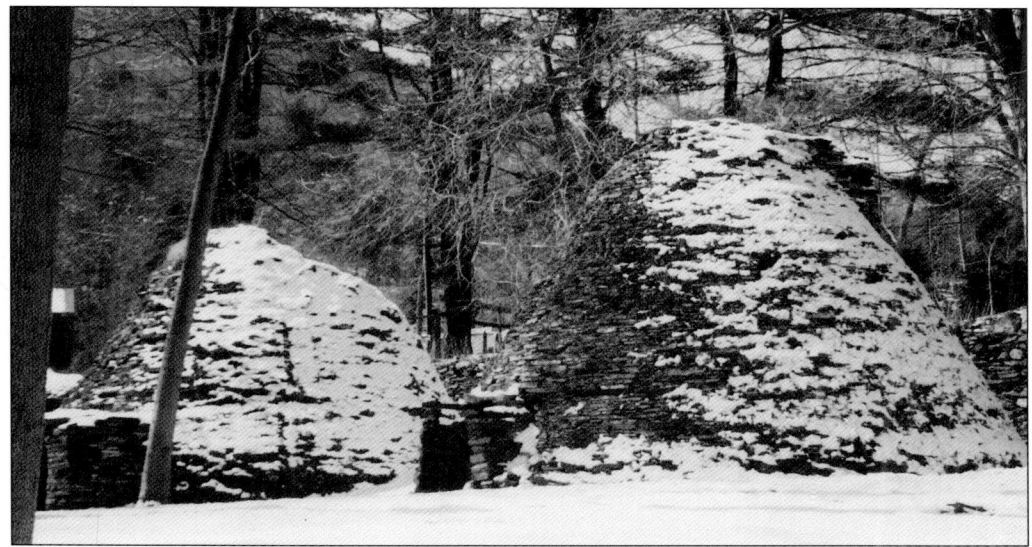

WASSAIC CHARCOAL KILNS. Located on Deep Hollow Road, these unique beehive kilns transformed wood into charcoal, which was used to fire the Noah Gridley and Son Iron Works established in 1825. Charcoal was the preferred fuel because of its low sulfur content. Men employed as colliers—those who felled the trees, cut them into lengths, and tended the open pit fires—deforested the hillsides. Iron was mined mainly from open pits, which today are filled with water. (JG.)

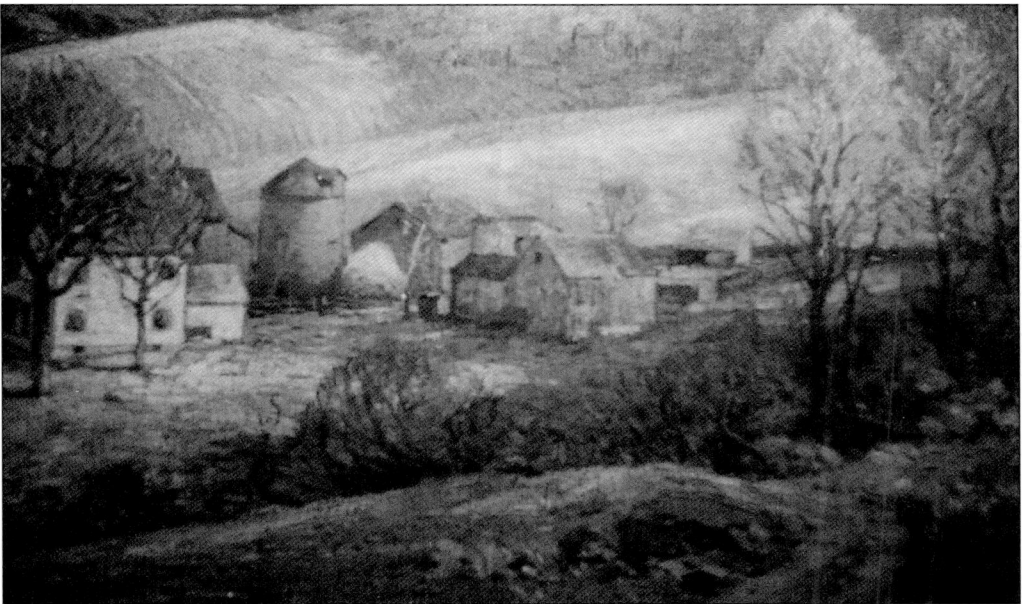

BATES FARM ON DEEP HOLLOW ROAD. This painting by Walter C. Hartson is of the William Bates Farm on Deep Hollow Road. A few years after the painting was completed in the late 1930s, the barn and outbuildings burned to the ground. Great-grandson Allen Merritt recalls that his grandfather Shedrick, who was born there, worked for the Gridley Iron Works as a young boy, hauling iron ore and also wood for the charcoal kilns; Shedrick later worked for Borden's. (AM.)

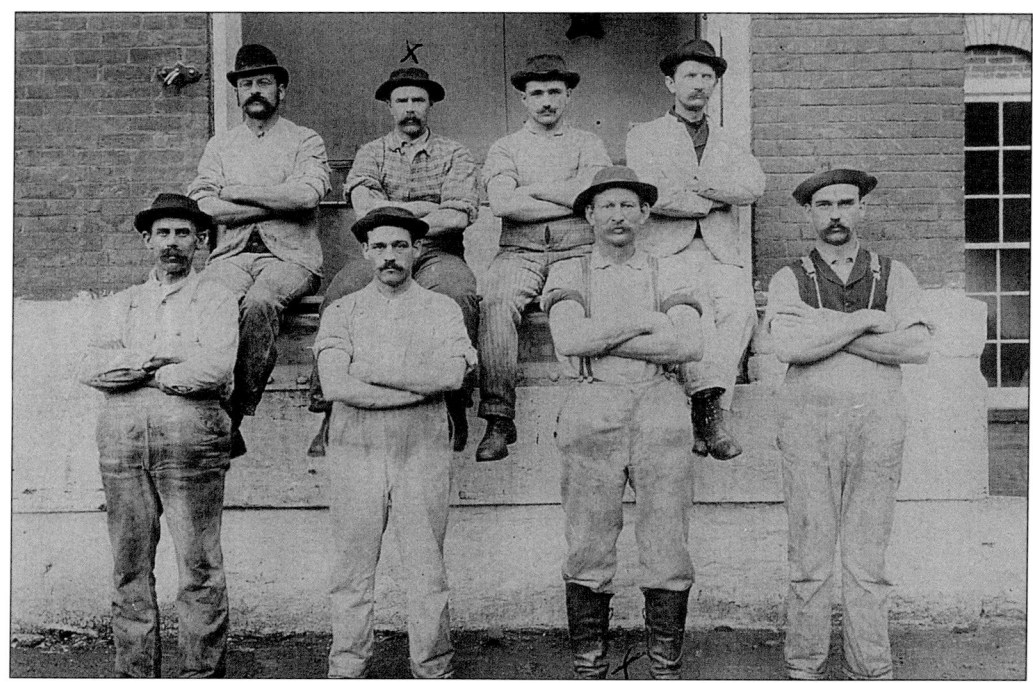

WORKERS AT BORDEN FACTORY. In this c. 1885 photograph of Borden workers, Shedrick Bates can be seen second from the left in the top row. In 1861, Gail Borden, encouraged by Noah Gridley, established the New York Condensed Milk Company. First contracting with the U.S. government to supply Union troops, by 1863, Borden had succeeded in having his factory produce over 14,000 quarts daily. By the 1920s, the Wassaic plant was used to receive and ship over 50,000 quarts of fluid milk daily. (AM.)

M.K. LEWIS DISCOUNT CARD. Love of a bargain and discount shopping are not late-20th-century phenomena. Before green and blue stamps and huge discount chains, M.K. Lewis was offering a discount card in 1904 to "Save you a dollar." The M.K. Lewis Store was built because Noah Gridley, the owner of the iron furnace and of considerable land in the area, wanted a store near the railroad station. (AM.)

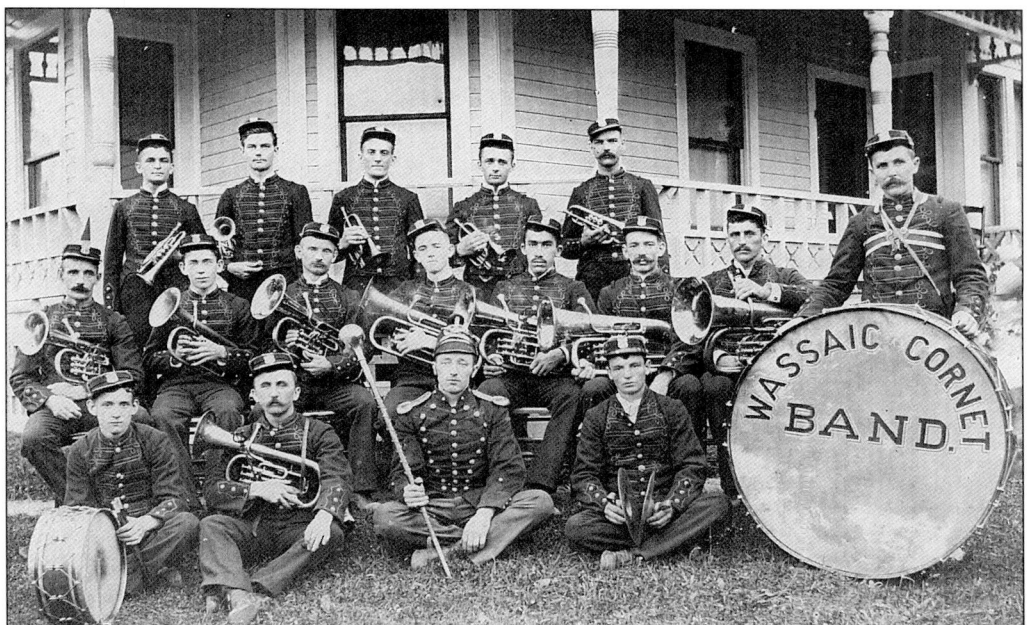

WASSAIC CORNET BAND. In 1896, there were no radios, no televisions, no tapes, no cds, but many small communities had their own bands that provided live music. Here the Wassaic Cornet Band members, all attired in their uniforms, sit on the steps of the Bowman House and look quite seriously at the camera. (PRH.)

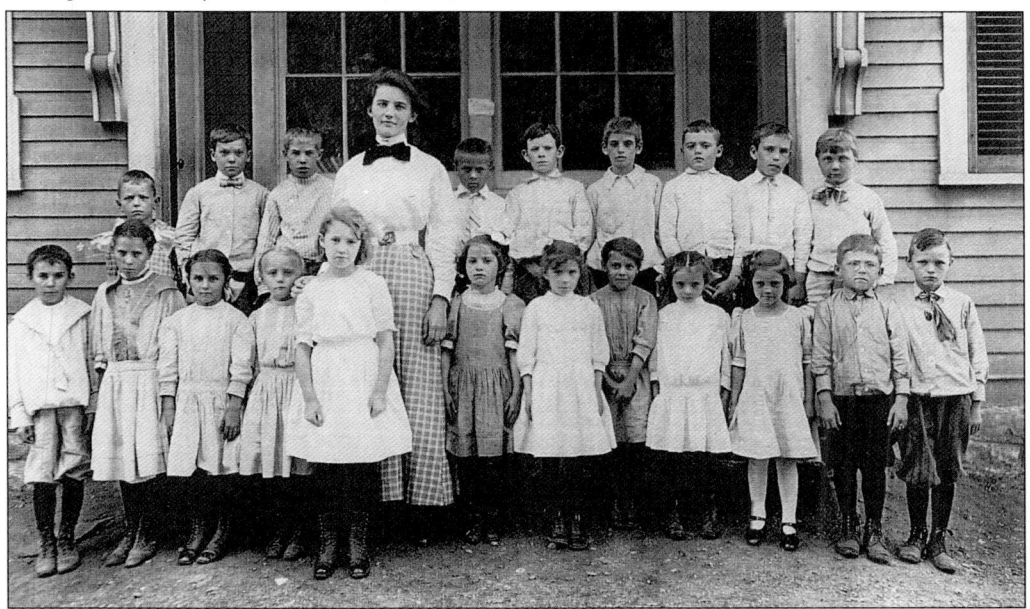

WASSAIC GRADE SCHOOL. This turn-of-the-century photograph shows the young teacher and her pupils in the Wassaic Grade School. Welthea Bates Merritt, who died at the age of 106 in 1998 and was the mother of Allen Merritt, is in the front row, sixth from the right. Note the starched and carefully ironed dresses of the girls, and consider the daily work demanded of women who also cooked, baked, and cleaned, all without today's modern conveniences. (AM.)

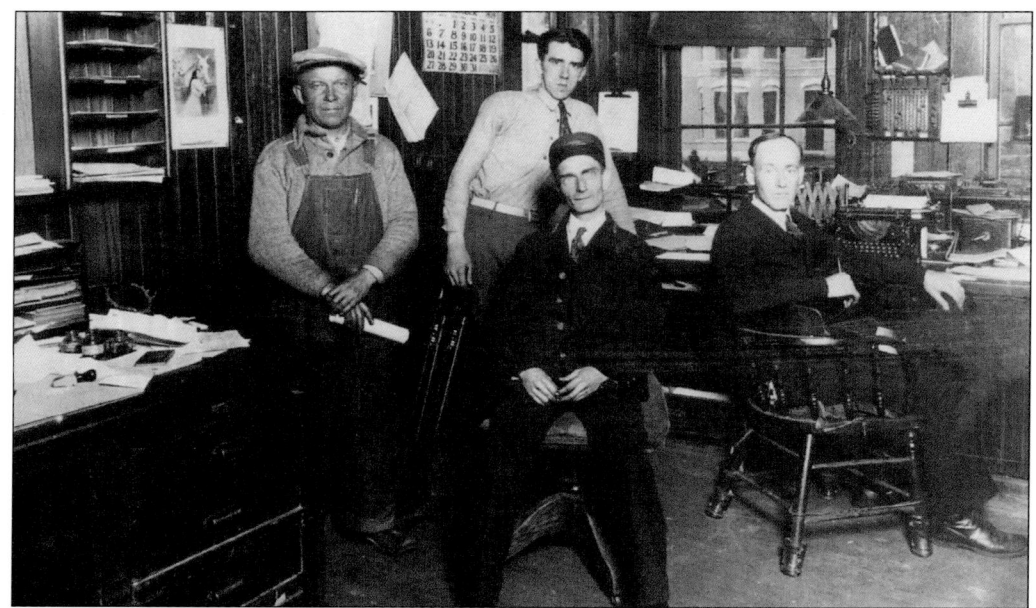

RAILROAD STATION AT WASSAIC, 1929. The coming of the railroad to Wassaic in the mid-19th century spurred the prosperity of the hamlet and created new employment opportunities. Think how bustling the activity in this tiny hamlet must have been to require four employees: Frank Struss, sectionman (track maintenance), standing left; William D. Sincerbox, station agent, seated center with hat; and Russell Maxfield, assistant station agent, seated left. The fourth man is probably a trainee. (HC.)

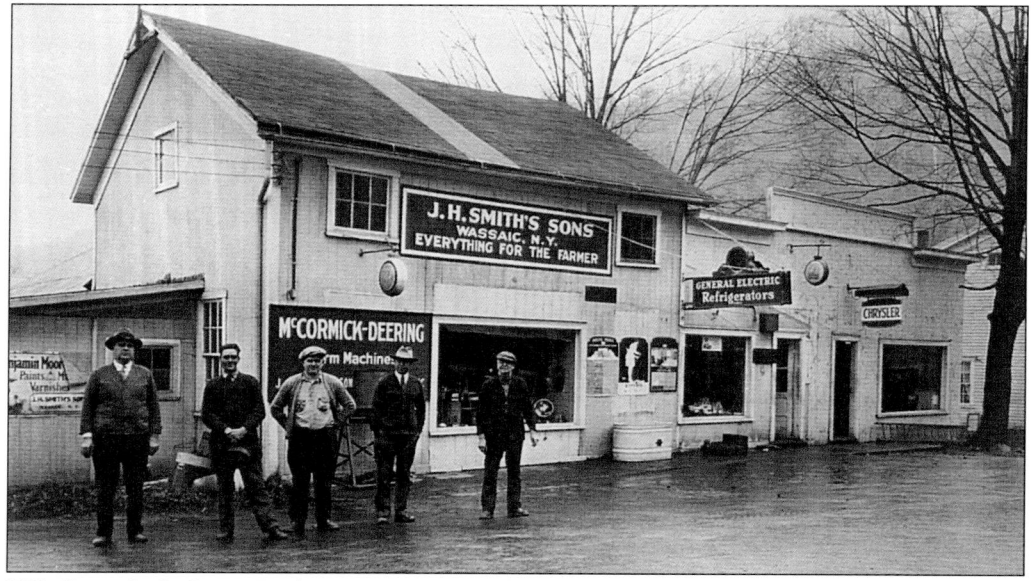

J.H. SMITH'S & SONS. In the 1940s, J.H. Smith's Sons advertised "Everything for the Farmer." Those pictured include A.W. Ketcham (father-in-law of Kenneth Hoadley, current Amenia Town Historian), Thorval Hansen, Stewart Cline, and Jack Ketcham. McCormick-Deering sold farm machines, and the Chrysler sign indicated the growing importance of the automobile. (KH/AHS.)

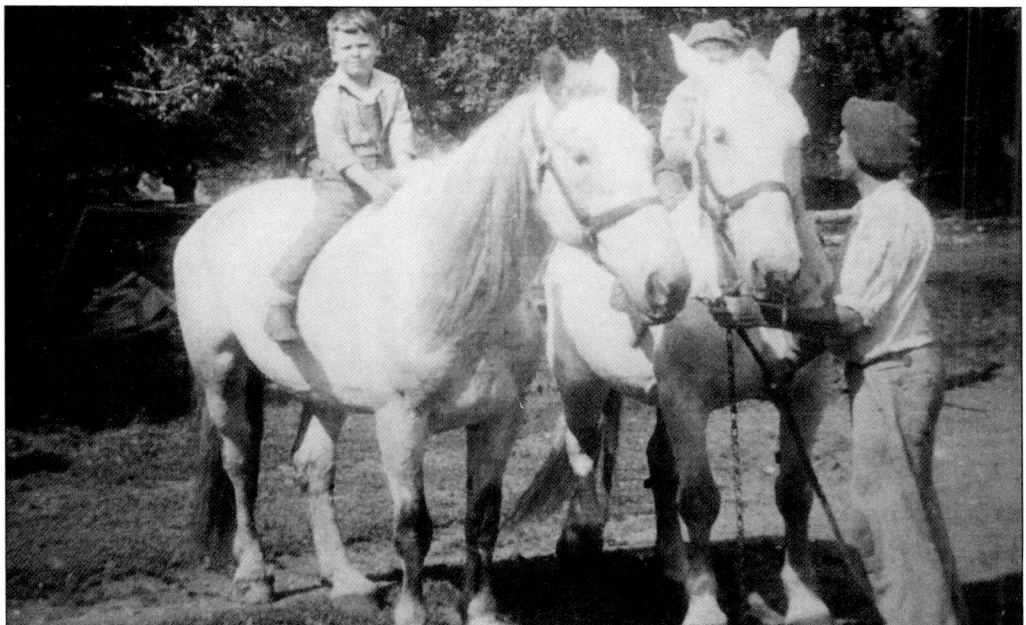

NORMAN BENSON WITH HORSES. Norm Benson is seen as a child seated on one of the family plow horses. The demand for milk by Borden's Condensed Milk Factory transformed the nature of agriculture from sheep, beef, and wheat to almost exclusively dairy. Borden's also provided a steady and predictable income to the farmers. However, after WW I, the economic base of Wassaic began to change again when New York State built the Wassaic State School, acquiring, among others, the farm of Norm's grandfather. (NB.)

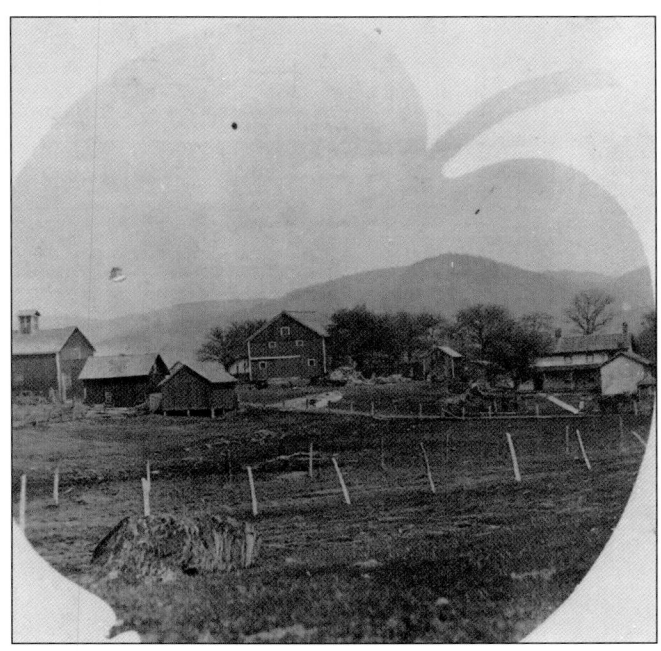

SITE OF STATE SCHOOL. In 1925, New York State bought two large farms in Wassaic from J. Henry Smith and Hadley H. Benson (and later part of a third) because of a need to house those labeled as the "feeble-minded" or "mental defectives." Today not only has the terminology changed, but also immeasurably higher expectations are often fulfilled. During the Depression, families came from western and northern New York and Vermont to find jobs at the State School, which became a self-sufficient community, providing employment opportunities for men and women. (NB.)

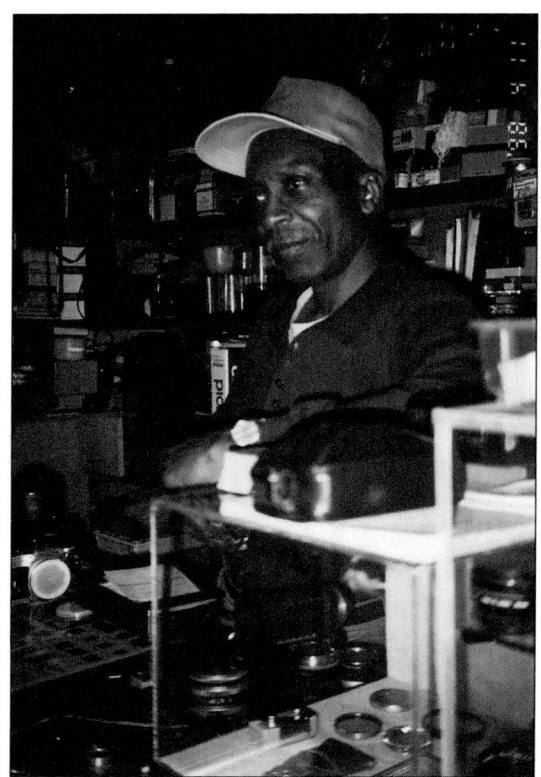

THEO MOODY. Theo Moody headed the recreation program at the Wassaic Developmental Center (now called the Taconic Developmental Disabilities Service Organization, TDDSO), and retired in 1994 after 34 years of service. He is shown with his many cameras, having turned an avocation into a business. While Mr. Moody was still at the center, Hollis Shaw, then its director, together with state, regional, and local leaders undertook a lengthy planning process in order to be ready to face whatever changes the future may bring. (JG.)

RALPH VINCHIARELLO. Shown here at a recent regional conference at the TDDSO, Ralph Vinchiarello has been a member of the Board of Visitors for over 18 years. He also serves on the surrogate decision-making panel for clients at Hudson River Psychiatric Center and on the merger committee of the New York State Association of Boards of Visitors. He was a member of the Dutchess County Legislature and Amenia Town Supervisor. (JG.)

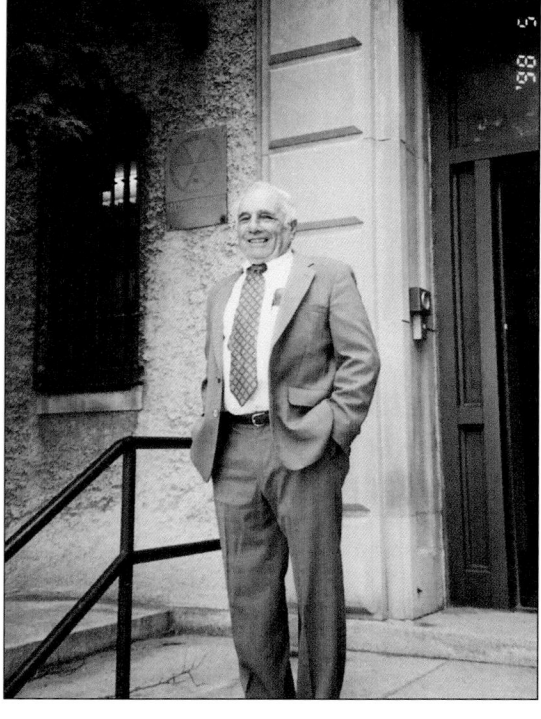

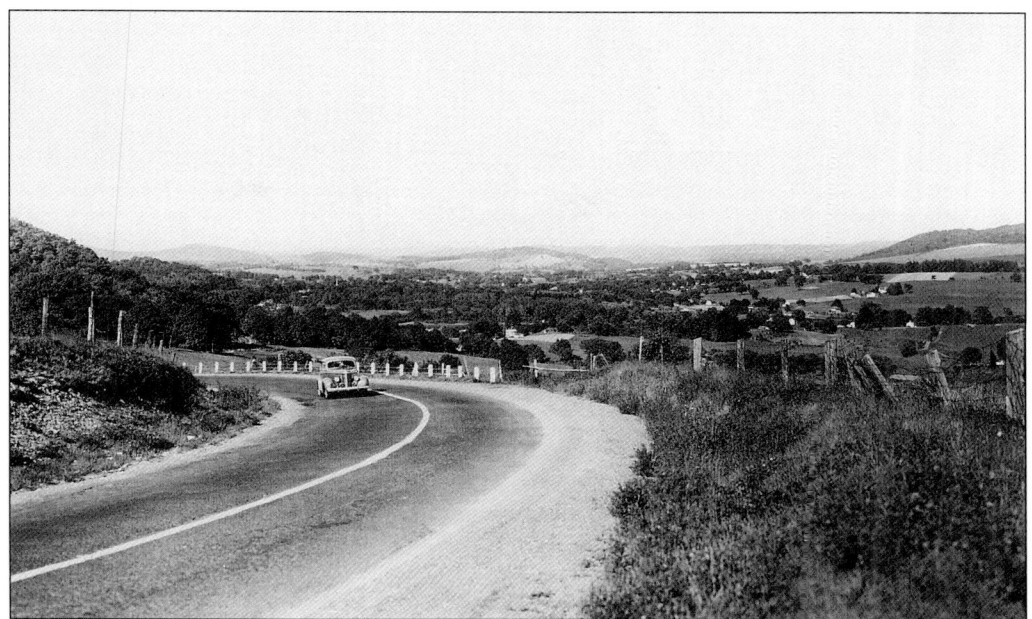

DELAVERGNE HILL. This 1930s photograph shows Delavergne Hill, a landscape seemingly unchanged since the early Huguenot settlers gave their name to the hill. Its natural beauty has always been one of the attractions of Amenia. In the bowl-shaped valley, there is a golf course, restaurant, and banquet facilities, and a conference center is planned for the future. It will also be the site of the summer program series of the Hudson Valley Philharmonic. (AML.)

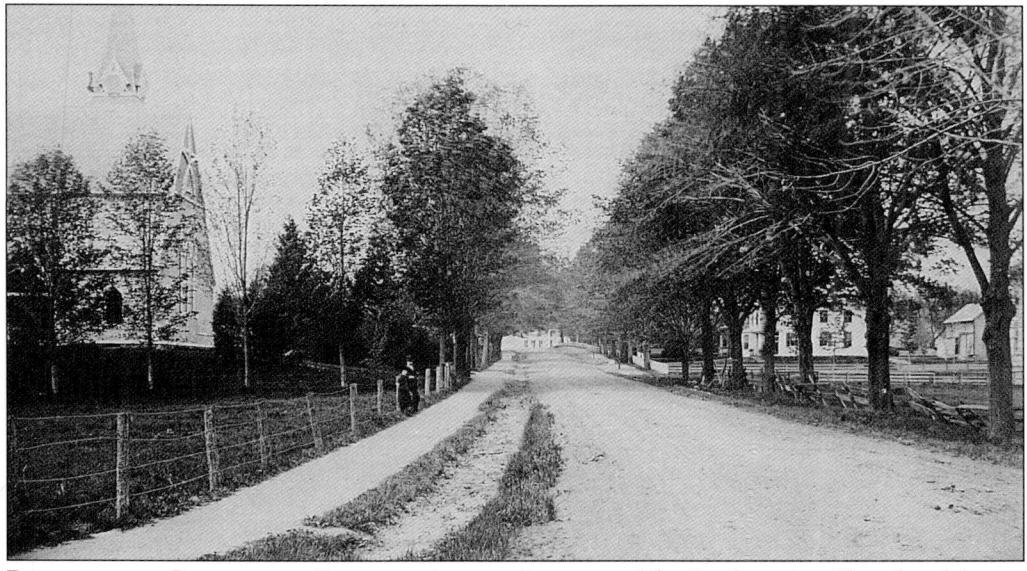

PRESBYTERIAN CHURCH AND LAWN OF AMENIA SEMINARY. The Presbyterian Church celebrates its 250th anniversary in 1998. Based on recently found records, a two-volume church history has been compiled. Nearby, the Amenia Seminary was established in 1834-35 under the aegis of leading Methodists. The first co-educational academy in New York State, it flourished for over 50 years until 1888, attracting students from all over the United States even before the coming of the railroad. Joel Benton wrote its history in 1906. (KH/AHS.)

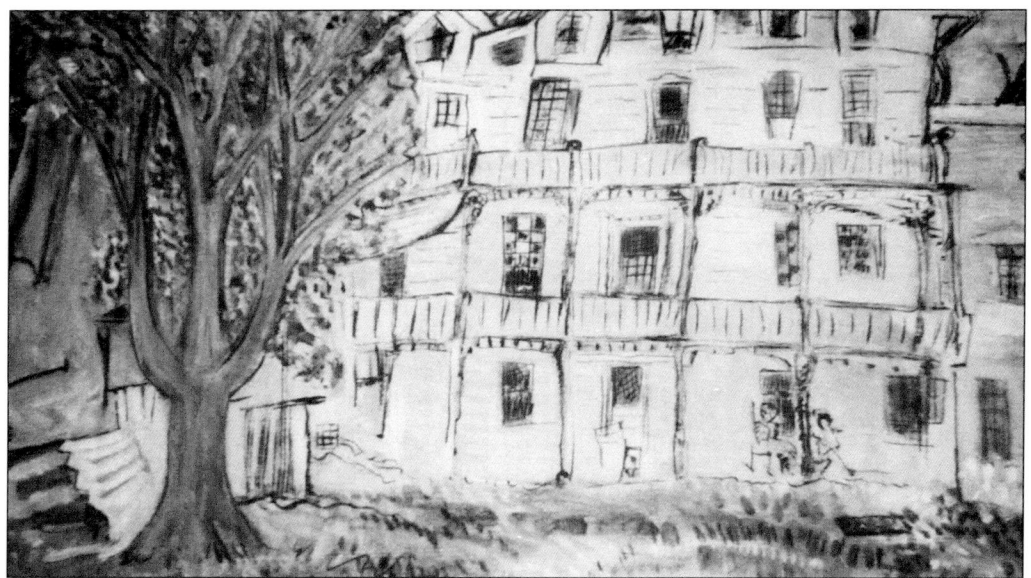

AMENIA INN. This painting, completed in 1946 by Amy Spingarn (who had also photographed the Amenia Conference in 1916), shows the Amenia Inn, which was across from the Amenia Railroad Station. The route of the new railroad led to prominence for the hamlet to be called Amenia. It became the commercial center and boasted a number of inns/hotels including several of the Kosher boarding houses which catered to visitors from New York City before Route 17 made the Catskills an easy destination. (MQ.)

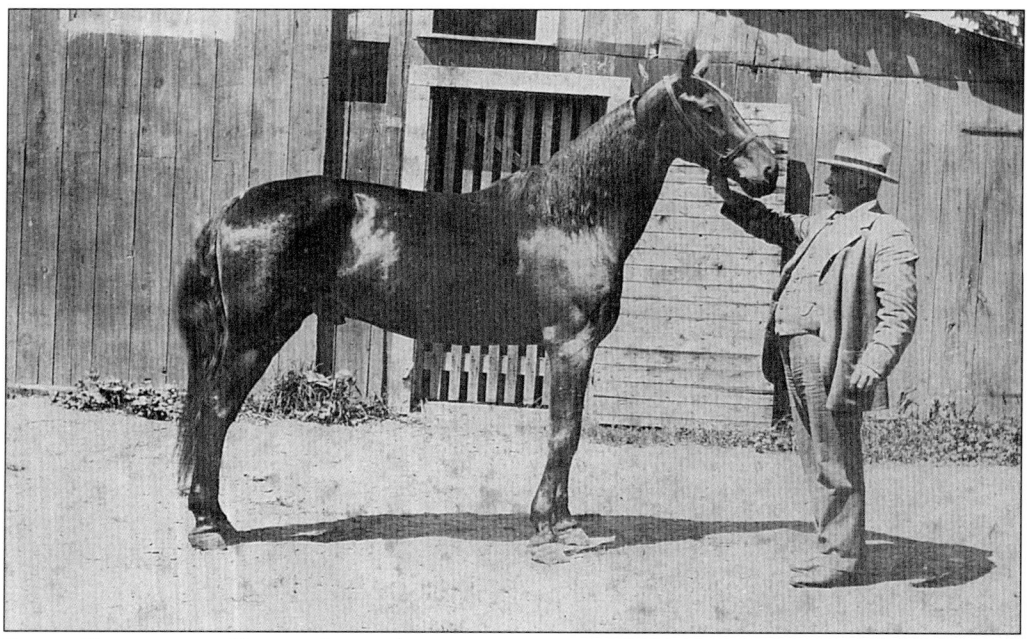

PETER PRATT AND HORSE. From about 1875, Peter Pratt ran Pratt's Hotel. His first love was, however, horse racing. In the 18th century, the Delavergne family had lived on the site and operated an inn. About 1925, the inn became known as the Delavergne Farms Hotel. (KH/AHS.)

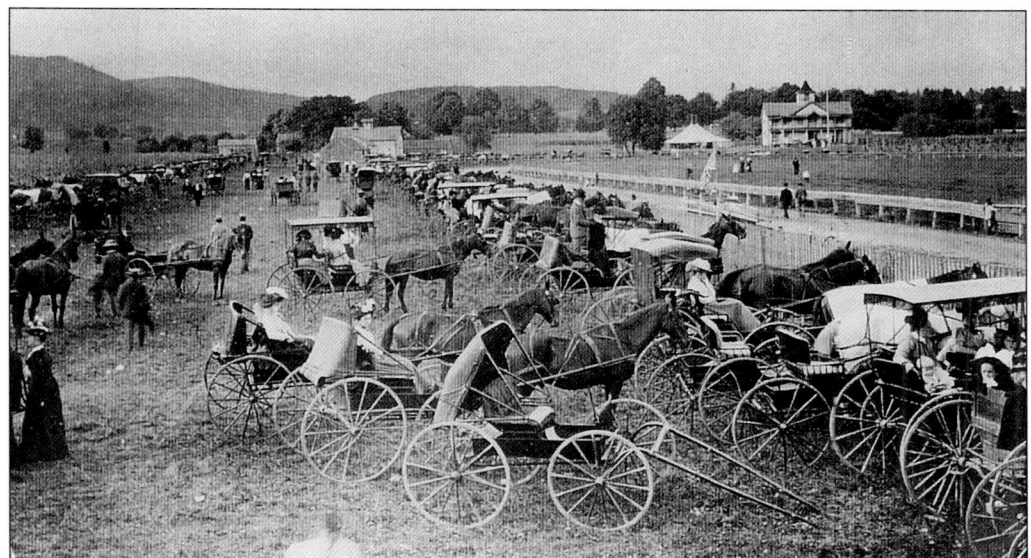

AMENIA FAIRGROUNDS. This photograph, which dates from c. 1902, shows the former fairgrounds, now the site of Ames Plaza. It is not unlikely that Peter Pratt spent time here at the race meets. In 1881, the great Vamburgh Circus performed at the fairgrounds, which also served as its winter quarters. Here, among other animals, one could have seen "the largest Elephant in this country, the only two-horned Rhinoceros in America, a herd of Camels, and a living Nondescript!" (KH/AHS.)

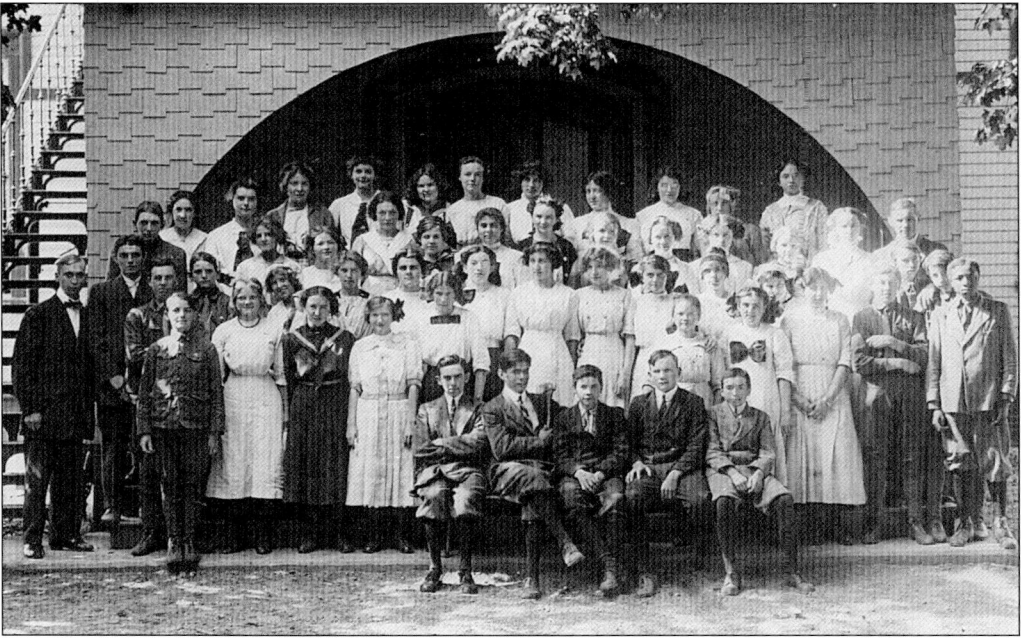

AMENIA HIGH SCHOOL. Shown in this image is an Amenia High School class c. 1916-18. Note the preponderance of young women among whom is Ella Bates, aunt of Allen Merritt. Until the latter part of the 19th century, public schooling was limited to the lower grades, thus making necessary the existence of academies such as the Amenia Seminary. (AM.)

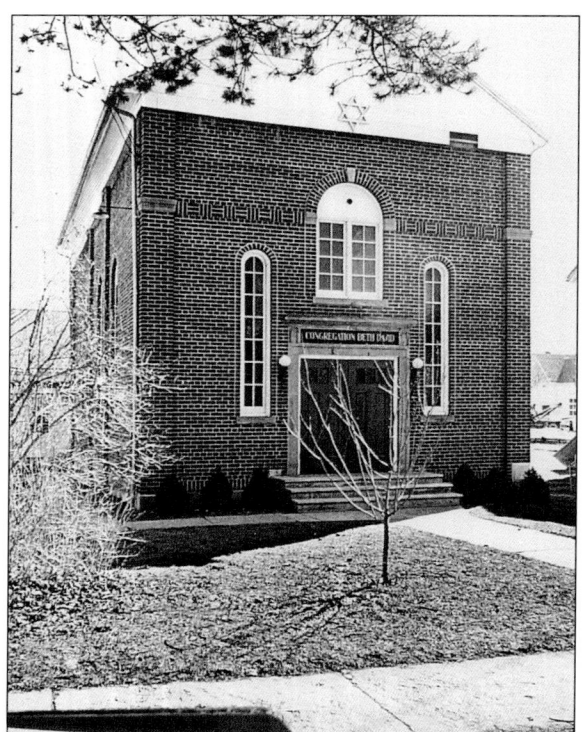

BETH-DAVID SYNAGOGUE. Beth-David Synagogue was built in 1929. Twelve to 15 families of Russian ancestry had come from Connecticut in the early part of the 20th century in search of better education for their children and better housing. Among the original families were the Shoifets and the Rothsteins. The father of Jacob Shoifet (Millerton mayor) came in 1916 as rabbi and slaughterer. The Rothstein family operated boarding houses on Leedsville Road and Lakeview House, from which could be seen the man-made Lake Amenia at the bottom of Delaverge Hill. (KH/AHS.)

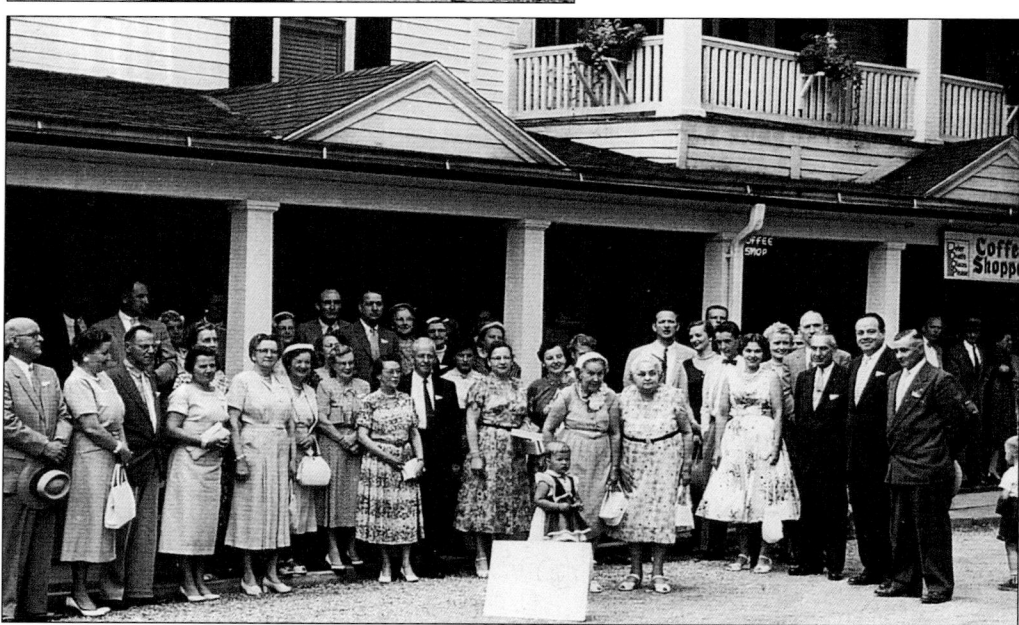

DELAVERGNE FARMS HOTEL. This photograph, taken c. 1956, shows one of many occasions celebrated at the hotel. Among those present was Robert J. Blinn, supervisor of Amenia and chairman of the Dutchess County Board of Supervisors. Unfortunately, the hotel in the center of the hamlet, the scene of local celebrations and the destination of many visitors, burned to the ground in 1974. (KH/AHS.)

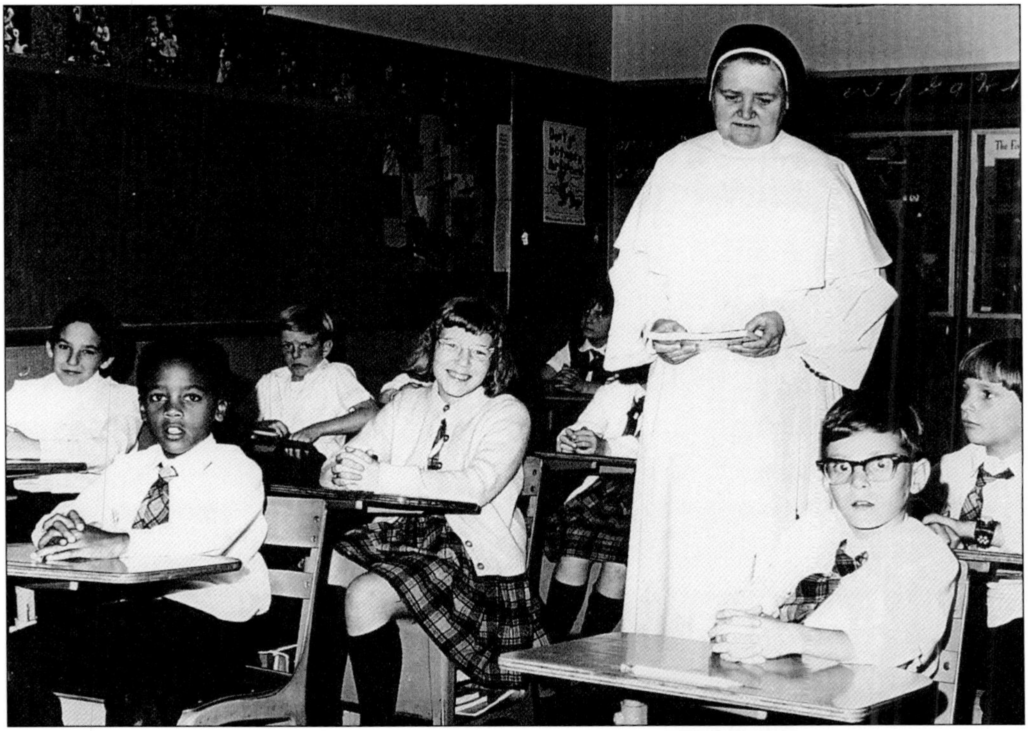

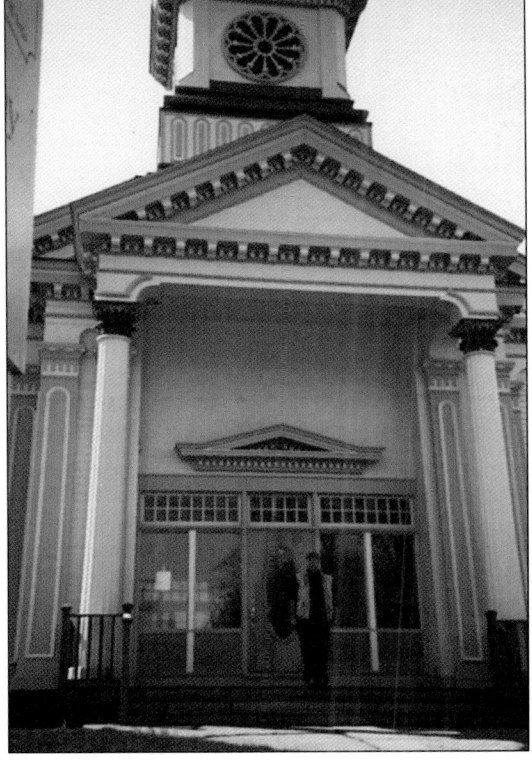

IMMACULATE CONCEPTION SCHOOL. Seen in this image is a class in the Immaculate Conception School in 1971. The school was built in 1958 adjacent to the church, which dates from 1887. Driven by the potato famine and lured by the promise of employment in the iron ore beds, many Irish Catholics arrived in Amenia mid-19th century. The first church built in 1868 was struck by lightning and destroyed by fire. Today, the Immaculate Conception Parish is one of the largest in Dutchess County. (KH/AHS.)

BAPTIST CHURCH BUILDING WITH ANN LINDEN. Ann Linden, a former art teacher, owner of the Red Hen Sign Co., and ardent supporter of local historic preservation and restoration efforts, stands in front of the Baptist church building, which she has recently purchased. In 1851, the Baptists, formed as a separate society in 1790, had erected this building on South Street. In 1959, it was converted into a supermarket and its 60-foot spire removed. Other uses have included apartments and an antique store. (JG.)

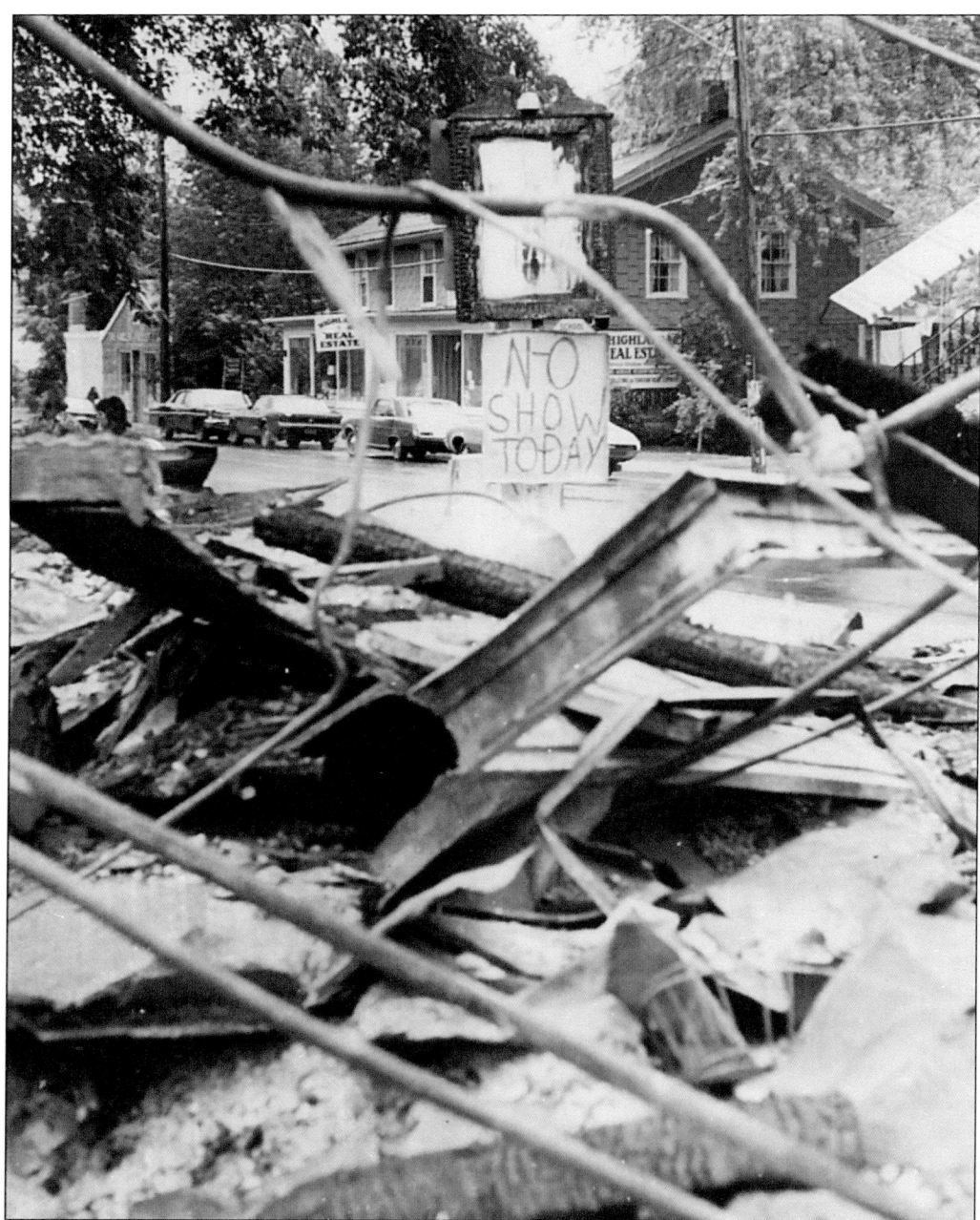

1974 Fire. A June 1974 fire destroyed the Amenia Theatre on East Main Street just a week after the Delavergne Farms Hotel fire. As the sign said, "No Show Today." Fire has continued to change the appearance of this hamlet and others as familiar landmarks are consumed by flames. This particular building (then known as Taylor Hall) was the first home of the Amenia Fire Company. In 1895, members of the newly formed fire company met there and voted to adopt the name of Amenia Hose Company No. 1. In 1899, the members voted to build a new firehouse, which was completed by 1900. During the same period, the constitution and by-laws of the Harlem Valley Firemen's Association were adopted. (AM/AFC.)

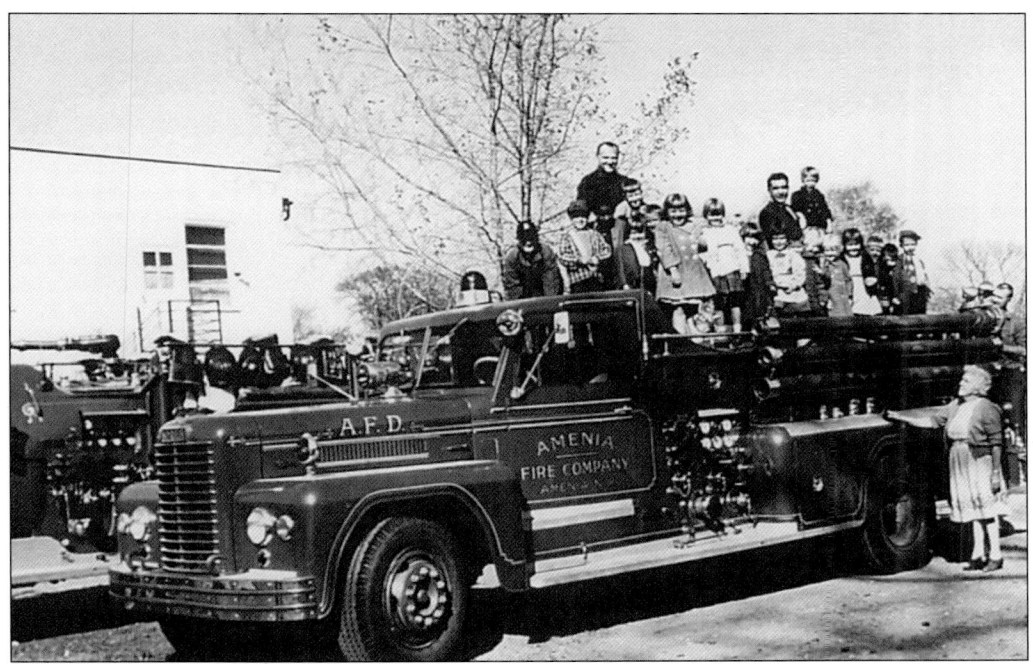

AMENIA FIRE COMPANY/ELEMENTARY SCHOOL. This is a 1960s photograph of Miss Staunton and her class enjoying a visit with the Amenia Fire Company. For more than a century, the fire company has responded to various emergencies, saving lives and property not only in Amenia, but throughout the valley. Andy Murphy, a Fire Company trustee, is proud of the Amenia firefighters who traveled to upstate New York to help during a recent devastating ice storm. (KH/AHS.)

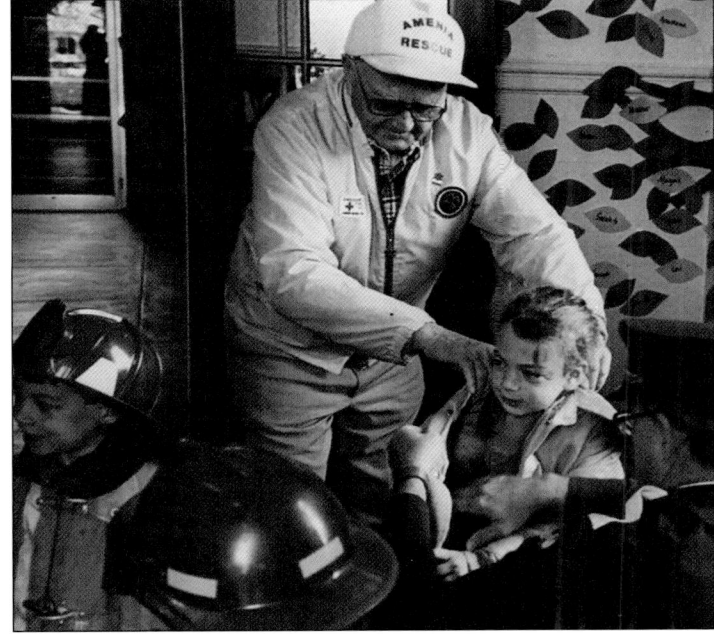

PAUL THOMPSON. Paul Thompson and his son Philip are shown in 1996 taking part in a program on safety given at the Amenia Elementary School by the Fire Company. Mr. Thompson founded the Amenia Rescue Squad and has been a volunteer firefighter for over 50 years. An active railroad employee, he was a station agent, telegrapher, and traveling freight agent. He was also elected town supervisor and is now a town justice. His work on behalf of the community has been truly remarkable. (ASM/AFC.)

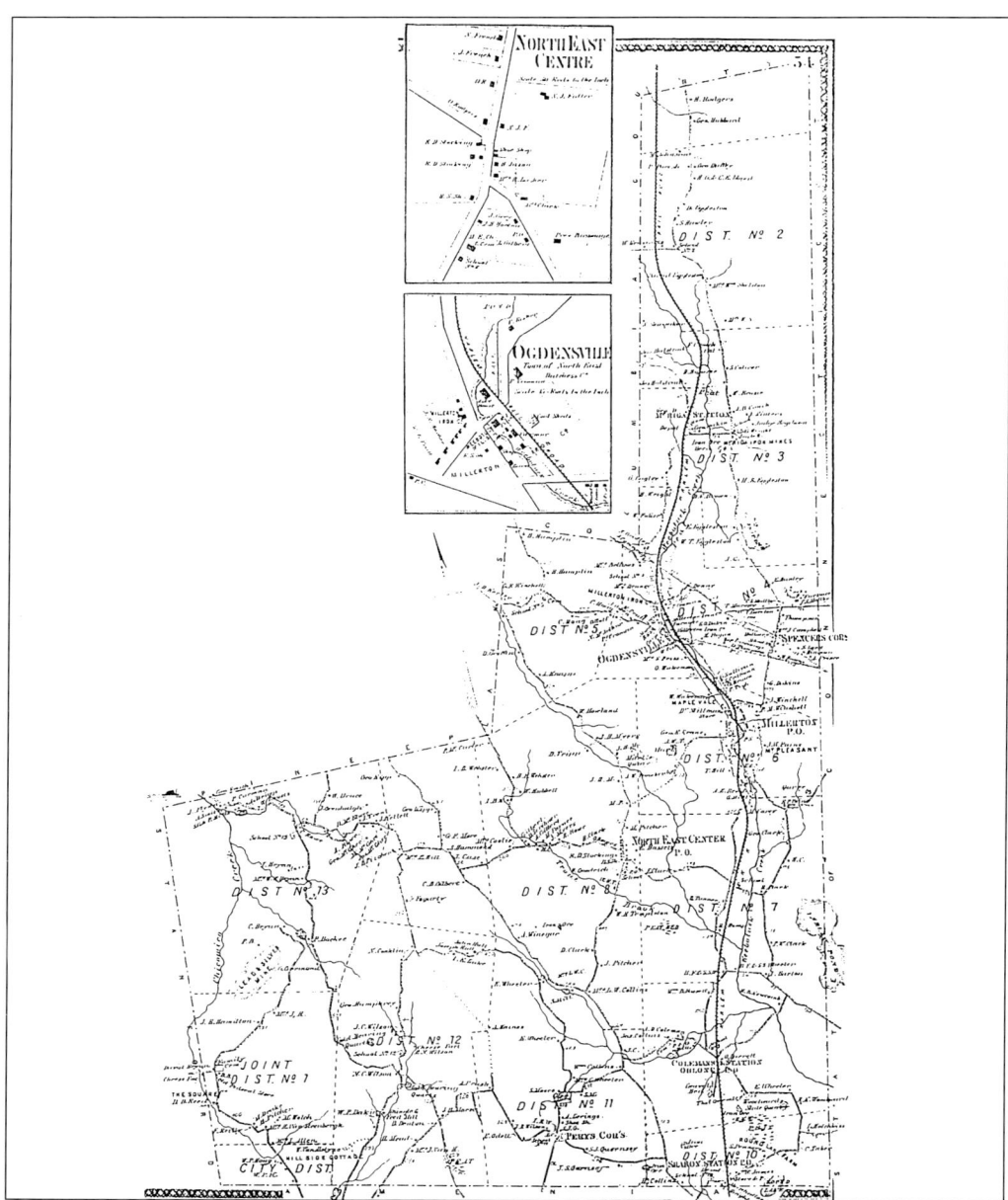

Map. This 1867 map of North East, one of the original towns of Dutchess County, includes its hamlets and the village of Millerton. Before the coming of the railroad in the mid-19th century, there were a number of thriving hamlets: Spencer's Corners, one of the earliest areas to be settled; Mt. Riga in the "chimney" (the approximately 2-mile-wide area stretching along the Connecticut/Massachusetts border to Ancram), the site of iron mines, holiday camps, and a railroad stop; Ogdensville (later known as Irondale) also the site of the iron industry; and North East Center where the first town meeting was held in 1823 after Pine Plains had been separated from North East and North Amenia had been ceded to it. When the railroad arrived in 1851, what had been farmland and orchards became the village of Millerton, which grew to be the community and commercial center of the town. (DCHS.)

Four

NORTH EAST AND MILLERTON

North East is named for its location in the extreme north east section of Dutchess county. In the mid-18th century, the land claims of the Schaghticoke Native Americans settled at Wechquadnach on the shore of Indian Lake were not usually recognized, and they were forced to withdraw across the border to Connecticut. At about the same time, families came from New England to obtain better land and religious freedom.

With the coming of the railroad, the village of Millerton was founded in 1851 and incorporated in 1875. Station stops were also established by the Harlem Line at Mt. Riga, which had been a source of iron ore from the late eighteenth century, and at Shekomeko by the Newburgh, Dutchess, and Connecticut lines, a predecessor of the Central New England.

The economy of North East was based on agriculture and mining. Multi-crop farms gave way to dairy farms, which became part of the agri-business promoted by companies such as Borden's and Sheffield's. Today, some farms still flourish but often through breeding thoroughbred horses or growing organic produce. A line of ore beds stretched from Spencer's Corners to Boston Corners, and to the west at Irondale there was the Millerton Iron Company. By the end of the 19th century, the mines and furnaces had been closed.

North East continues to be a desired destination for those in search of natural beauty and the advantages of country living. Residents and visitors can enjoy the amenities of a thriving village and recreational opportunities like Indian Lake, Rudd Pond, and the Harlem Valley Rail Trail.

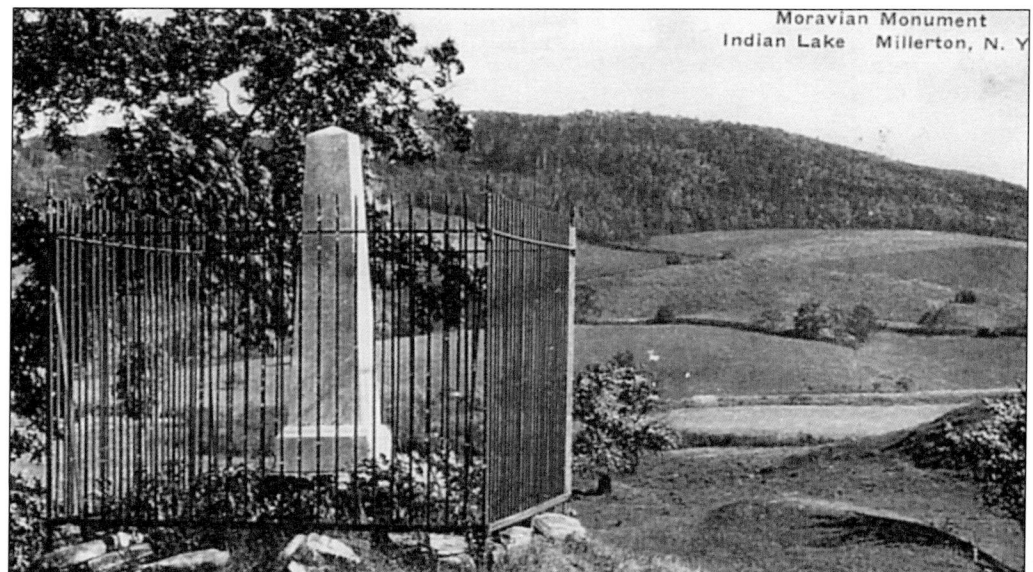

MORAVIAN MONUMENT. Erected by the Moravian Society in 1859 on the eastern shore of Indian Lake, this monument commemorates the mid-18th century Moravian mission at Wechquadnach, a Native American village on the western shore. Here, Brother David Bruce earned the love and respect of the Native Americans. After the death of Brother Joseph Powell in 1774, the mission apparently declined. (BS.)

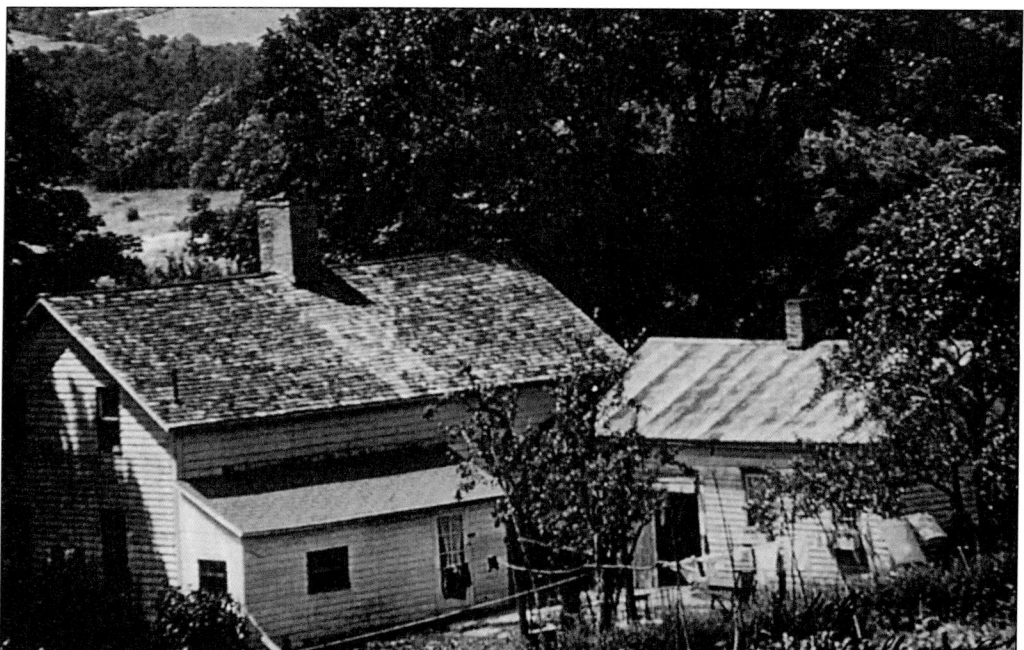

YOUNG HOUSE. This 1940s photograph shows the Young house on Boston Corners Road, which was originally built in the late 1700s. Elsie Young Albig recounts that Revolutionary War hero Ethan Allen participated in its "raising." The smaller wing on the right was once a one-room schoolhouse at White House Crossing. (NEHS.)

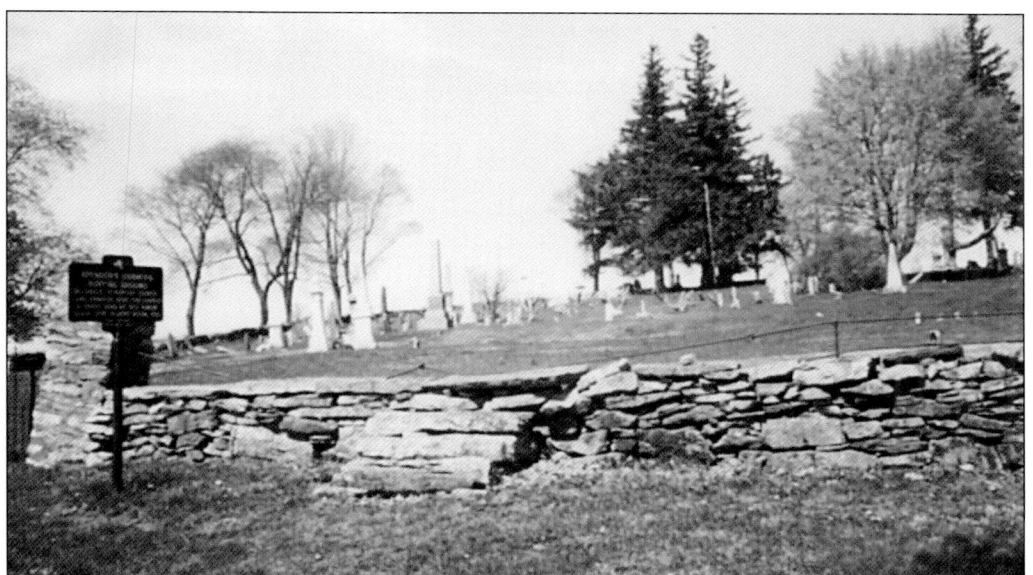

SPENCER'S BURYING GROUND. The land for this burying ground and for the first Baptist church building was donated by Simon Dakin, an early Baptist who came from Putnam County. In 1773, the first covenant meeting of the Baptists took place at his home near Spencer's Corners, and in 1778, he declared slavery to be contrary to the gospel. By 1795, the hamlet had a post office following the establishment of a post route between Sharon and Rhinebeck by Alexander Neely and Israel Reynolds. (JG.)

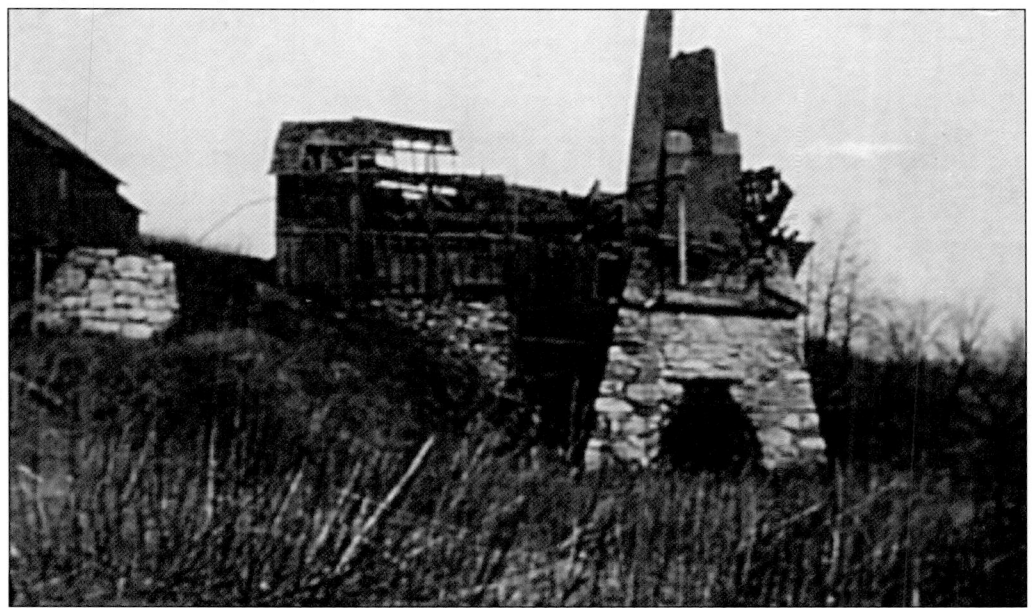

MALTBY FURNACE. This 1930s photograph from a family album shows the remains of one of the oldest iron furnaces in the area. According to tradition, ore was discovered on the original Dakin farm c.1770 and was used to produce cannons during the American Revolution. In 1846, the mine was rediscovered and in 1861 sold to Caleb S. Maltby. The Maltby Furnace produced high-grade pig iron with which to manufacture railroad car wheels. It was closed in 1893. (JJB.)

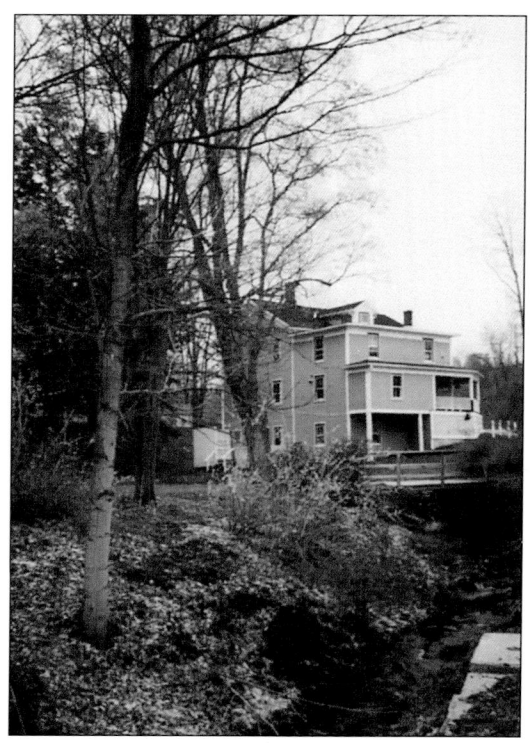

SHEKOMEKO GENERAL STORE. This general store was known as R.D. Berline, Store and Post Office in the 19th century, when the hamlet of Shekomeko, named after the creek, also included a feed store and a plaster and sawmill. During the American Revolution, John MacDonald from Scotland oversaw the excavation of lead from mines in the vicinity. From 1869 to 1934, the railroad provided service to the hamlet, also the site of a freight house and milk depot. (JG.)

IRONDALE MILL. This is the site of the gristmill that Deacon James Winchell erected in 1803. Winter services for the Baptist church were held at his nearby house. The hamlet, once known as Ogdensville, was also the location of a school, stores, a post office, and the Millerton Iron Company, built in 1854 by Julius Benedict. The Iron Company came to a fiery end in the early 1880s. In the 1960s, Lois and Virgil Martin restored the building, opened an antique shop, and were valued members of the community. (JG.)

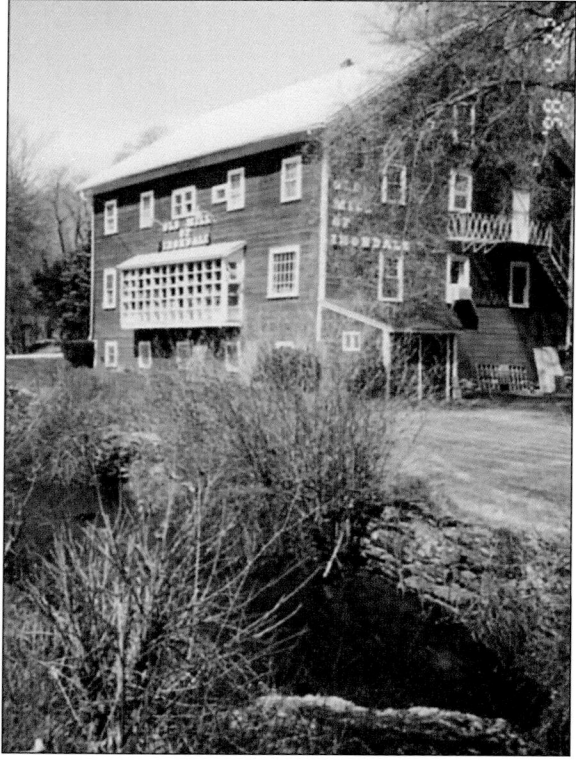

BOCKEE-SMITH BURYING GROUND AT FEDERAL SQUARE. Federal Square, located in a part of North East that was originally in Amenia, was settled by Jacob Bockee and his son Abraham, of Huguenot ancestry, who came to Dutchess mid-18th century. Isaac Smith came from Long Island in 1767-68 and his daughter Catharine married Jacob, Abraham's son, who emancipated his own slaves and was an early abolitionist. (JG.)

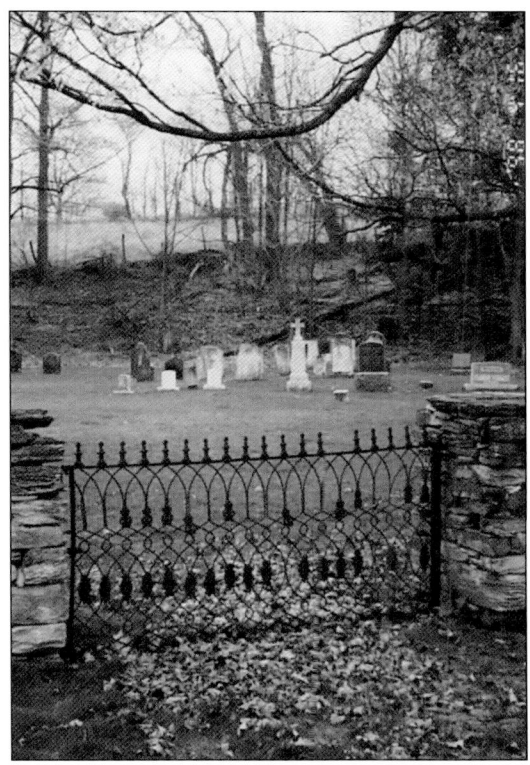

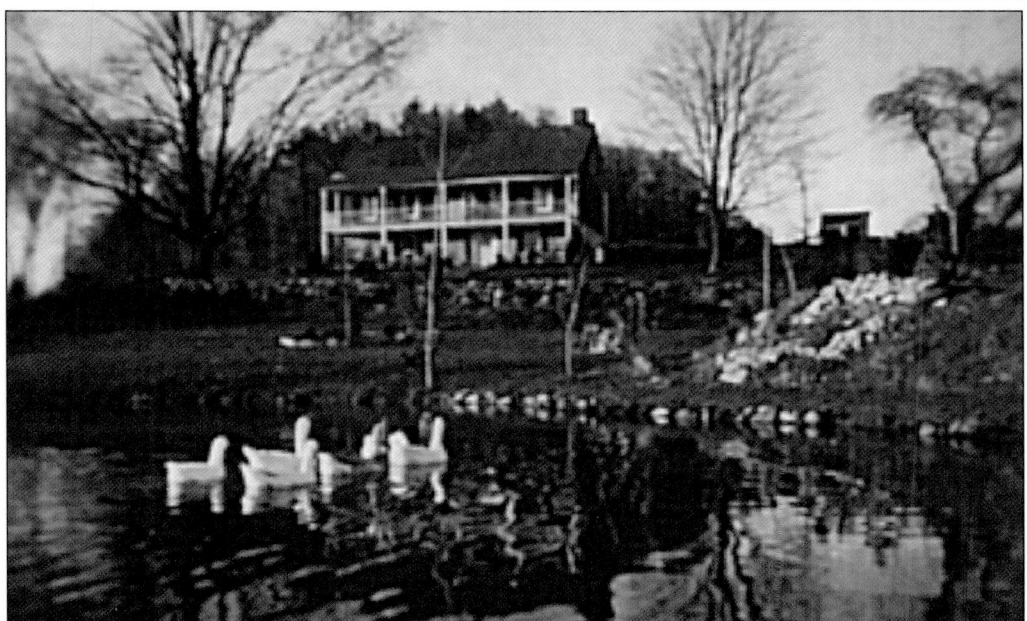

EZRA CLARK HOUSE. On Mill Road, just a little north of the Coleman Station Historic District, the house was built in the late 1700s by Ezra Clark, supplier of lead to the Revolutionary War forces. Constructed of brick with walls two feet thick, it is a beautifully preserved example of Hudson River Dutch vernacular architecture. (NEHS.)

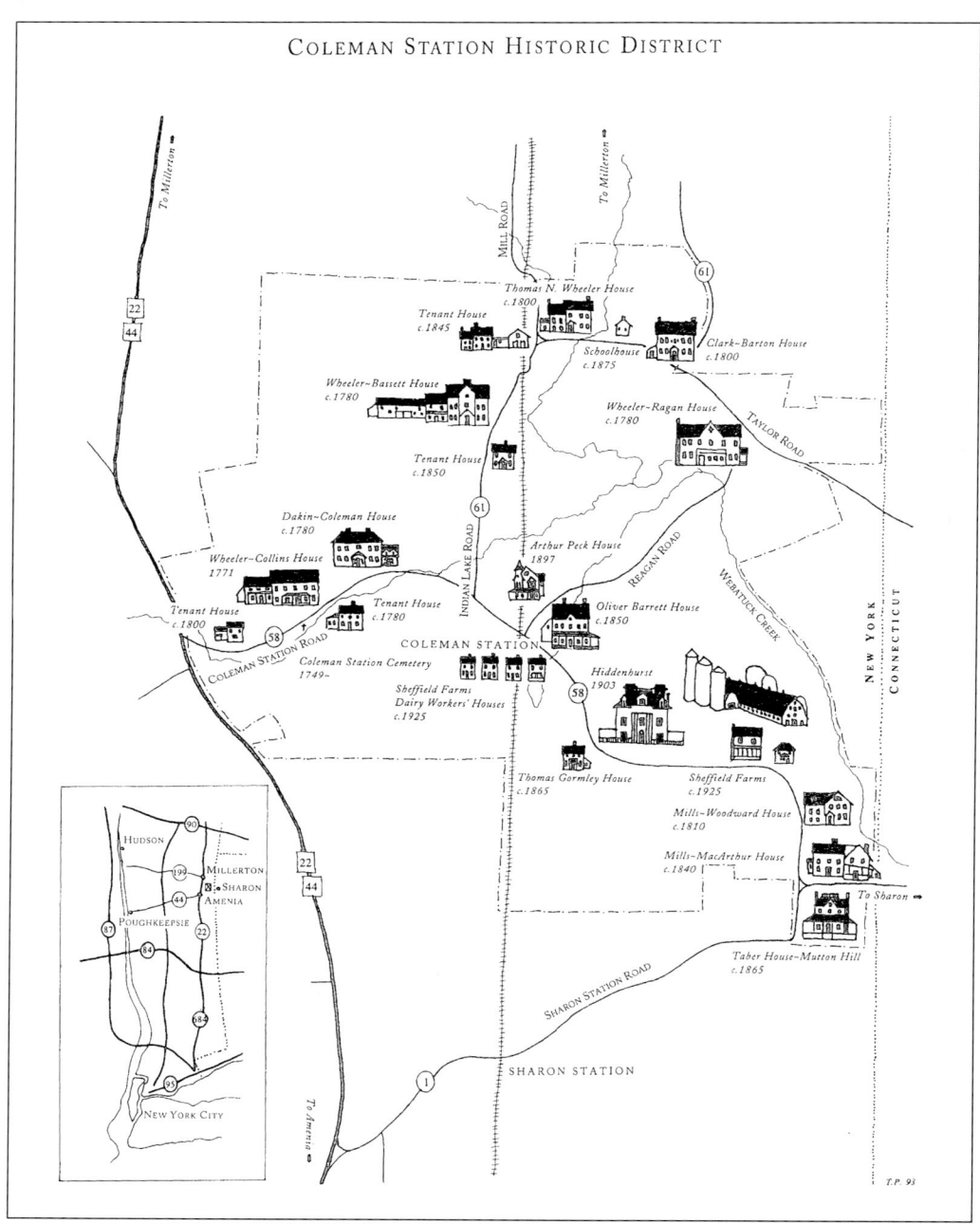

MAP OF THE COLEMAN STATION HISTORIC DISTRICT. This map of the historic district shows a defined area, which has continued to function as an agricultural community for more than two hundred years. Farms and tenant houses date from the late 18th to the mid-19th century when the railroad arrived. A schoolhouse was erected *c.* 1875. Hiddenhurst, an estate built for a New Yorker in search of a country retreat, was completed in 1903. The 20th century also saw the construction of Sheffield Farms, part of the dairy industry, which even provided worker housing. The district is a microcosm of history: individual farmer, dairy industry, and country place for the city dweller. (RQ.)

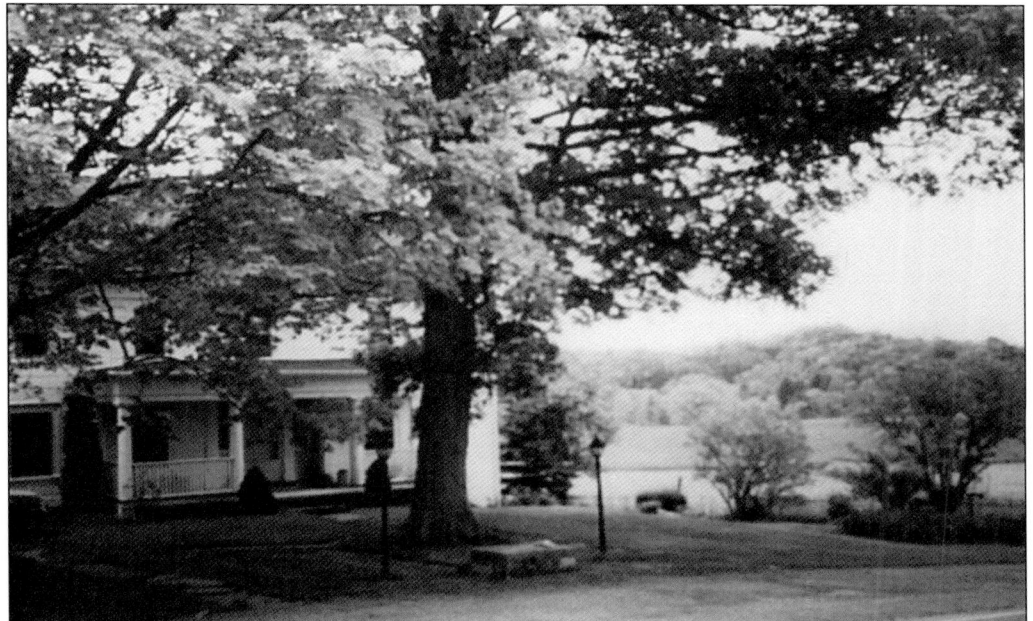

WHEELER-COLLINS HOUSE. This house on Coleman Station Road is the only house in the historic district with a date inscribed on it, 1771. It is a significant structure in this two hundred-year-old agricultural community where the landscape and buildings continue to be in harmony with history. A descendant of the original Collins family still lives there. (JS.)

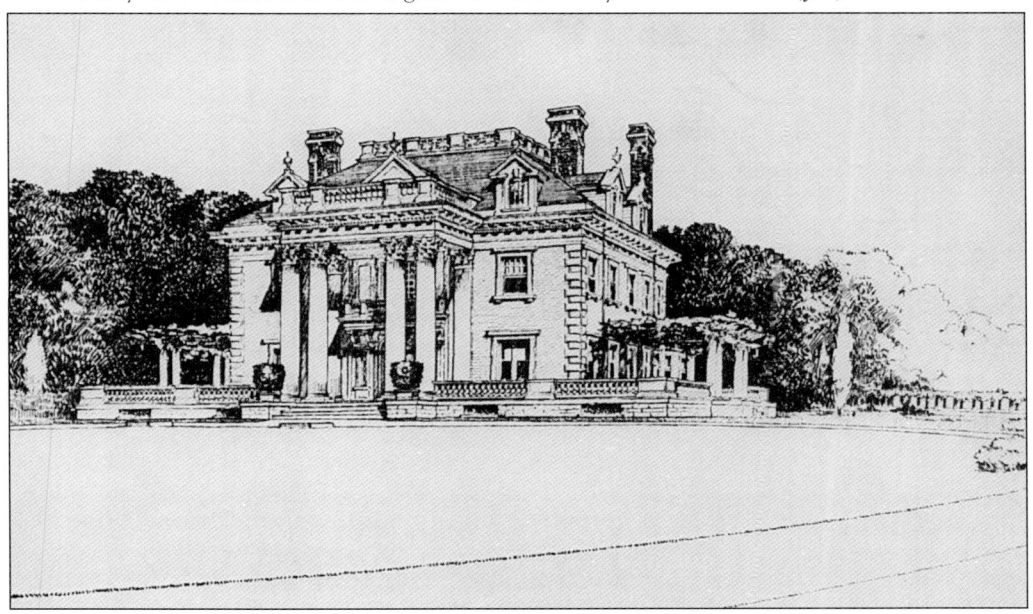

HIDDENHURST. This was the country estate of paint manufacturer and horse breeder Thomas Hidden. At the turn of the century, he was among the wealthy New Yorkers who sought the "salubrious airs" to be found in the foothills of the Berkshires. Hiddenhurst became his principal residence, and in cooperation with the Harlem Railroad, he built a new stone station (Sharon Station) to serve his transportation needs. (RQ.)

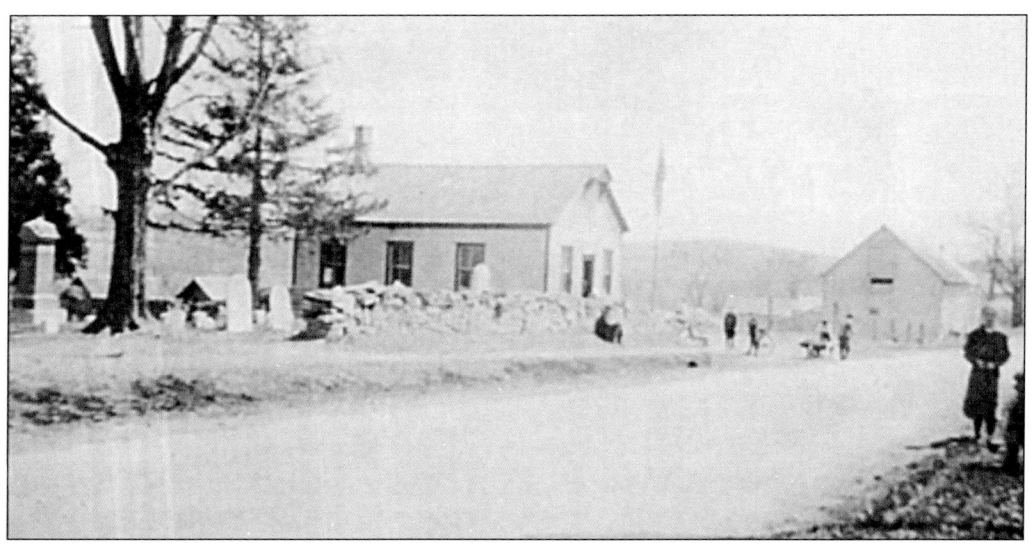

NORTH EAST CENTER SCHOOL #8. This school on Route 22 once stood in a busy hamlet. According to an article in the 1976 NEHS Yearbook, the school was begun in 1839 and ready for occupancy in 1840. It continued as a school for almost a hundred years, educating the children of the area, including three generations of the family of Village Clerk, Beverly Hosier Gordon. Today it is a residence. (NEHS.)

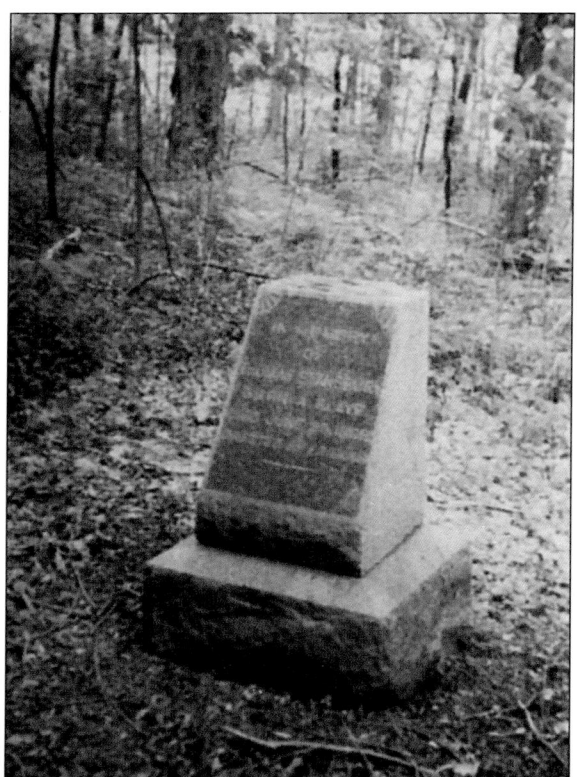

NORTH EAST CENTER CEMETERY. Next to the school is the burying ground and foundations of the old Methodist church, which in 1847 had 64 members and housed a library with 250 volumes. In the cemetery stands a granite monument engraved: "Thomas Stansbury, Born a slave Died June 30, 1899 Erected by his friends," a remarkable tribute to a highly respected man who, as a boy, had run away from a plantation in Maryland in order to find freedom. The church itself moved to Millerton as the village grew in importance. (JS.)

CULVER FARM FIELDS. On Downey Road at the intersection of CR 61 is this farm that was the site of the Moravian Mission Burying Ground near the Mission House. Two stones with "Powell" (i.e. Brother Joseph Powell) were found and given by the Culver family to the Moravians in Bethlehem. Mr. Culver was North East Supervisor from 1947 to 1961 and a very active community member. (JG.)

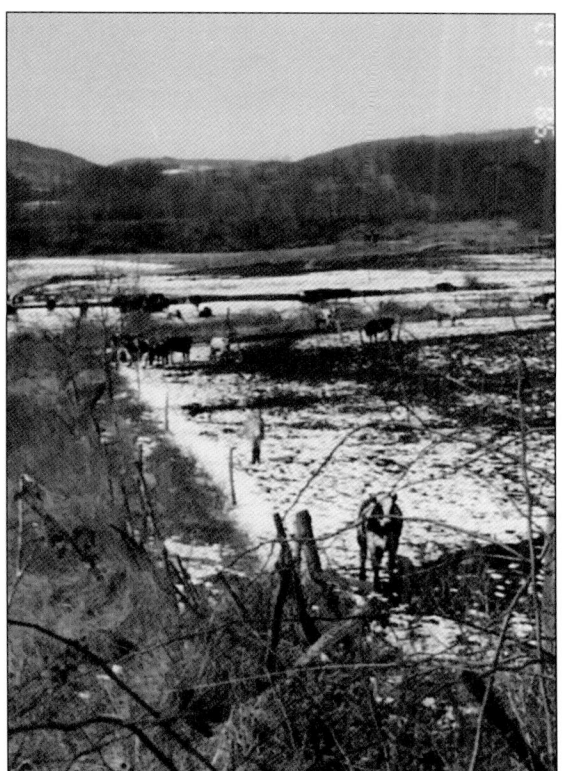

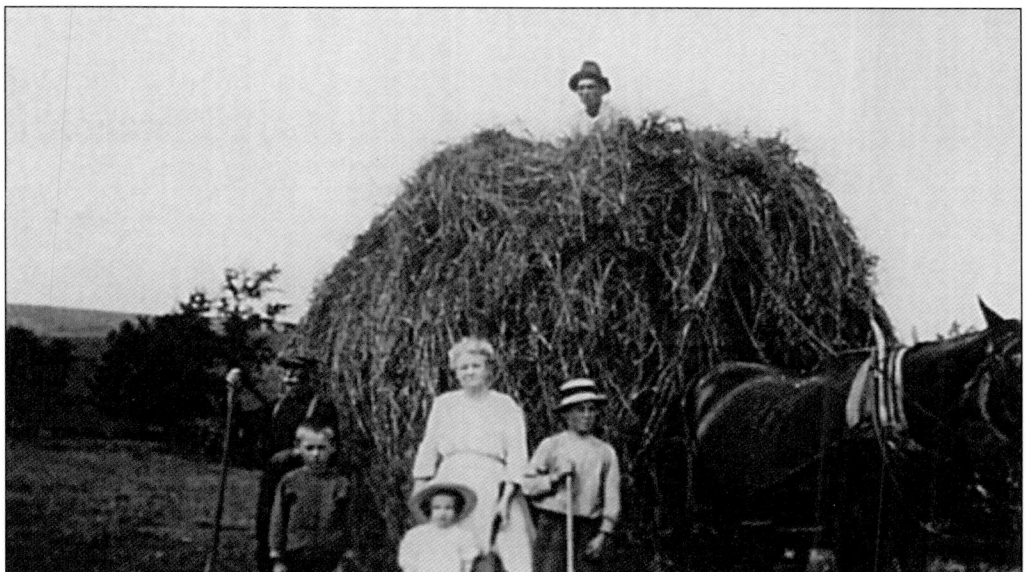

DOWNEY FARM. This photograph, which dates from c. 1920, shows the Downey family standing in front of a wagon filled with hay that they had apparently just finished raking. Ed Downey's grandfather and grandmother emigrated from Ireland in the 1880s, met and married in America, and raised 13 children. At first tenant farmers, the family acquired the farm in 1897 after some years of hard work. (ED.)

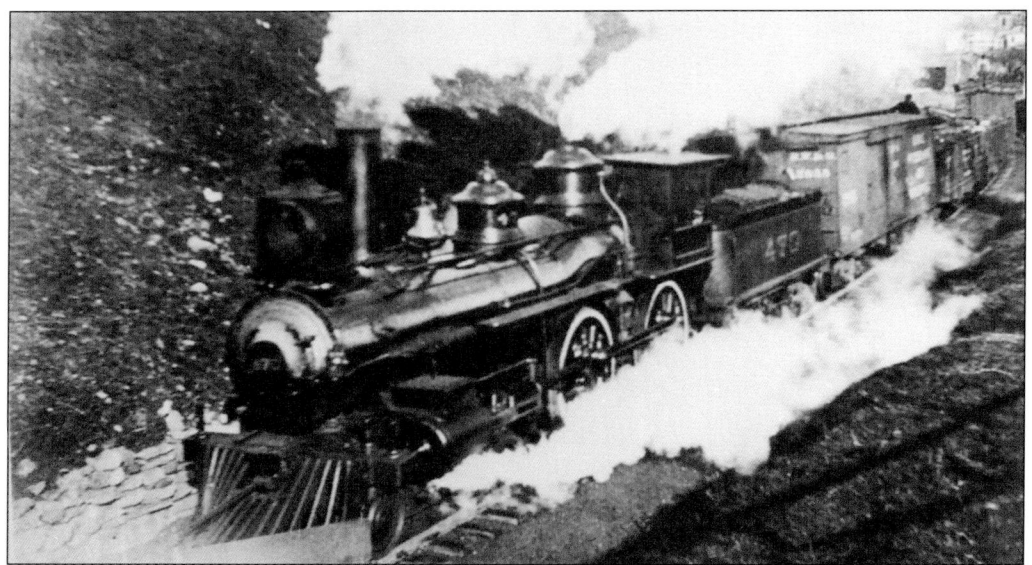

GOING THROUGH THE ROCK-CUT. A train with the village of Millerton barely visible in the upper right-hand corner is a graphic reminder that without the train there would have been no Millerton. The extension of the railroad through the Harlem Valley led to myriad changes, including the establishment of the village. Before the coming of the railroad, there were no houses or buildings in what is now the center of the village. (NEHS.)

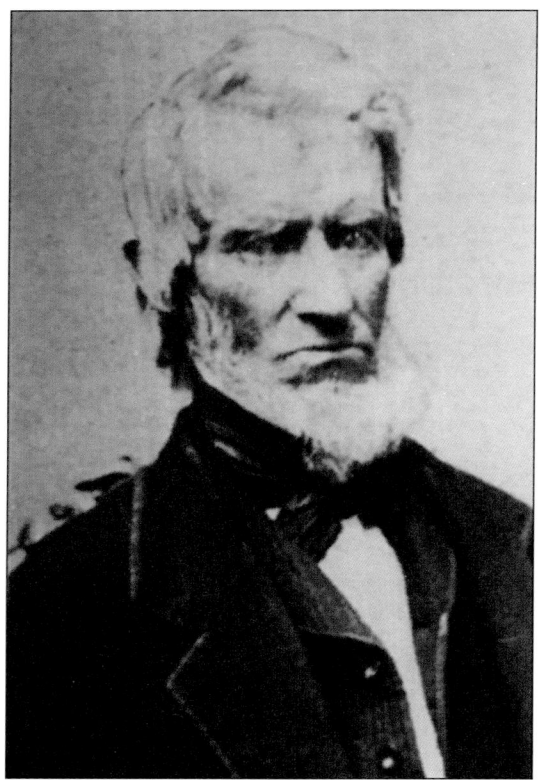

COL. JOHN WINCHELL. In 1851, Col. John Winchell, Walter Wakeman, and Alexander H. Holley (later governor of Connecticut) laid out the present village of Millerton. Much of the land had belonged to the Winchell and Wakeman families. Colonel Winchell's grandfather Lt. James Winchell, a soldier in the American Revolution, had come from Turkey Hills, Connecticut, in 1760. Colonel John Winchell and his son James, known as "Colonel Jim," laid out the trees to line the village streets. (NEHS.)

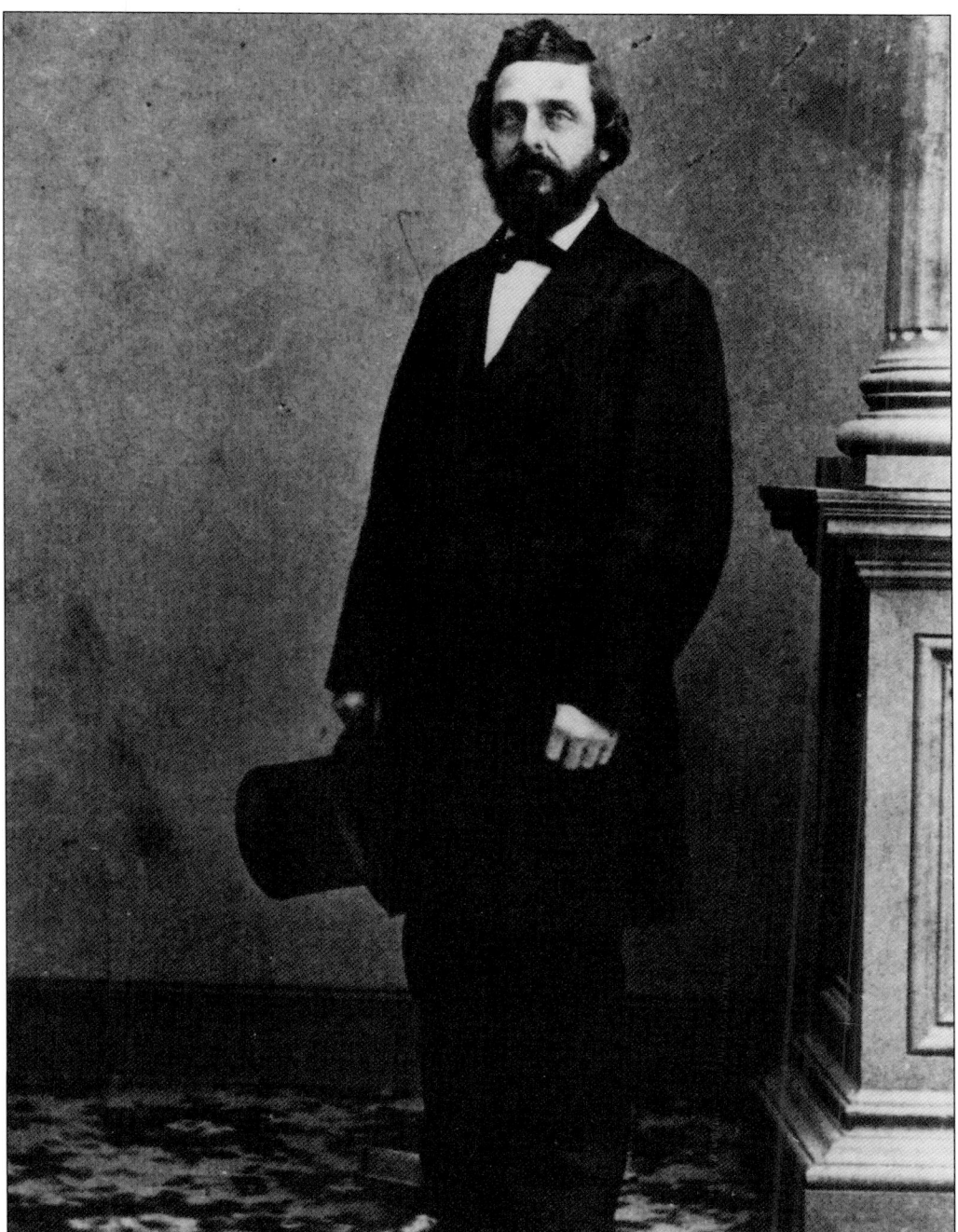

SIDNEY MILLER. This formal portrait of Sidney Miller was done by Brady. The decision was made in the Wakeman house to name the village "Millerton" after Miller, a civil engineer and major contractor, who had overseen the construction of the Harlem Railroad between Dover Plains and Chatham. The new center was soon seen as the location for up and coming businesses; entrepreneurs moved as close as they could to the new depot. Families and churches also relocated to Millerton, abandoning Spencer's Corners and North East Center. (NEHS.)

MILLERTON HOTEL,

OPPOSITE RAILROAD DEPOT,

MILLERTON, N. Y.

HORSES AND CARRIAGES
TO LET,

PASSENGERS CONVEYED TO ANY POINT.

N. E. WHEELER, Pro'r.

M. PULVER, Clerk.

MILLERTON HOTEL ADVERTISEMENT. This advertisement dates from the turn of the century. One of the first buildings to be erected in the new village, it was completed in 1852 and run by "Colonel Jim" during the time when hordes of rowdies, scavenging for food and drink after the Morrissey-Sullivan fight, overran the village. This rampage finally resulted in the establishment of civil order in what had been "Hell's Acre," once the refuge of pirates, cock fighters, horse thieves, and "skippy girls." (NEHS.)

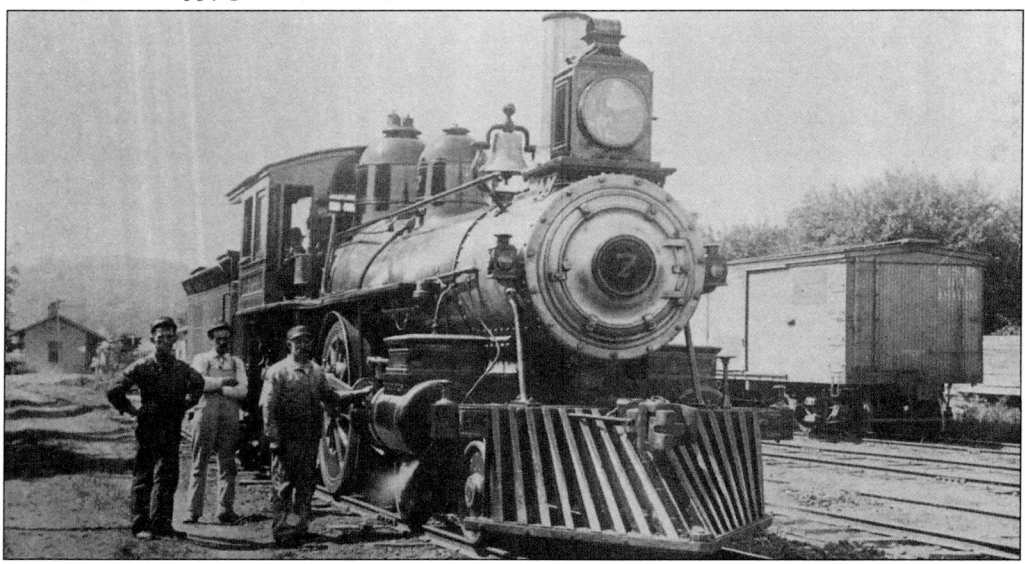

NEWBURGH, DUTCHESS, AND CONNECTICUT RAILROAD CREW. This 1899 photograph is a reminder that Millerton was not only on the Harlem Line, but was also served by the N, D, and C (Newburgh, Dutchess and Connecticut), which was consolidated into the Central New England at the beginning of the 20th century. This east-west connection allowed Harlem Valley residents to reach Dutchess Junction to board the New York Central to New York or take the ferry to Newburgh and proceed to points west. (NEHS.)

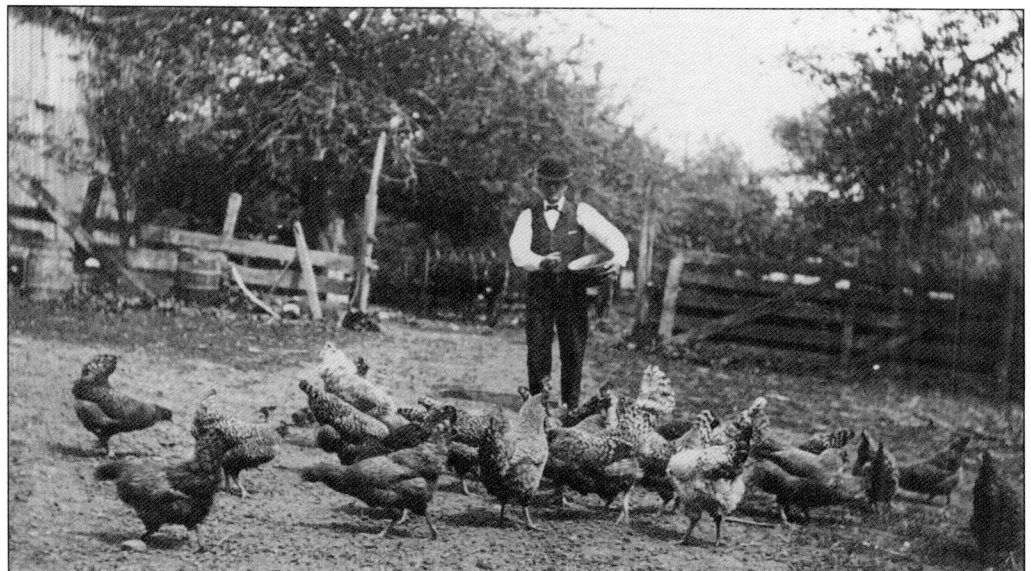

JOHN R. WINCHELL FEEDING THE CHICKENS. The grandson of Col. John Winchell and son of "Colonel Jim," John R. continued the family farming tradition. In the 18th and early 19th century, farmers were often almost completely self-sufficient. They grew grain to feed the cows or sheep, which in turn supplied milk and meat as well as hides and wool for clothing. Chickens laid eggs and appeared themselves, roasted, surrounded by home-grown vegetables on Sunday dinner tables. (NEHS.)

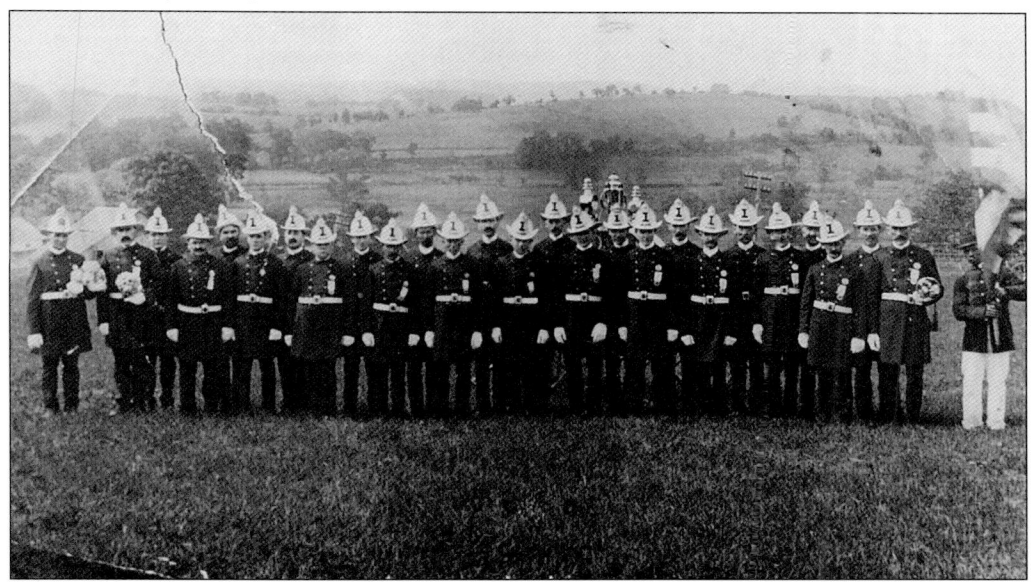

FIREMEN WITH NEW UNIFORMS. In 1901, members of the fire company organized in 1892 received their first uniforms and were all Number One! A disastrous fire in 1891 demonstrated the need for a village water works instead of having to rely on a bucket brigade that could stretch from the Webatuck across the railroad tracks to the scene. The newly established fire company was named the E.H. Thompson Hose Company in honor of the president of the Millerton National Bank. (BS.)

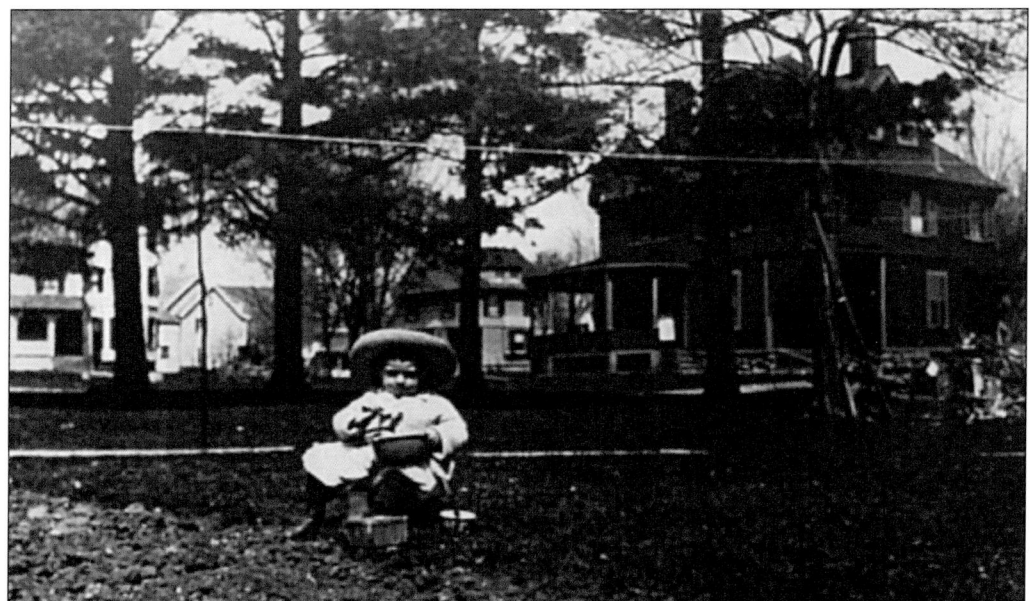

JANET JENKS BURNETT IN FRONT OF HOUSE. Janet Jenks is seen c. 1914 in front of the house on Park Street where she was married and near the house where she still lives. Her great-grandfather and grandfather had once run "Lord's Tavern" on State Line Road in Spencer's Corners, and her grandmother Marion Rogers Traver ran the former Dakin Inn. Toward the end of the 19th century, Mrs. Burnett's family moved from Spencer's Corners to the village of Millerton. (JJB.)

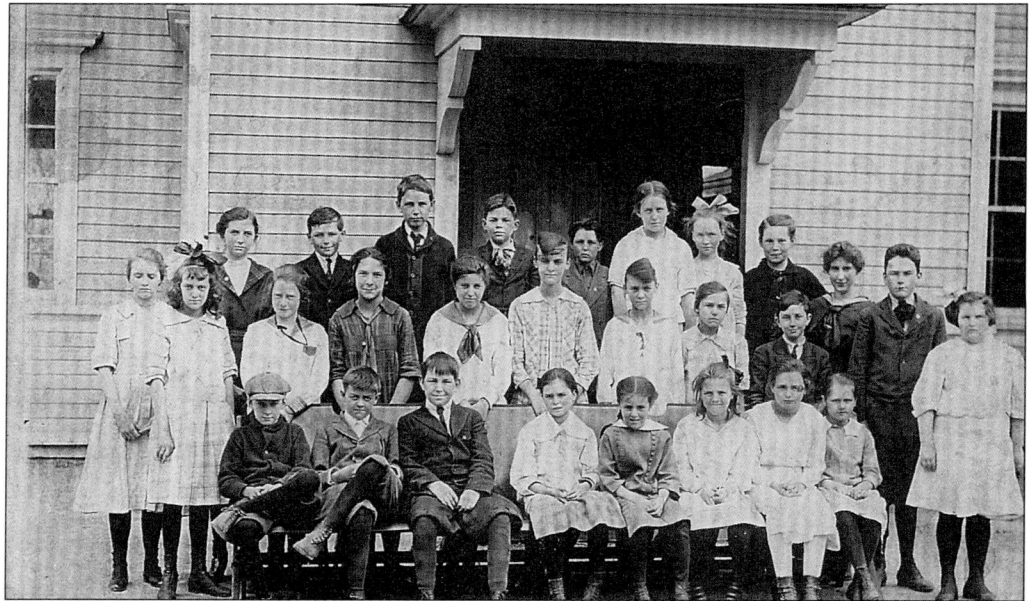

MILLERTON UNION FREE SCHOOL. This photograph shows a 1915 class in front of the school that was located at the approach of Checkerboard Corner. Built in 1884 and added to in 1889, 1895, and 1900, the Union Free School was established in 1896 when every hamlet still had its own one-room schoolhouse. Four years later a high school was approved. (BS.)

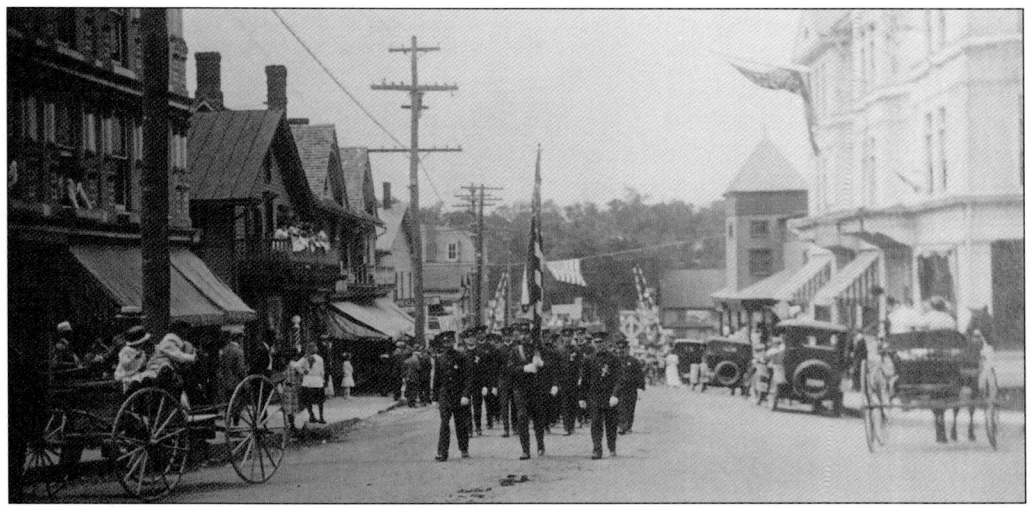

JULY 4TH PARADE. Shown in this image is a 1917 July 4th parade on Main Street in Millerton. America had just joined the war effort. Three modes of transportation are indicated: raised railroad gates, horse drawn traps, and automobiles. The building on the right is the Shaffer and Shufelt building, located where Riley's Furniture is today. (NEHS.)

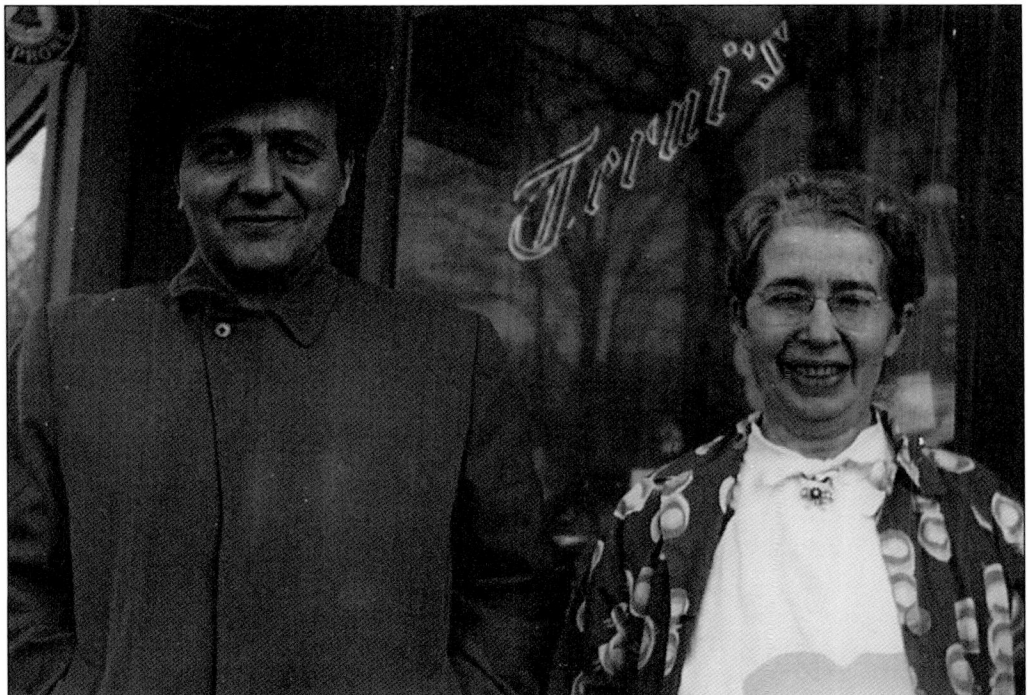

TERNI'S. This is a 1956 photograph of Assunta Terni with her son Arthur. Paul and Assunta Terni, originally from Italy, bought the former Brown property in 1919 and began to sell fresh fruits, vegetables, ice cream, and candy. In 1926, they expanded to open the United Cigar Store in the annex. In 1927, Mr. Terni died, but Mrs. Terni and her sons Arthur and Stephen continued the business. In 1934, Art opened the Sports Store. Today, Philip Terni, a grandson, runs the family business. (PT).

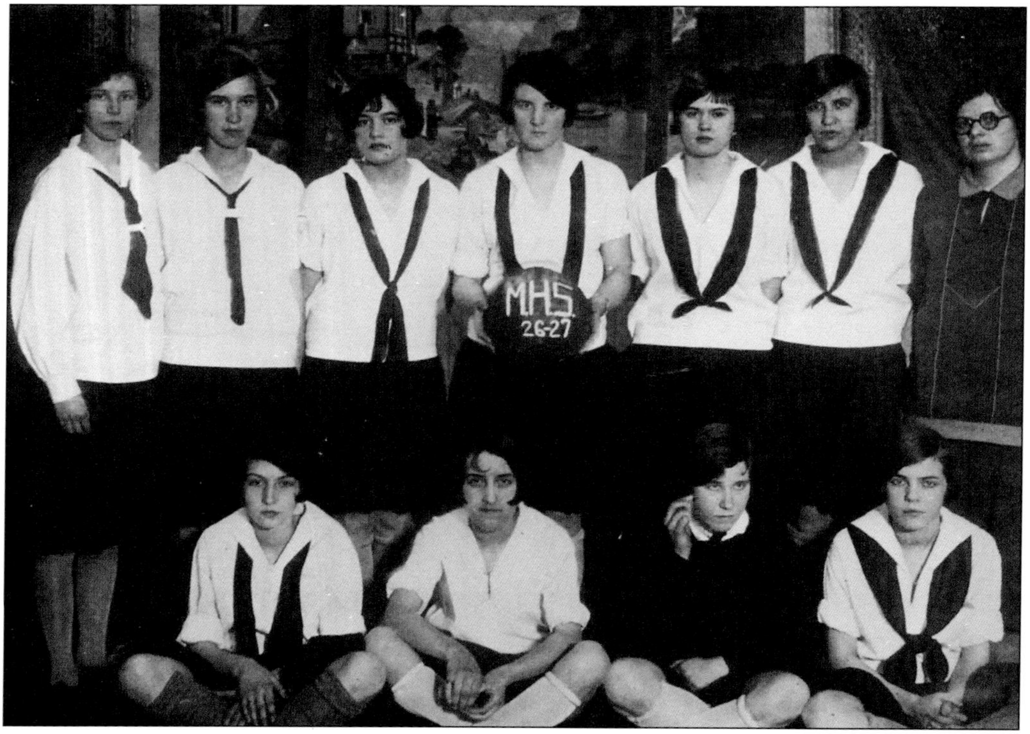

GIRLS' BASKETBALL TEAM. This 1926-27 team dressed in their middy blouses recalls a fashion statement of an earlier time. To the right of the young woman holding the ball is Violet Simmons, who became a much respected and loved teacher. Sandy Berger, now on President Clinton's staff, recalls her fondly. Once she arranged to have her Webatuck class speak with then Supreme Court Justice Thurgood Marshall. (NEHS.)

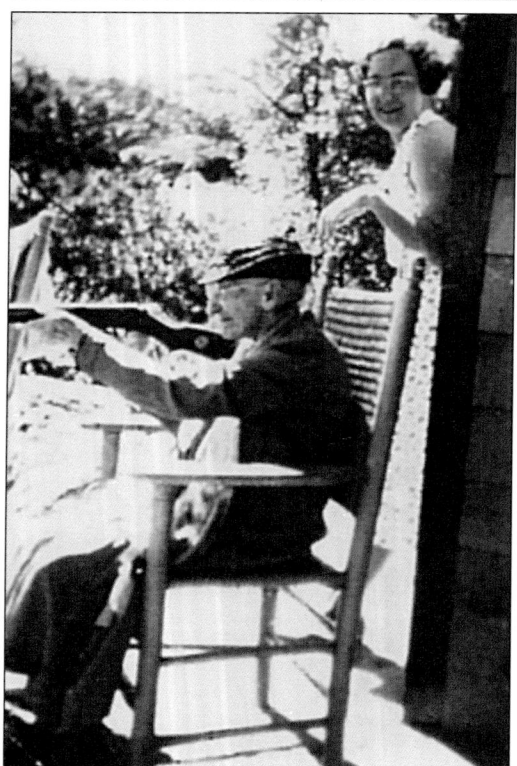

MARION TRAVER SHOOTING TIN CANS. This 1930s photograph of Mrs. Traver, a diminutive sharp-shooter and Millerton's own "Annie Get Your Gun," with her granddaughter Janet Jenks (Burnett) was taken at the family camp at Mt. Riga. Mrs. Traver, originally from Scotland, reputedly a marvelous baker, also enjoyed picking wild strawberries growing along the Central New England Railroad tracks. (JJB.)

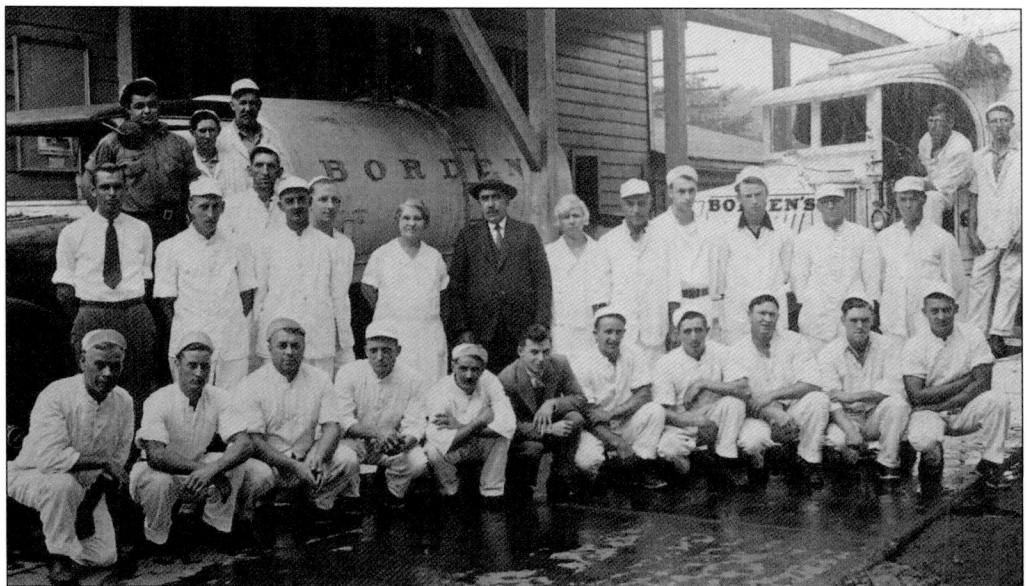

BORDEN'S MILK PLANT EMPLOYEES. Shown here in a 1932 photograph are workers at the Borden's Milk Plant in Millerton. The company, which had originated in Wassaic, had plants up and down the Harlem Railroad line. Its demand for milk transformed a varied subsistence type of farming into an agri-business involving the dairy farmer, plant worker, and freight handler. (NEHS.)

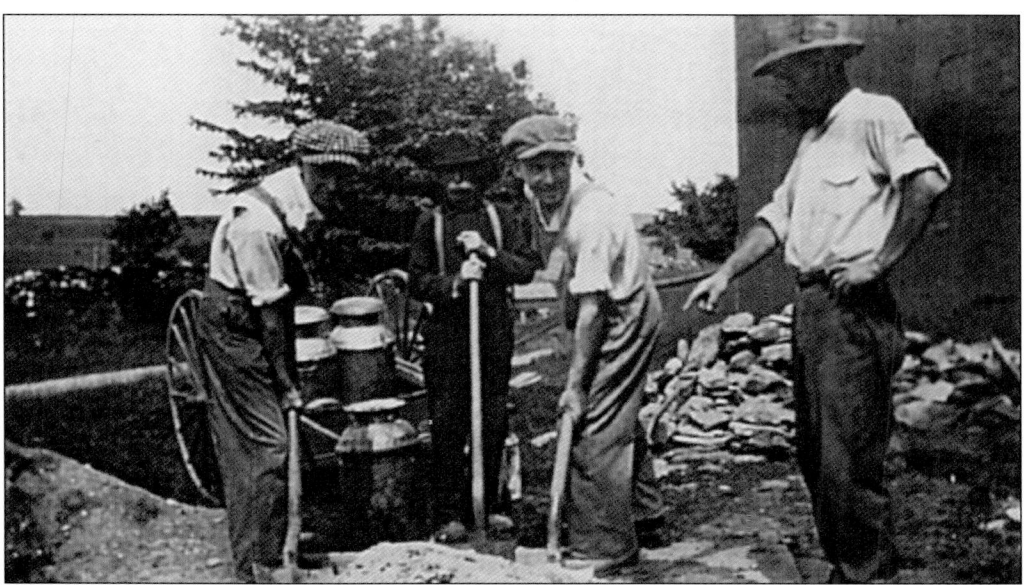

DOWNEY MEN WITH MILK CANS. Like other farmers, the Downeys also turned to dairy farming and sold milk to one of the local milk processing companies. After WW II, they established their own dairy business: milking the cow, pasteurizing the milk, bottling it, and finally delivering it to the doors of their neighbors. They were in control from production to retail. (ED.)

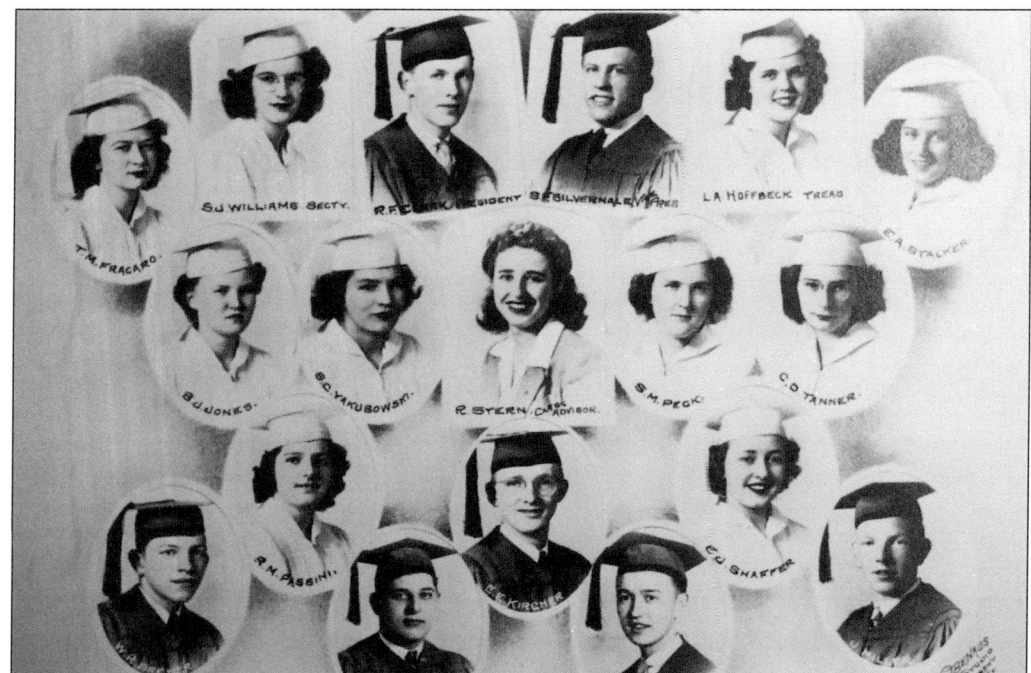

MILLERTON HIGH SCHOOL CLASS OF 1944. A formal photograph of the graduating class, it includes seven young men and ten young women. The war may have decreased the number of the former, but it seems that in general there were always more female than male high school graduates. Little could they imagine how greatly the world they would encounter as adults would differ from pre-war Millerton. (NEHS.)

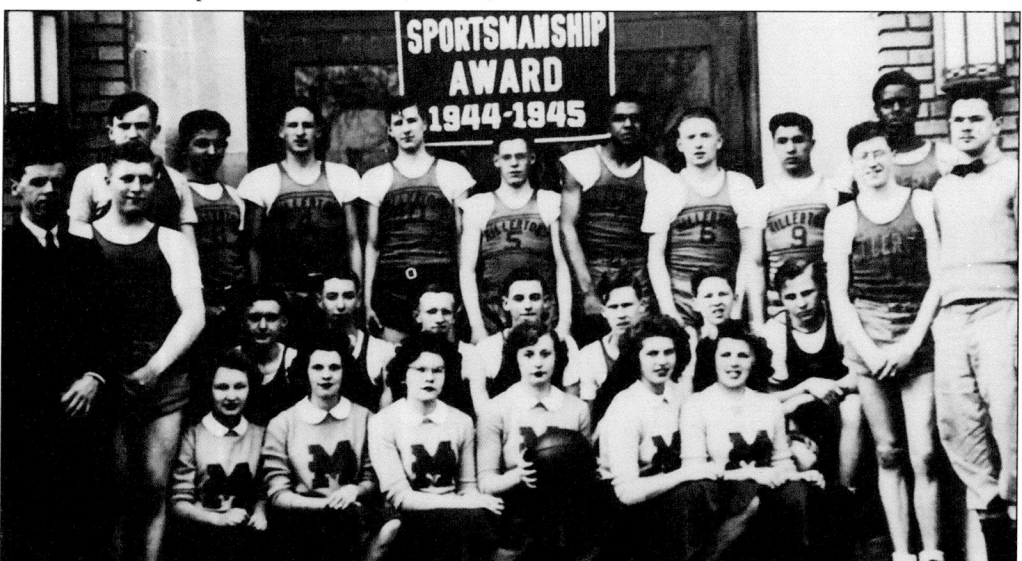

SPORTSMANSHIP AWARDS. Shown here in a 1945 photograph are athletes and cheerleaders. School has never been "all work and no play." Elsie Young Albig can be seen as an enthusiastic cheerleader, extreme right in the front row. Now she is head cheerleader for the NEHS and the town's historical resources. (NEHS.)

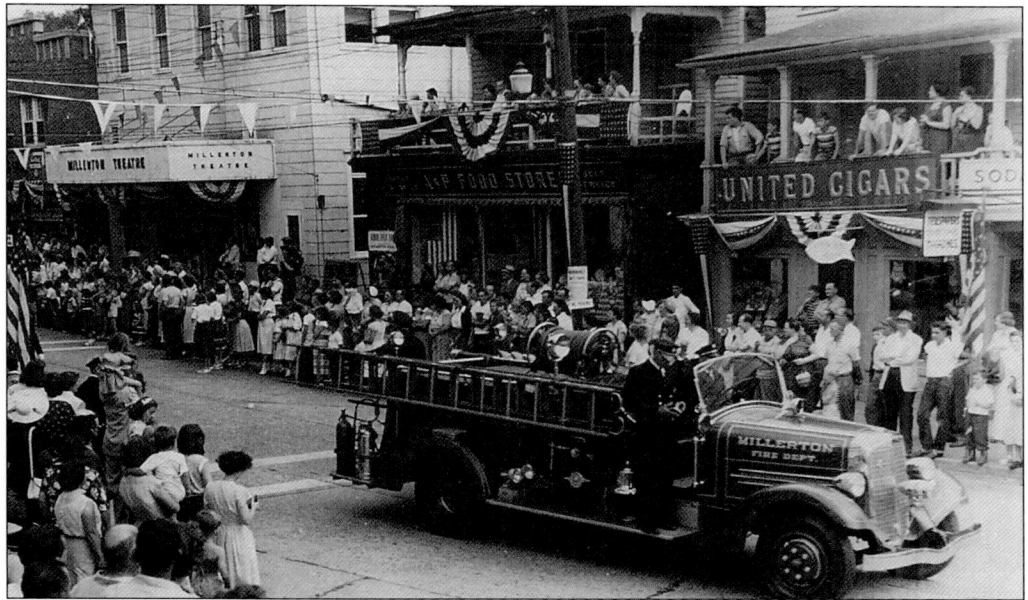

CENTENNIAL PARADE. Pictured here in 1951 is the Millerton Fire Department engine proceeding down Main Street, past the Millerton Theater, and about to go by Terni's. Crowds of people are happily celebrating the centenary of the establishment of the village. This photograph captures the pride and neighborliness of small town America. (BS.)

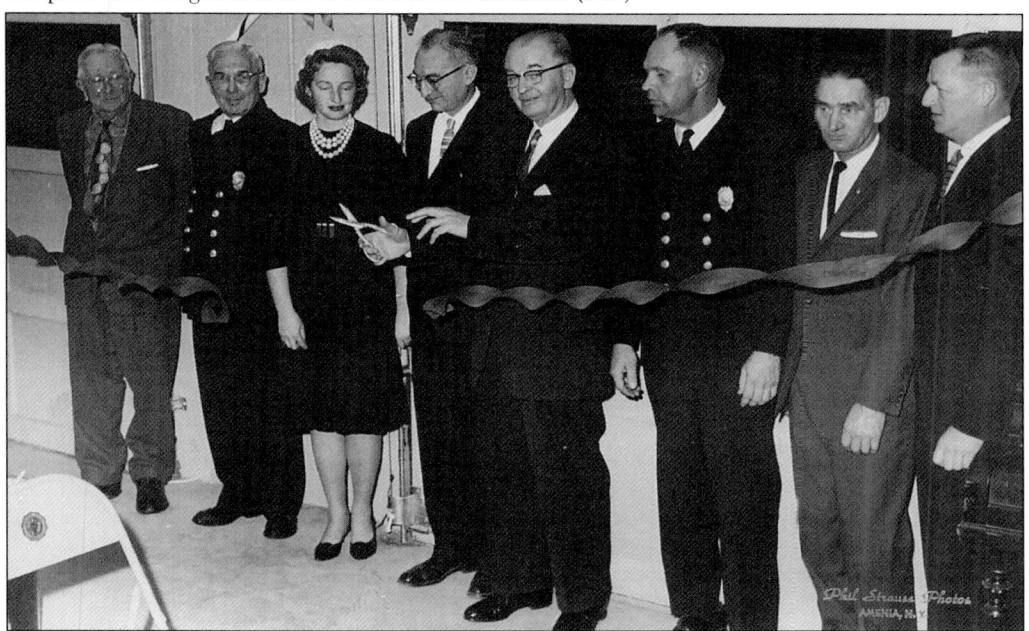

DEDICATION OF THE NEW FIREHOUSE. The new firehouse was dedicated on December 29, 1962. Shown in this image is the ribbon-cutting ceremony. William Gormley (fifth from the left) was mayor of Millerton. In 1992, the department celebrated its 100th anniversary. Bernie Silvernail, fire department historian who has provided many of the photographs in this book, had completed 42 years of service then. The year 2000 will see his 50th anniversary. (BS.)

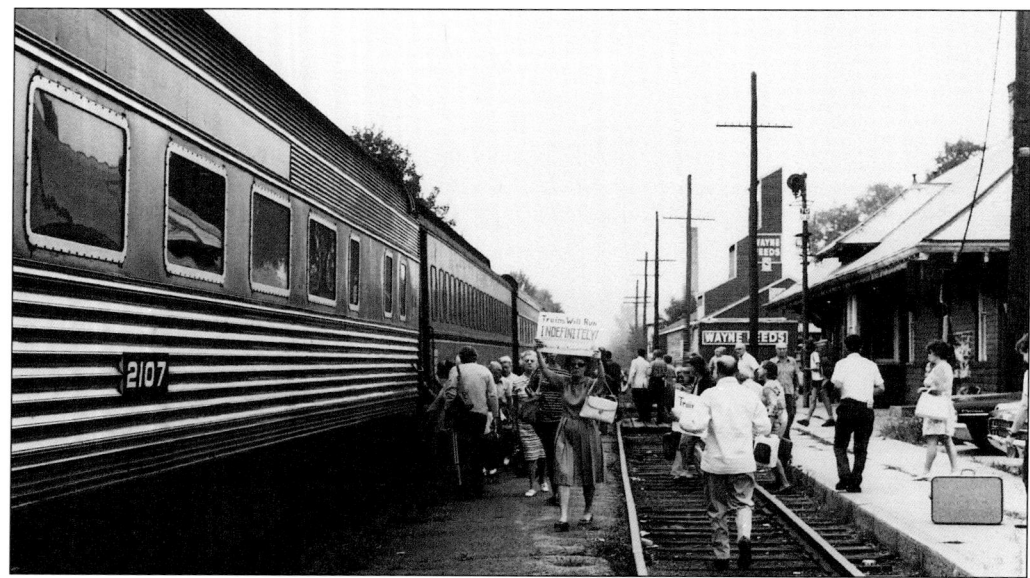

LETTIE CARSON. In this photograph by Heyward Cohen, accomplished railroad photographer, Lettie Carson is holding up a sign on Labor Day 1971: "Trains Will Run Indefinitely." Under her leadership, the Harlem Valley Transportation Association waged a gallant but ultimately unsuccessful 12-year fight to retain passenger service north of Dover on the Upper Harlem Railroad Line. Subsequently, a federal ruling stated that railroad service could not be stopped without the operators' first showing that abandonment will not harm the surrounding "human environment." (HC.)

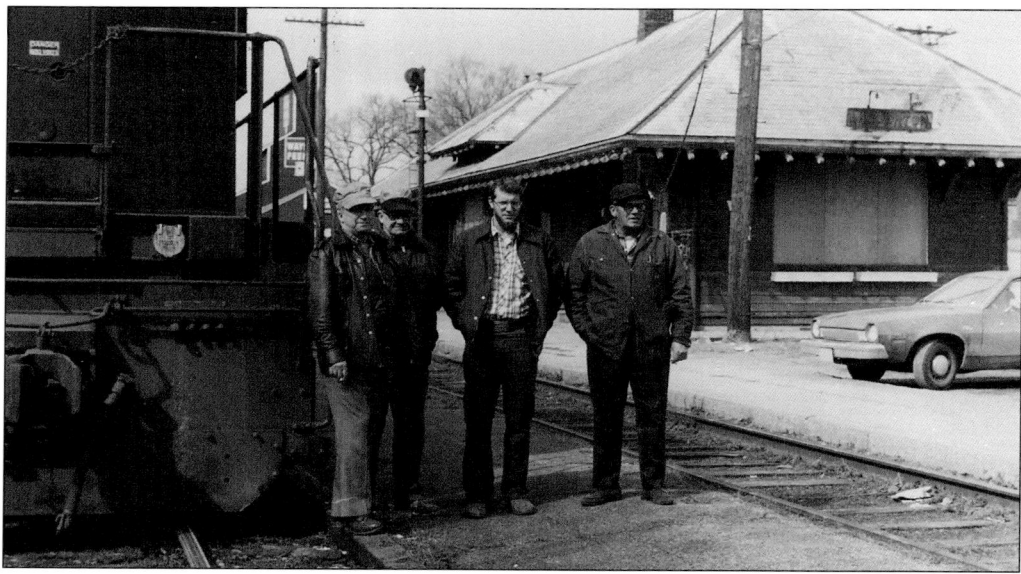

TRAIN CREW. This crew of a freight train includes locomotive engineer Ray Duvall; train conductor Walter Morris, a Millerton resident; and George Smith, now employed as a Metro-North engineer on the Harlem Line. The railroad continued freight service north of Millerton to Chatham until April 1976 and from Wassaic to Millerton until 1980. The tracks were removed in 1981, and a rail trail established during the 1980s. (HC.)

ELSIE YOUNG ALBIG AND DIANE THOMPSON. Seen here in front of the library, where the well-cared-for records of the North East Historical Society are stored, are Diane Thompson, vice-president of the society, and Elsie Young Albig, an active member whose various slide shows always draw an enthusiastic audience. They both credit "Chet" Eisenhuth, former town historian, for his dedication to preserving the town's history. (JG.)

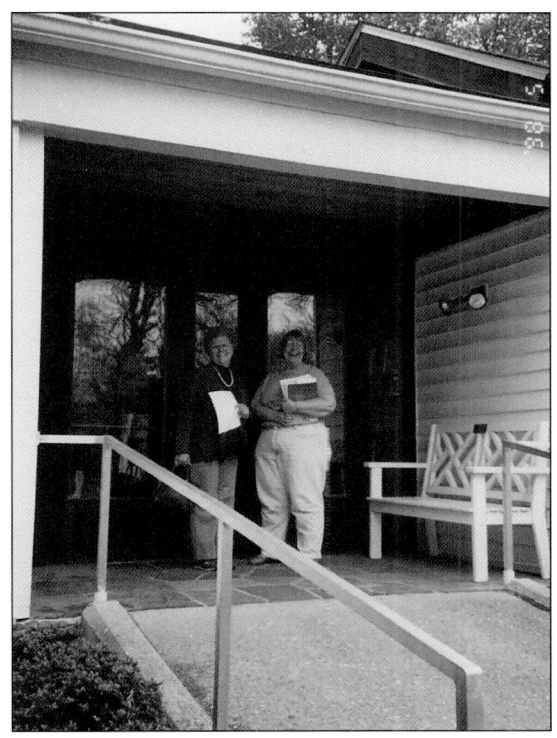

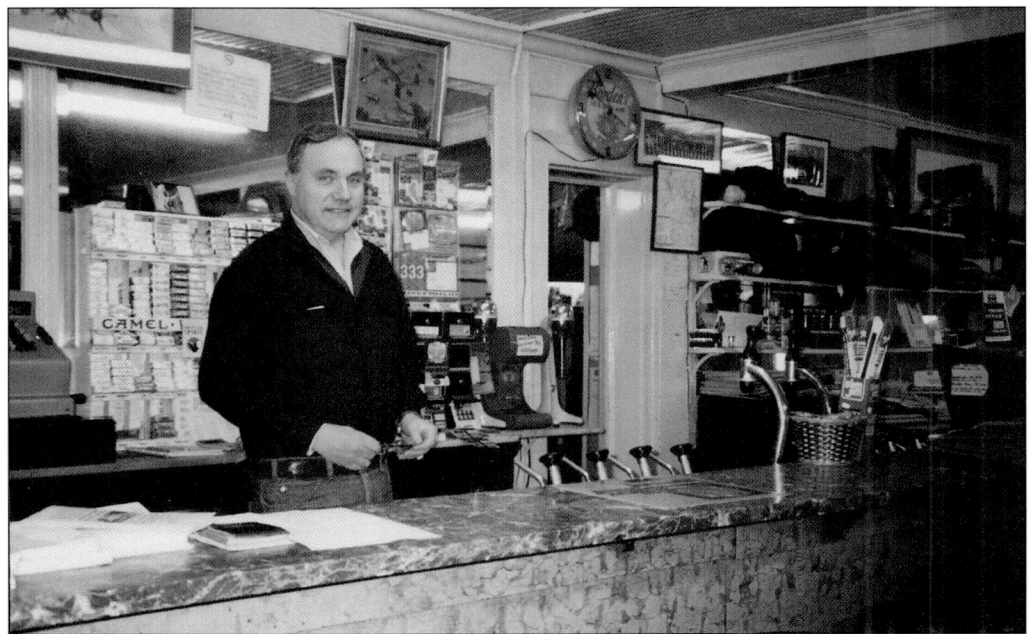

PHIL TERNI. Phil Terni is the third generation of the Terni family to manage their stores. This continuity of service provides a sense of place even to those who return to Millerton after an absence of 30 years. The railroad tracks, which caused the village to be established, have been replaced by the Harlem Valley Rail Trail, and Millerton continues to flourish. (JG.)

MAP OF PINE PLAINS. French's *Gazetteer* of 1860 listed statistics for Pine Plains that had, according to the previous census, a population of 754 males and 699 females. With an animal population of 407 horses, 711 oxen, 678 cows, 5,723 sheep, and 2,117 swine, humans were outnumbered by more than 7 to 1. Of the 272 families enumerated, 150 were property owners i.e. freeholders. The remainder rented or worked for a family that provided housing. General farming was the principal industry supporting grist- and sawmills and small businesses such as general stores and blacksmiths. The Harris Scythe Works in Hammertown was the biggest mill in town with 50 "hands." The 1876 map of Pine Plains shows a sparsely settled town that was just beginning to show signs of growth influenced by the coming of several railroad lines after the Civil War. (DCHS.)

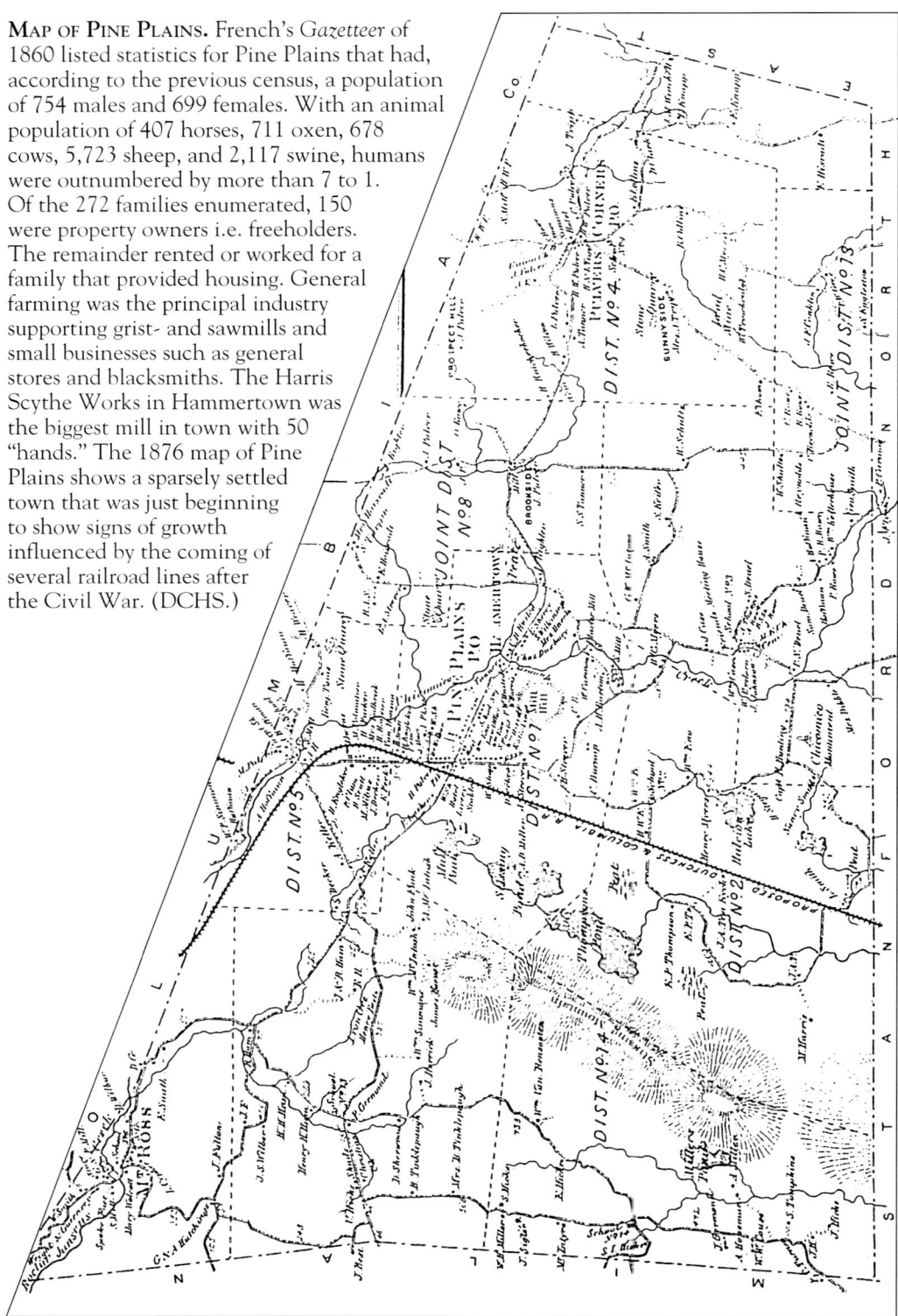

Five

PINE PLAINS

Stissing Mountain near Pine Plains hamlet overlooks a rich plain watered by the Shekomeko Creek and three lakes, the source of the Wappinger Creek. In the 18th century, Palatines settled on territory inhabited by Schaghticoke/Mahicans. A Native American village, Shekomeko, was the setting for dramatic efforts by Moravian missionaries to convert Native Americans c. 1742.

History lives along two modern highways that intersect at Pine Plains hamlet, the town center. NY 199 roughly follows the old Salisbury Turnpike that linked Livingston mines in Connecticut with the Hudson. A modified country trail system that passed the Shekomeko Native American village and the home of Morris Graham, delegate to the Provincial Convention of 1775 and leader of a Revolutionary War regiment, is now NYS Route 82. The names of the mid-trail hamlet and town were inspired by a pine grove in the hamlet that served as a Native American burial site. Town history is linked to North East from which it was separated in 1823.

Borders drawn in 1706 for the Little Nine Partners Patent lines influenced growth for more than a century as original leaseholds kept land in the hands of patent holders' heirs. As it was primarily farm and mining country tied to rural Columbia County, only a few small settlements dot the landscape: Mt. Ross, Pulvers Corners, Hoffmann's Corners, and Bethel.

The coming of the railroads after the Civil War attracted visitors to relax at lakes and connected residents to larger Dutchess towns. Flagging down a train in the tiniest hamlet accessed the world. With increasing development, it becomes even more important to appreciate Pine Plains for its unique environment worthy of study and protection.

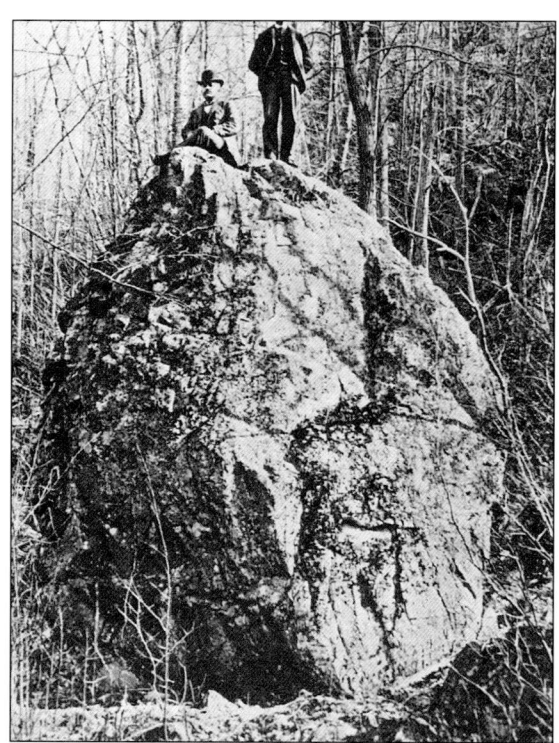

STISSING MOUNTAIN "METEOR." Stissing Mountain has always been something of a mystery; not part of a chain, but representing a single geological event eons ago, it hovers over the quiet waters of nearby lakes like a protective guardian. Its mystery has spawned folklore and some tall tales—like the one promulgated by the creator of this turn-of-the-century postcard explaining this huge Stissing rock as "a rare calciferous meteorite." (LNPHS.)

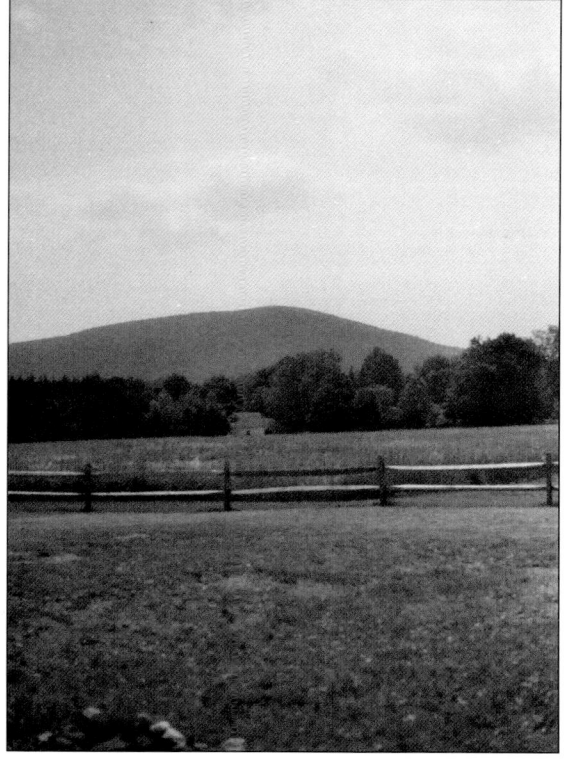

STISSING MOUNTAIN VIEWSHED. During the Roosevelt era, Stissing Mountain's height and viewshed made it valued as a lookout for spotting forest fires. Townspeople saved the 1939 WPA-built spotting tower from destruction by convincing the Department of Environmental Conservation to give it to them. The Nature Conservancy granted funds to purchase an acre of land around it. The tower affords the best view of the nearby lakes and the whole region in the Hudson Valley. (JG.)

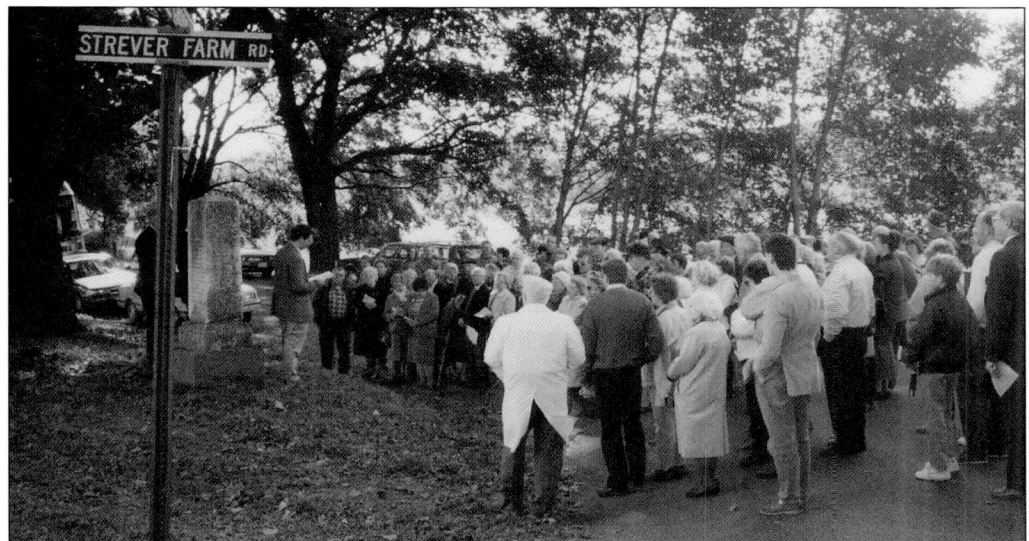

MORAVIAN MONUMENT PILGRIMAGE. In 1990, Supervisor Scott Chase and the Historical Society welcomed Moravian pilgrims to a monument to Gottlob Büttner raised on Edward Huntting's land in 1859 by Pennsylvania Moravians. It memorializes missionary martyrs who c. 1742 converted northeastern Mahican groups to Christianity. Christian Henry Rausch and Gottlob Büttner from Bethlehem began a mission in Shekomeko Native American village. It became Büttner's graveyard when persecution by liquor-selling squatters took its toll. (JG.)

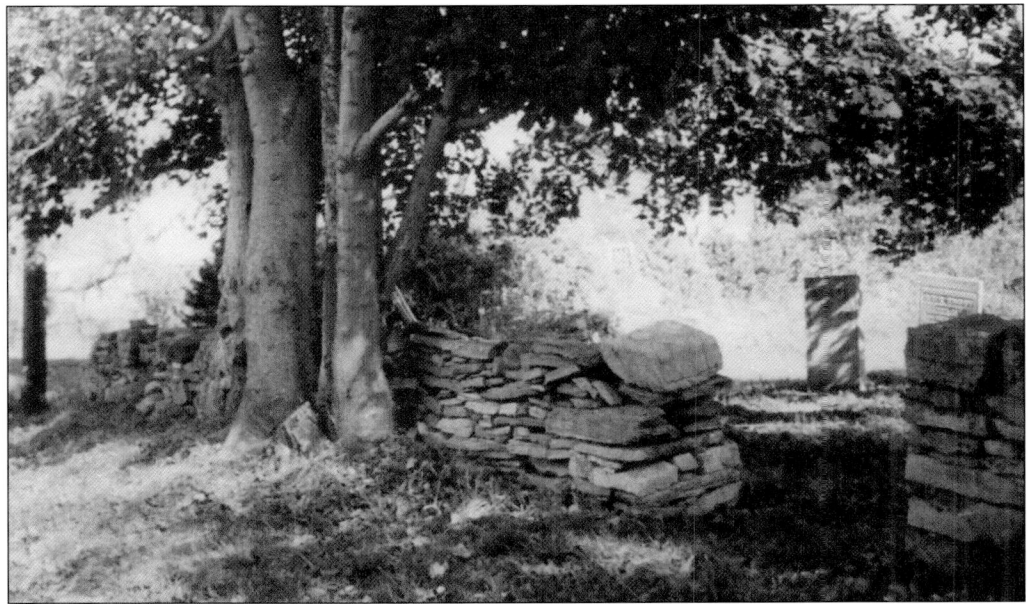

BETHEL CEMETERY. The town's oldest settlement is Bethel, a farm hamlet near historian Isaac Huntting's home on Carpenter Hill Road. Its history is embodied in twin cemeteries linked to local families and three former houses of worship. Lutherans built "Round Top," the first church, c. 1744-69. Friends, led by Charles Hoag, began a Meeting here in 1803, later adding a school where Quaker scholars Deborah and Jacob Willets taught. A Union Church advertising "free seats" was built in 1839. (JG.)

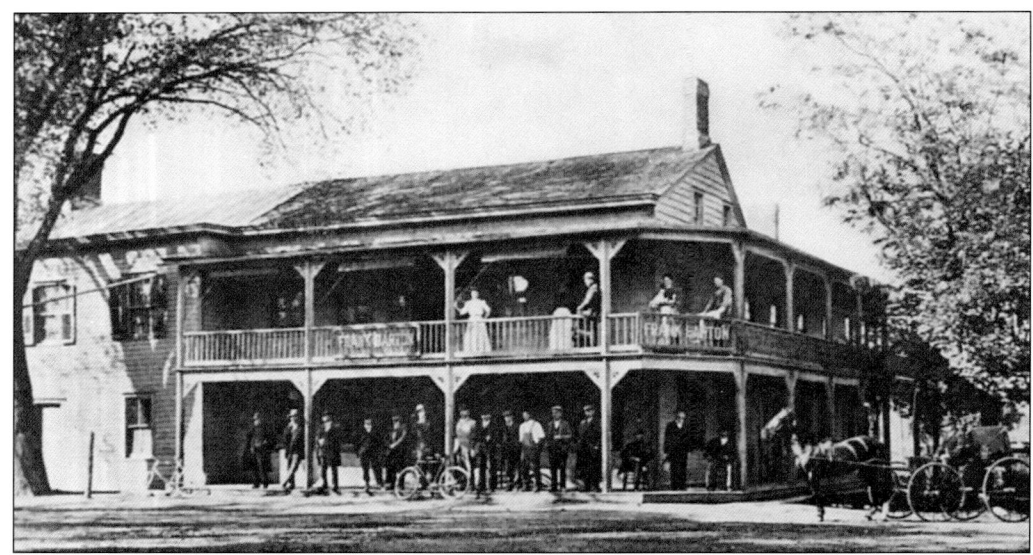

STISSING HOUSE. This restored hostelry, one of the town's oldest structures, dates to 1782 when Red Hook's "Capt." Cornelius Elmendorph opened his log house tavern. It has lodged, entertained, fed, watered both people and horses, held town meetings and elections, and rented out space under various proprietors. It has also died and been resurrected upon occasion. Whether called Husteds, Bowmans, Myers, Bartons, or Stissing House, a treasured phoenix sits at the crossroads of Church and Main Streets. (LNPHS.)

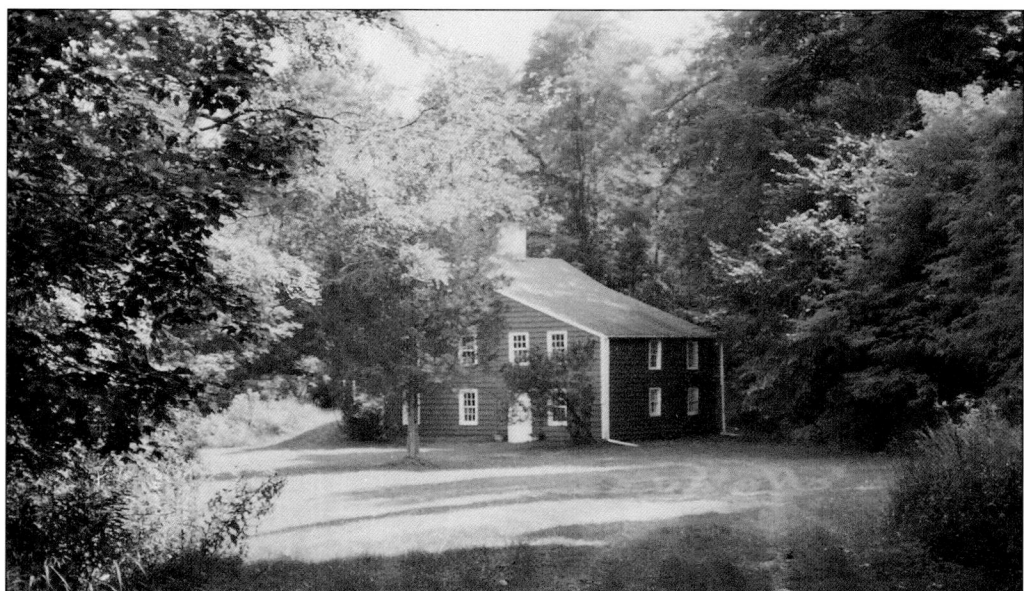

HARRIS-HUSTED HOUSE. This house overlooking the Shekomeko is all that remains of Hammertown, once a vital industrial hamlet. A gristmill and tannery, built c. 1776 by Peter Husted, were operating when John Harris, a scythe maker, came to Pine Plains c. 1783. He purchased creek property near the future route of the Rhinebeck Salisbury Turnpike for Harris Mills where the mowing machine's forerunner was proudly turned out with his imprint, "J.H." A noisy triphammer later named the hamlet. (DCTPA/JG.)

THE MELIUS-BENTLEY HOUSE. On Mt. Ross Road, near the hamlet hidden behind fencing, is the National Register farm built c. 1740 by the Melius family. Added to over the years by successive owners, farmhouses and outbuildings were built close to the roadside to ease winter chores. A closet bar beside the fireplace that could be locked to protect liquor supplies and valuables suggests tavern use as well. Roadside siting would have been an asset. The nearby historic barn burned in 1996. (JG.)

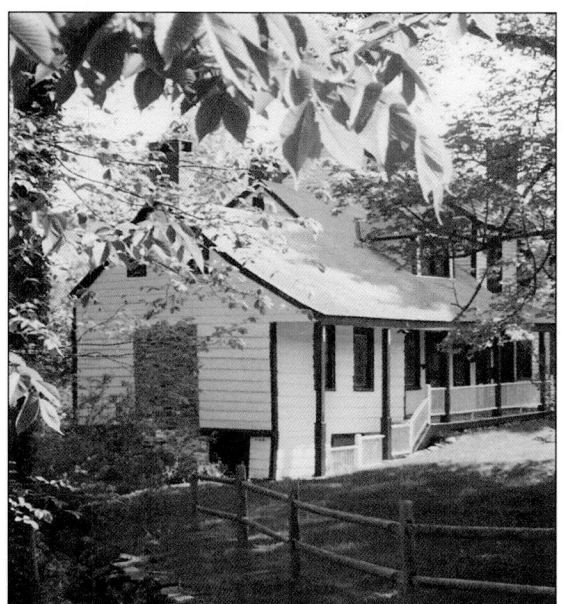

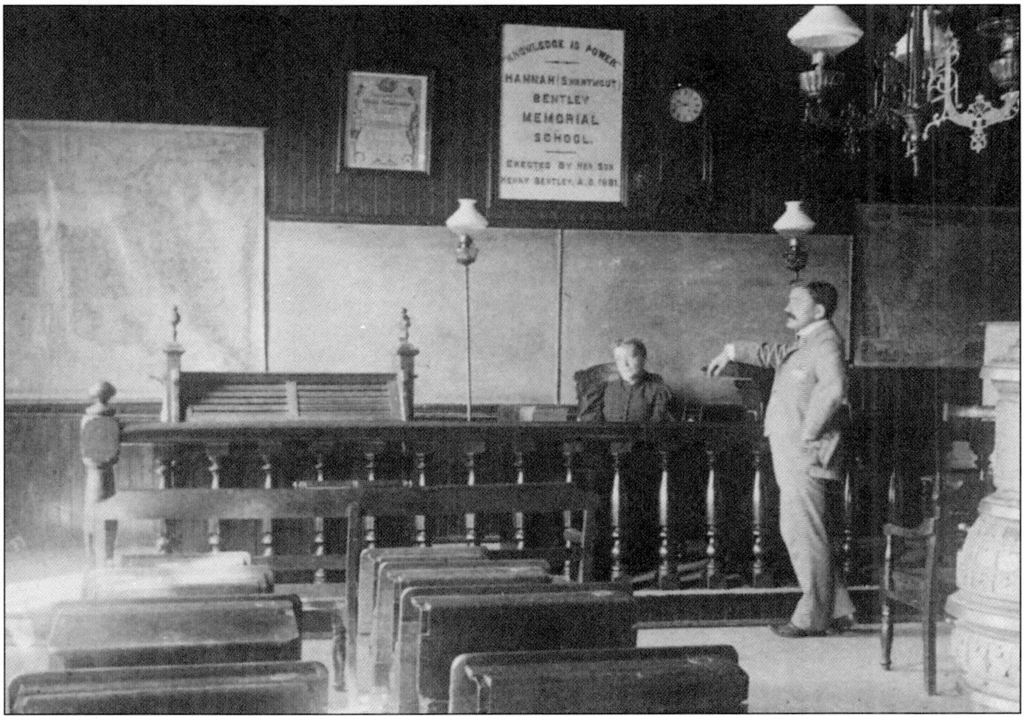

BENTLEY SCHOOL. The Bentleys, later residents of the Melius farm, endowed Mount Ross hamlet with a new public school. The building was the proud enterprise of donor Henry Bentley shown here with teacher Rose Fraleigh. The finely designed interior of the school was more reminiscent of a courtroom than the simple frame schools in other hamlets. A polished railing and platform separated the teacher from the pupils seated at oak and wrought iron desk-seats, bolted to the floor. (LNPHS.)

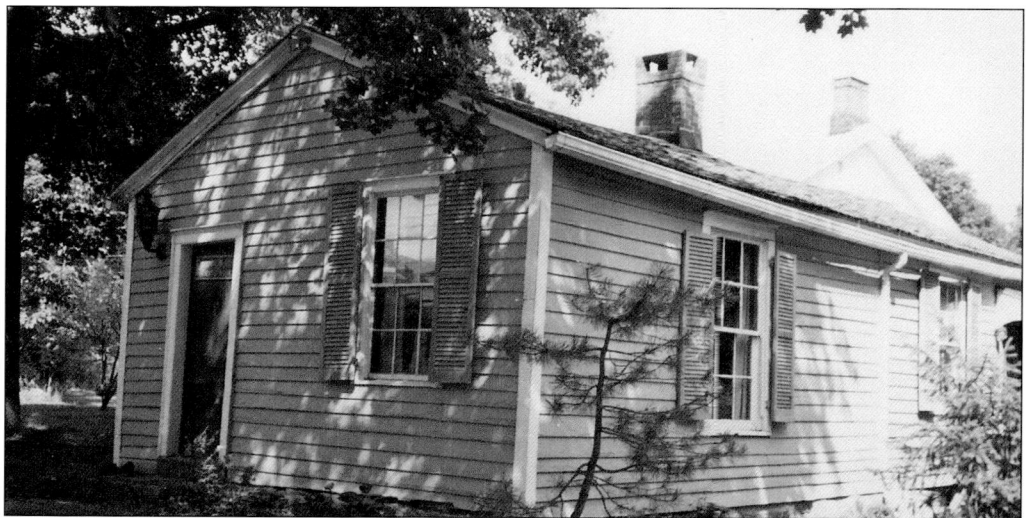

ENO LAW OFFICE. Stephen Eno's tiny yellow frame law office, built in 1814 by Rufus Bostwick, is a local landmark. Eno (1764-1854) came here at 27 to clerk in Philip Spencer Jr.'s law office after successfully educating himself to be a teacher. Despite a lack of formal education, he became a respected jurist and community businessman. His diary, passed down to descendant Janet Holden Adams, outlines the path of disciplined self-teaching that guided his successes. (DCTPA/JG.)

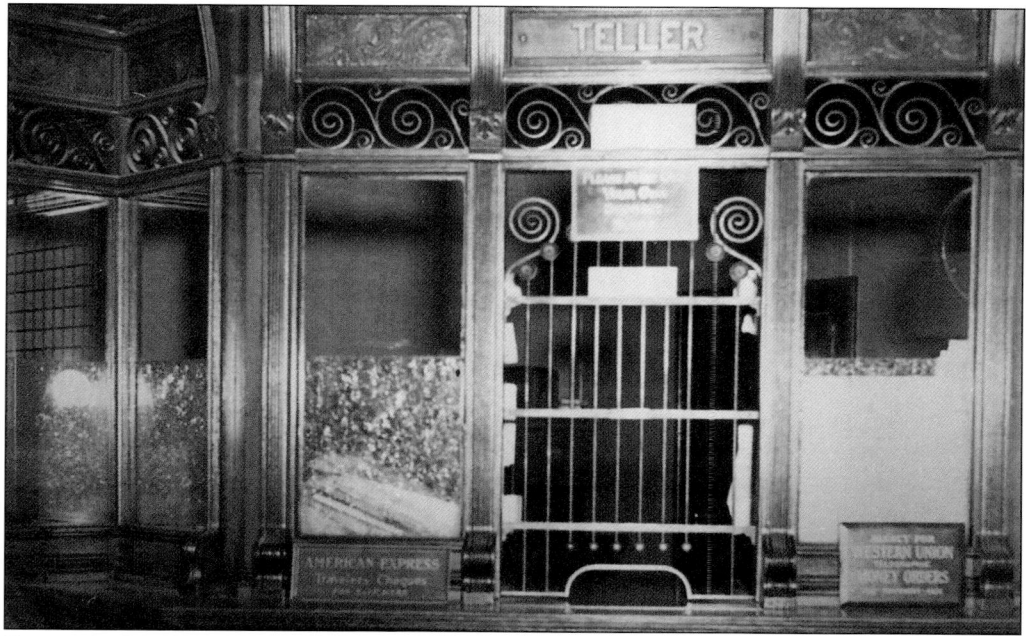

STISSING NATIONAL BANK. By 1839, Pine Plains felt the need for a local bank. Reuben W. Bostwick led in forming the Pine Plains Bank that year with capital of over $100,000—a tidy sum. The bank was humming along until the 1857 crash forced closure. A year later, it reorganized as the Stissing Bank, with $90,000 in assets and William S. Eno as president. It became a National bank in 1865 and has served customers through good times and bad ever since. (LNPHS.)

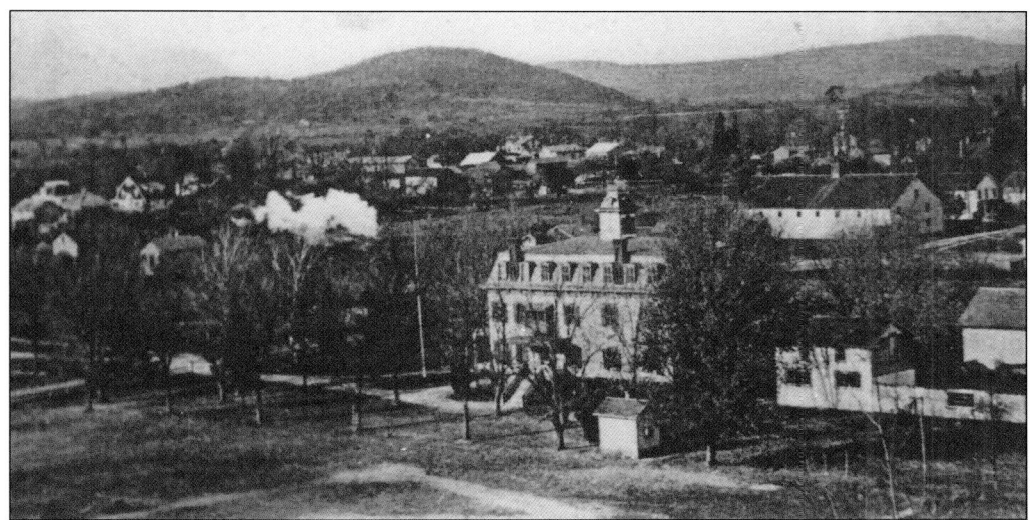

STEAMY PINE PLAINS. A turn-of-the-century postcard shows steam rising along the tracks. Rail service here, proposed as early as 1832, was slow in coming. Lines reached the rest of Dutchess County shortly after 1850, but northern tracks waited until after the Civil War. Multiple lines and 18 trains daily eventually came through town for freight and passengers, but the Central New England line was the one that counted. Pine Plains was on line with whistles, bells, and steam from wood-fired engines. (LNPHS.)

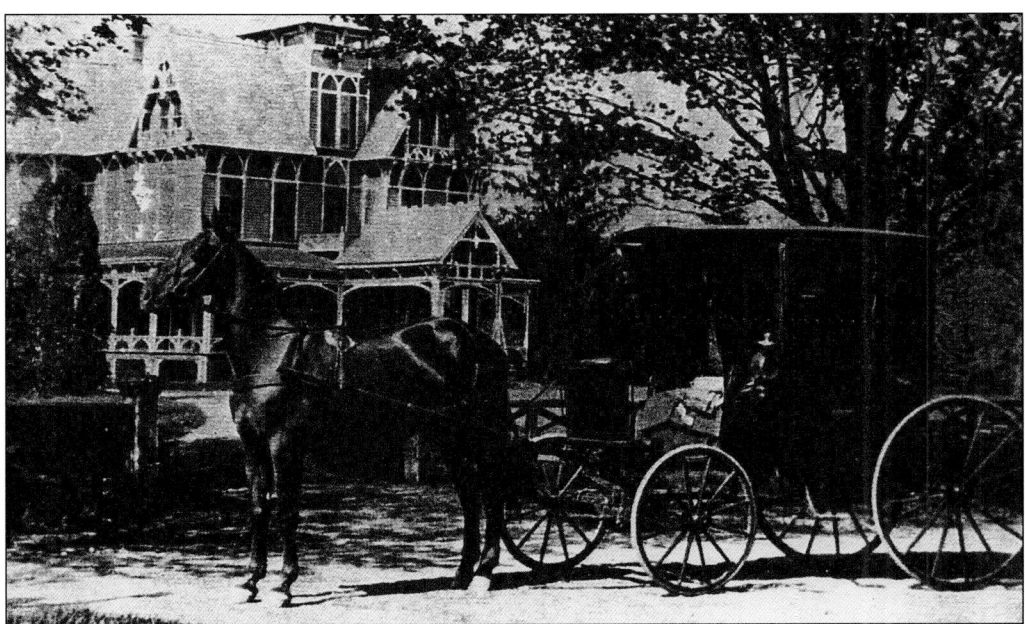

MR. OWEN'S HACK AT THE WILLIAM S. ENO HOME. Eno descendants became lawyers and businessmen. Grandson William S. Eno was both lawyer and businessman—and banker—and developer. His home is now a renowned bed and breakfast, "The Pines." Bill Owen, whose hack and long-lived horse "Duff" awaited outside Eno's Maple Street residence, had other business interests. A modest fleet of hacks provided local taxi service at the depot, delivered children to school, and carried housewives on errands. (LNPHS.)

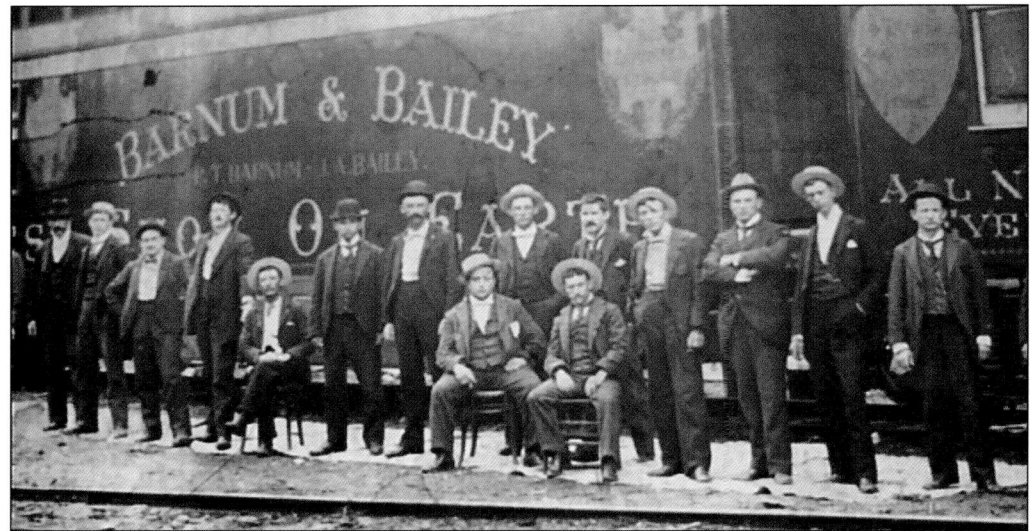

BARNUM AND BAILEY CIRCUS TRAIN. "Bread and Circuses" really do go well together. Some, like Van Amburgh's, actually started in Dutchess County. Performers, animals, and roustabouts traveled the rail lines from spring until fall, when owners boarded some menagerie critters with local farmers. Animal-boarder income was supplemented by earnings from helping unload, set up, and reload the trains. The arrival of Barnum and Bailey meant work, fun, and money in the pocket. (LNPHS/John Duxbury Collection.)

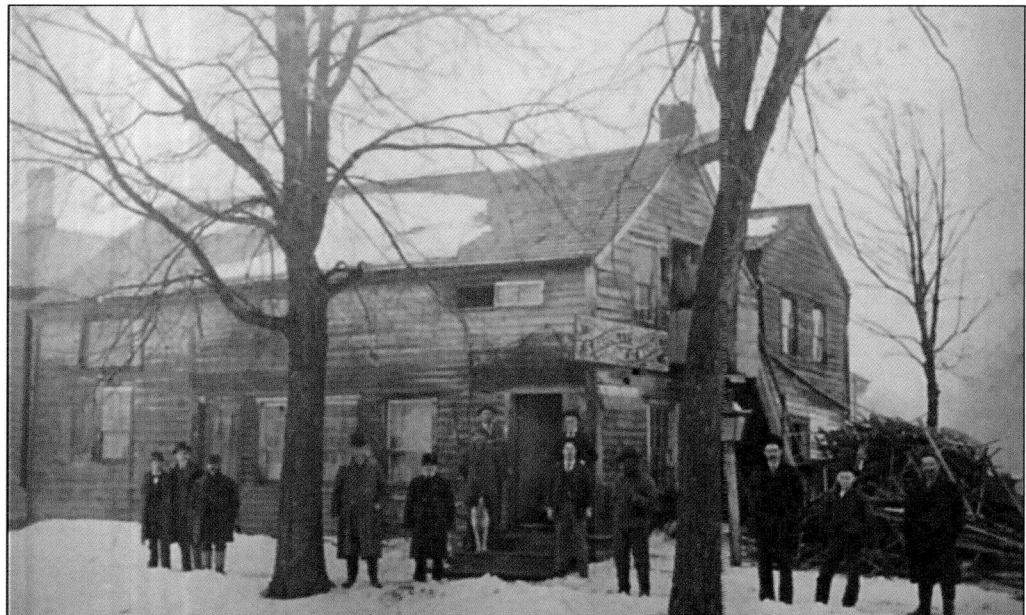

F.S. BARRETT'S MEAT MARKET 1897. Pine Plains, remote from commercial centers, depended upon itself. If one could not manufacture or buy an item locally, it meant a long wait or trip to Poughkeepsie. Local housewives commonly killed and cleaned chickens, but larger jobs required experts. Fred Barrett's meat market on the site of the present American Legion post was the town butcher. A hoist in the gable end of the barn near the tree helped to lift heavy carcasses. (LNPHS.)

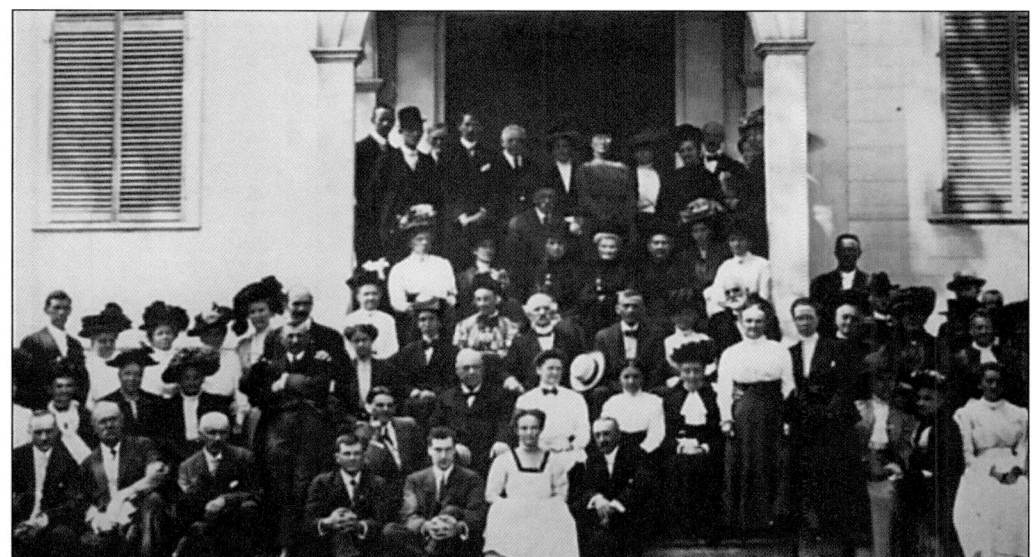

CHURCH STREET BAPTISTS. Church Street was aptly named for the collective presence of Methodists, Episcopalians, Presbyterians, and Baptists in the vicinity of Pine Street. Pine Plains Baptists formed a congregation, c. 1835, meeting first at the Brush home. At the turn of the century, a Baptist convention at the church posed for a portrait. When the congregation later disbanded, the building became home to the local Grange unit, incorporated in 1929. Today it houses Balsamos Antiques. (LNPHS.)

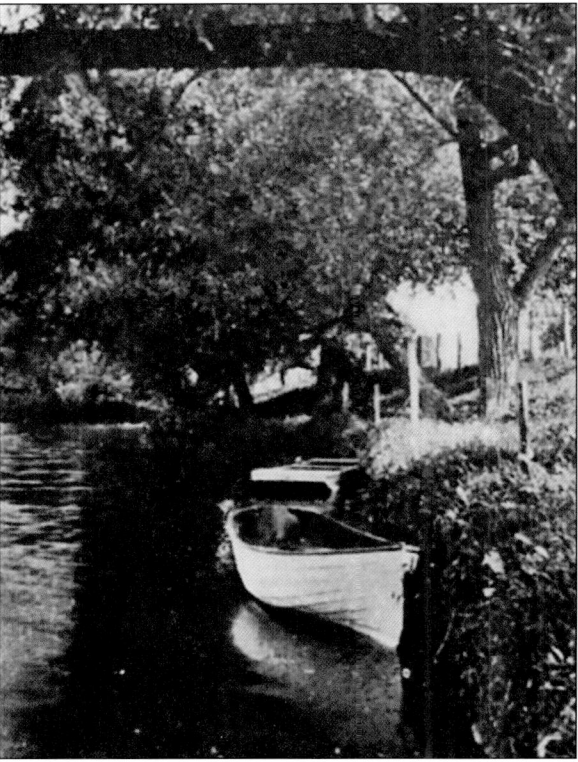

JACKSON CANOE ON STISSING LAKE. Harry Jackson, a jeweler who also sold sports equipment, was a booster and beneficiary of turn-of-the-century tourism. He also advertised himself as a craftsman. His fine photographs of scenery and sites around Pine Plains and northern Dutchess produced as postcards were a staple of the visitor services business and a valuable historical record. A canoe at the dock near his cottage on Stissing Lake invites visitors on a moonlight cruise. (LNPHS.)

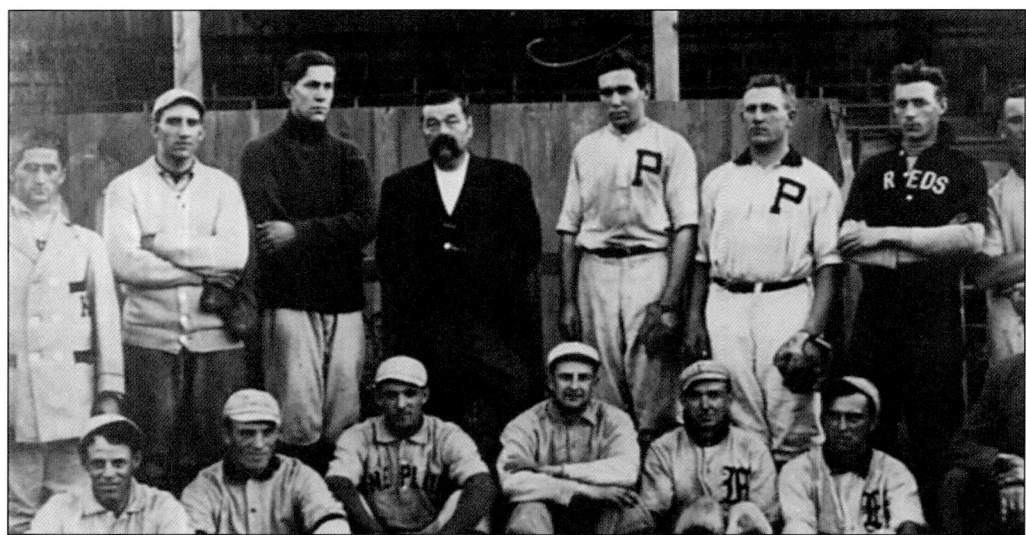

PINE PLAINS BASEBALL TEAM, 1907. Before big leagues came to power, every small town in the United States had its own baseball team. Local non-professionals and semi-pros played a summer schedule that attracted a dedicated set of rooters. Millerton was the arch-rival. The only emotion comparable to the passion felt by fans of yesteryear might be that of a mother of a wronged Little Leaguer. Charles Ketterer (with the mustache), owner of Ketterer's hotel, ran the team. (LNPHS.)

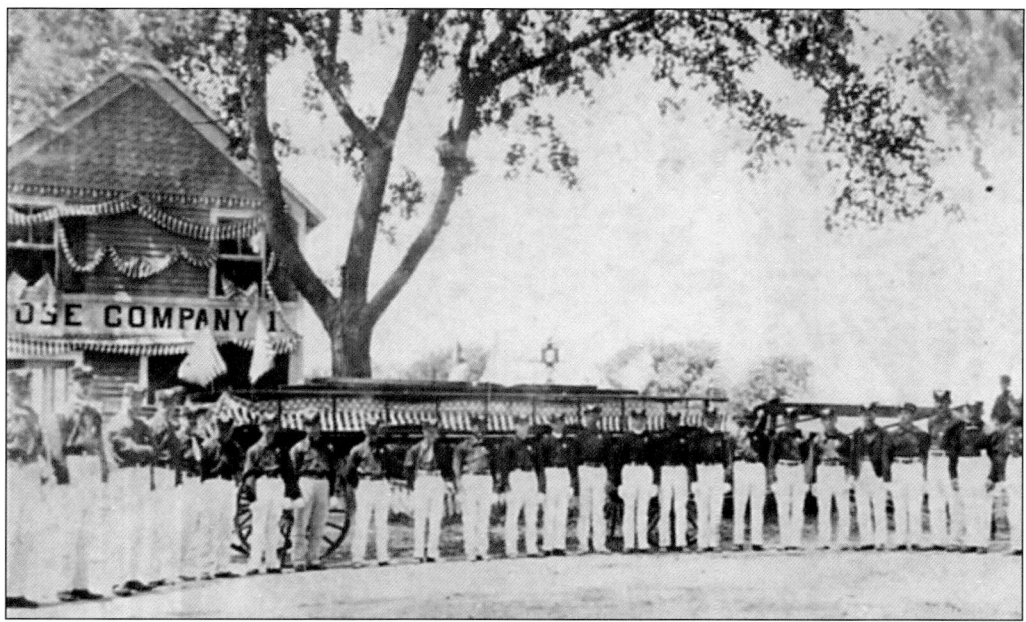

PINE PLAINS HOSE COMPANY. The year 1895 brought a new fire company and a new station that still stands, albeit changed, on Main Street opposite the library. Fire in rural communities is a great danger. Nineteenth-century farmers were on their own, supported only by buckets and ponds. In Pine Plains hamlet volunteer firemen have saved neighboring frame structures more than once. Improved training and equipment now enable volunteers to deal effectively with all kind of emergencies. (LNPHS.)

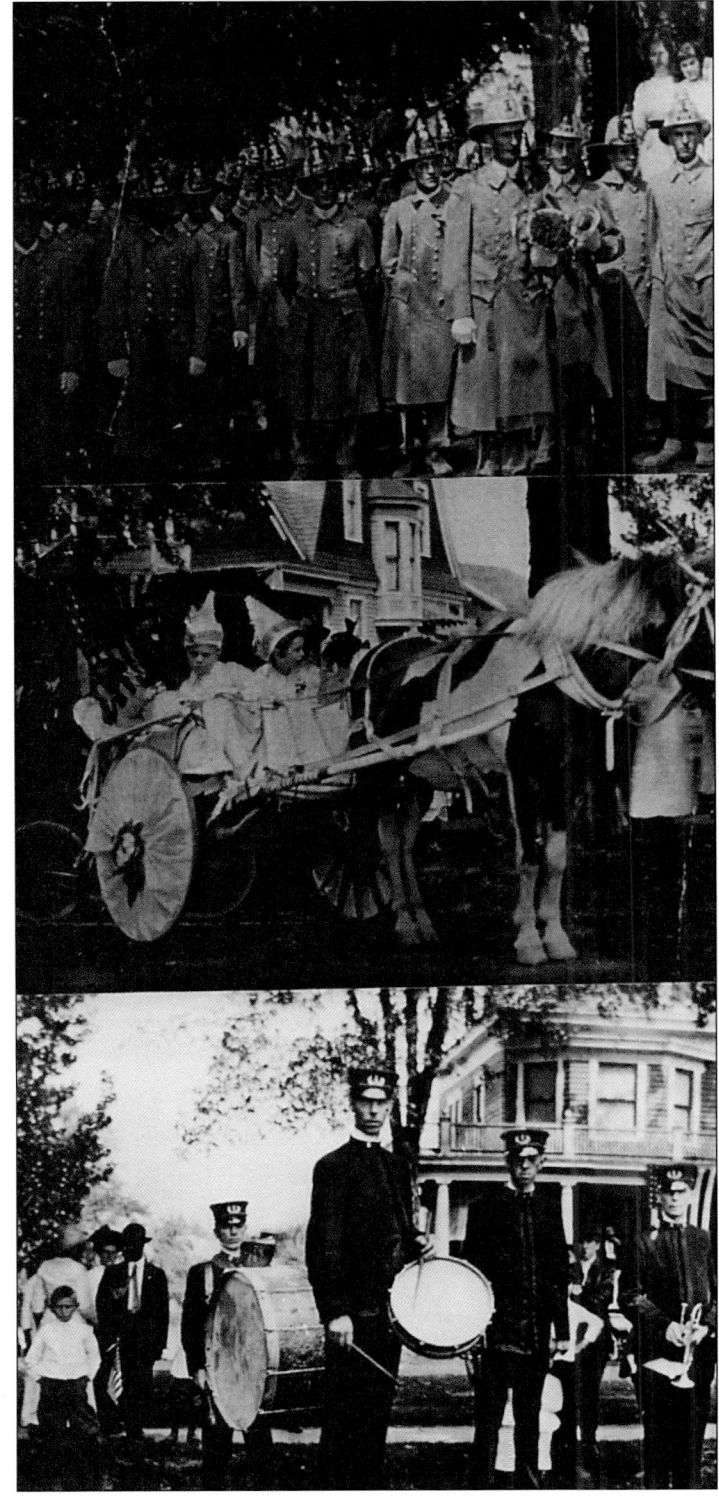

Firemen on Parade c. 1912. Three segments of a panorama photograph of a fireman's parade in Pine Plains show everyone prepared for a day of festivities. Firemen's Musters often coincided with national holidays and were the occasion for parades, games, demonstrations of fire-fighting techniques, and contests between fire companies to see which was best at its work. Kenneth Chase and Elizabeth Rudd, two of the youngest in the parade line-up, were strategically placed right behind the bass drum. Scott Chase's great-uncle Ken handled a two-wheeled, decorated pony cart like an expert. If body language is an indicator, one suspects that the pony interested him more than his lovely passenger did. Fire Companies served the community but they were also social groups. Fireman's bands were company public relations arms and platforms for those whose skills were more artistic than physical. The drum section bears this out. The bass drum, held up by Henry Corball, kept marchers in step. Henry Cahill, on the snare drum, could have played center for the Lakers, but chose to reserve his energy for fighting fires. (CC/SC.)

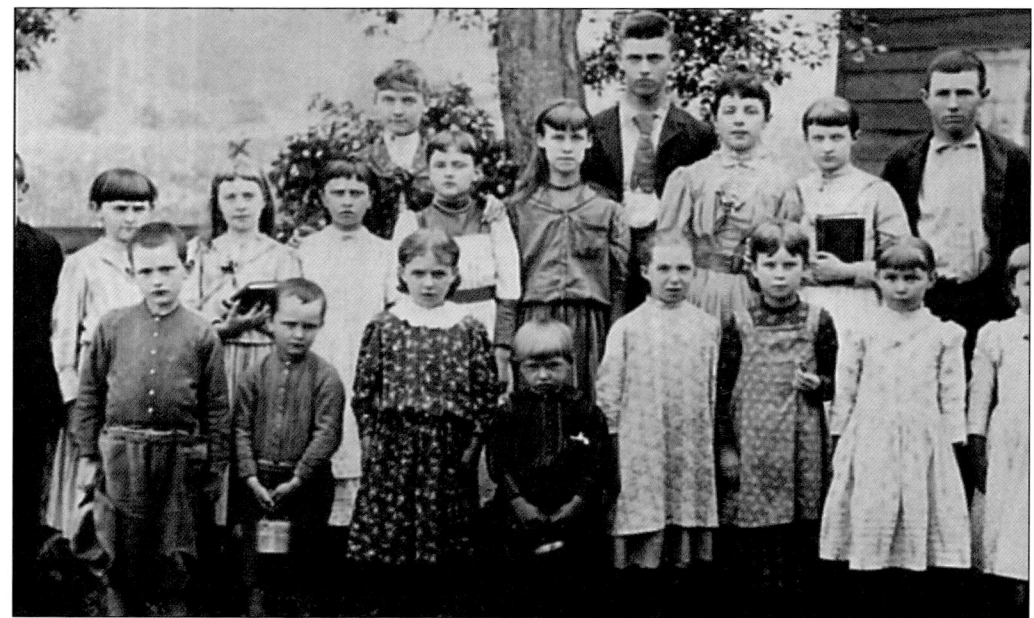

SMALL SCHOOL DISTRICTS. Through the 19th and part of the 20th century, most Pine Plains children attended small, rural elementary neighborhood schools. This 1889 Bethel public school taught by a young schoolmaster was in one of Pine Plains's 13 districts, some of which were "joint," crossing either county or town lines. Bethel had a private Quaker boarding school c. 1812 taught by the Willets, noted educators who wrote educational manuals on grammar and mathematics. (LNPHS.)

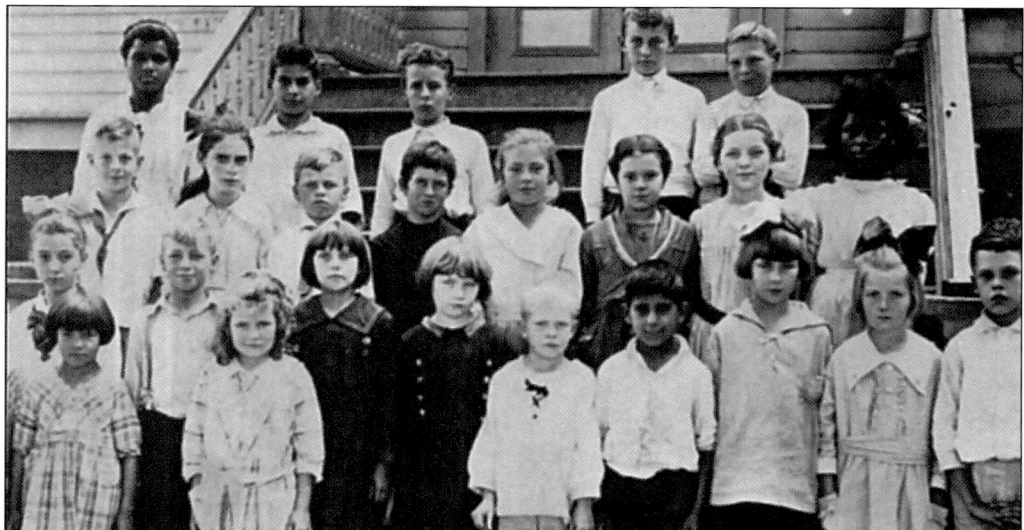

SEYMOUR SMITH SCHOOL CHILDREN. Seymour Smith Institute was created by a generous bequest to the community from Seymour Smith, who lies buried in the Pine Plains hamlet cemetery. Because of his own struggles to be educated in the face of poverty and lack of local educational resources, he resolved that other children would be better served. His entire estate went to create the school, bearing his name since 1874. Helen Cole (third from right) was among its fourth graders in 1921. (LNPHS.)

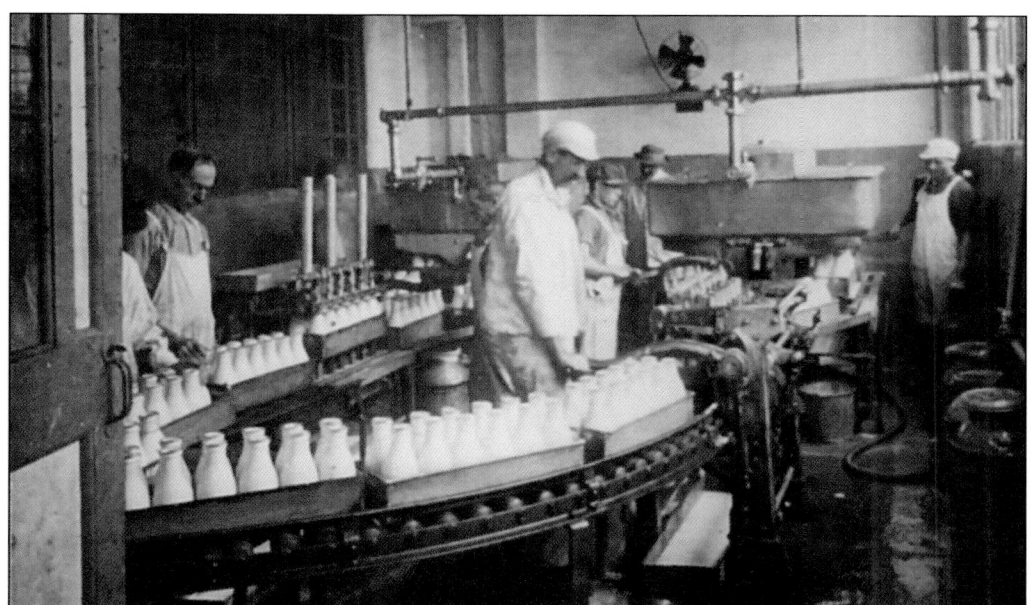

BORDEN'S BOTTLING PLANT. After the coming of the railroad, every hamlet in the Harlem Valley with dairy herds had a Borden's plant. The railroad also brought occasional grief. In 1897, a Borden's horse was killed on the trestle near the plant on Factory Lane. This modern, mechanized plant bottling milk and cream for city and regional markets closed after a general strike in 1957. Changes within the industry and curtailed railroad service drastically affected agricultural communities throughout the Harlem Valley. (LNPHS.)

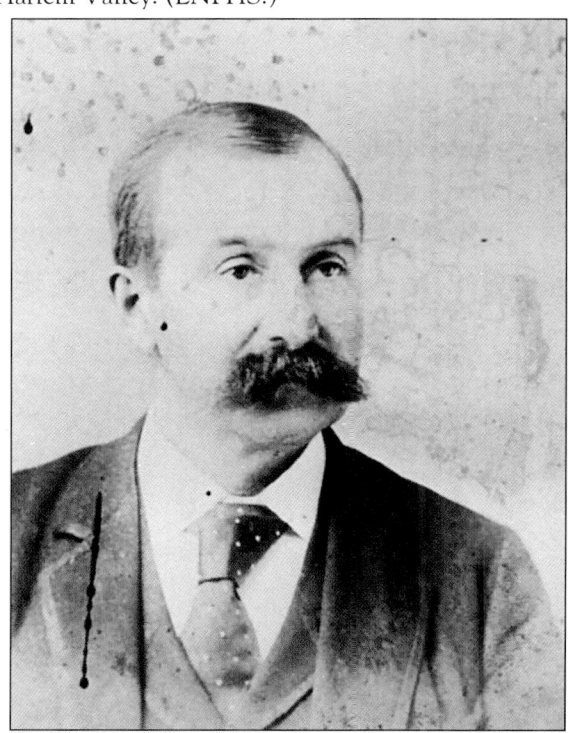

DR. HENRY CLAY WILBER, 1908. Dr. Wilber was the son of a country doctor, Benjamin S. Wilber, who preceded him in this community. Henry, one of ten children, was brought up on his father's farm at Halcyon Lake. He graduated from Bellevue Medical School in 1867 and came home to open an office on Main Street near the bank where he practiced for 52 years. When he died in 1919, a clock-tower landmark was raised to his memory by a grateful community. (LNPHS.)

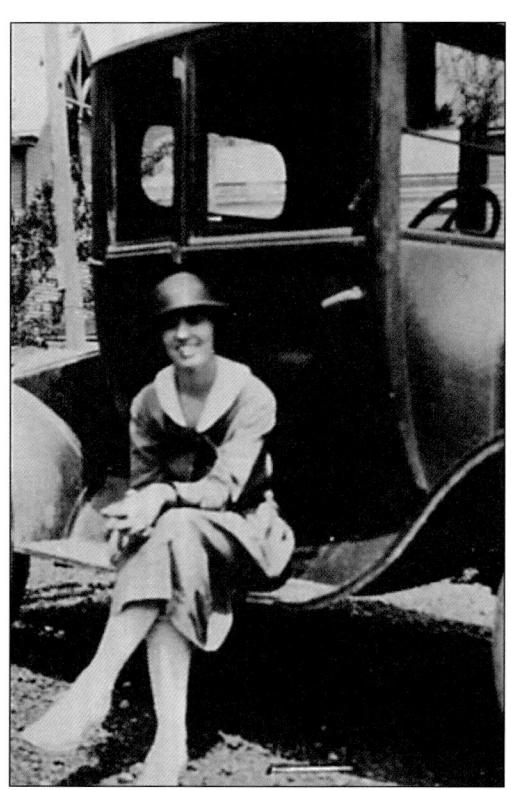

PUBLIC HEALTH NURSE READY FOR ACTION. Nurse Isabel K. Jordan and her trusty Ford were a welcome sight coming down the road. An album from the 1920s and 30s chronicles the growth of local-health delivery services. Government clinics and education programs, spearheaded by County Health Department nurses and school doctors, reached into the countryside and schools to educate families, mothers, and children about nutrition, vaccines, cleanliness, and first aid. (LNPHS.)

WELL-BABY CLINIC. The county nurse was a dynamo, bringing health services to a community dependent upon private physicians far from a hospital. Her office/clinic in Peck's store regularly scheduled "Well-Baby Clinics" providing basic examinations and educating young mothers in child development, parenting, and nutrition. Help in recognizing serious problems brought early treatment. Sometimes the clinic was also an operating room used by school doctor Dr. Oliver for minor surgery and tonsillectomies. (LNPHS.)

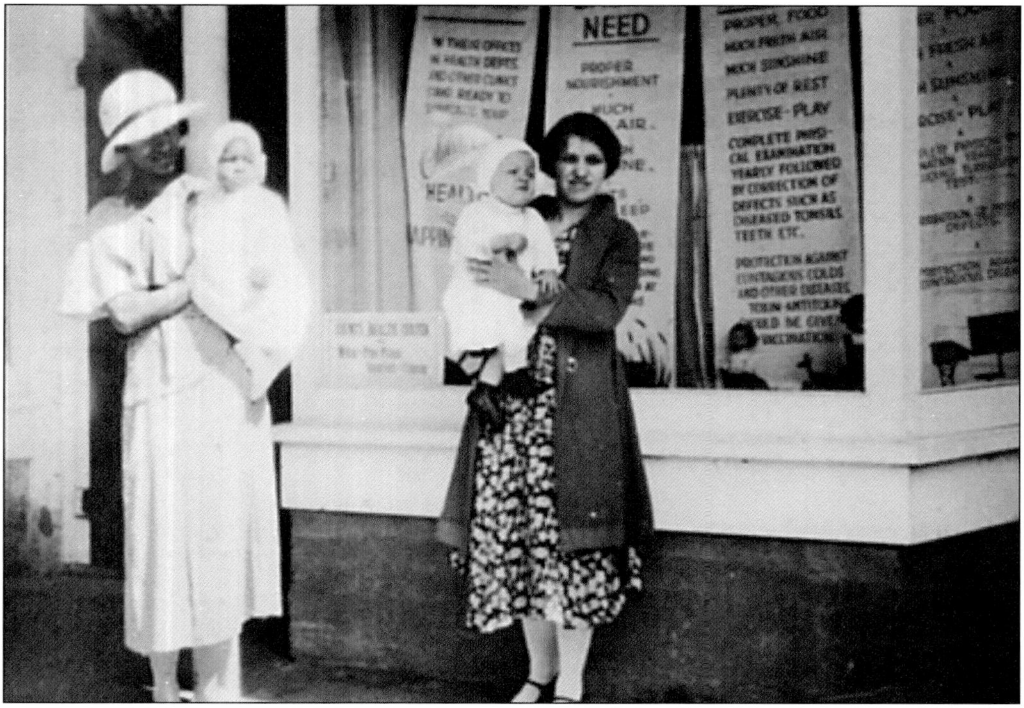

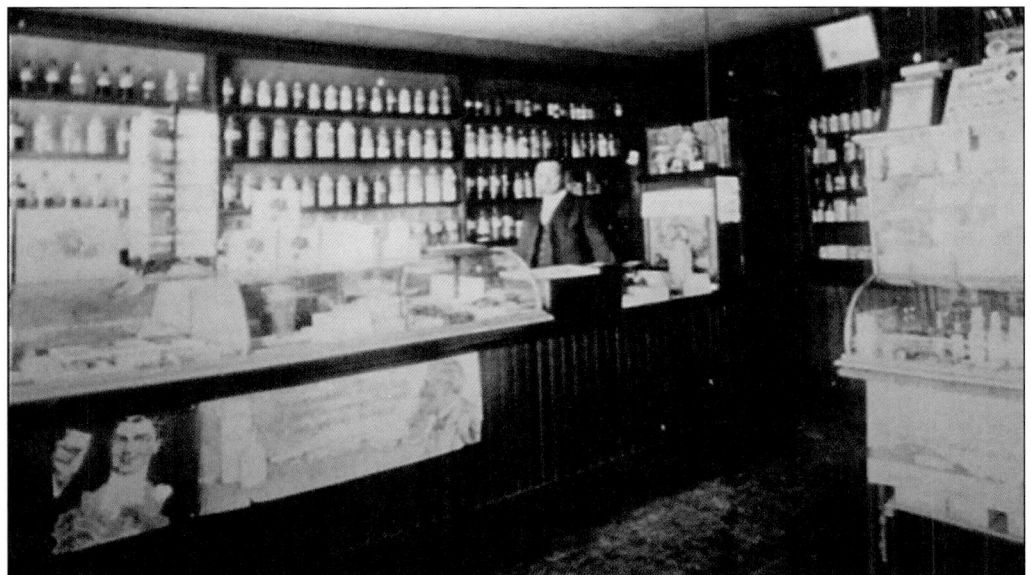

COLE'S DRUG STORE. The Cole family pharmacy served the community on Main Street across from the Wilber Memorial Clock for three generations. Dr. Charles Cole (1830-1884) opened the first store in 1881 in the family residence after ill health forced him to limit his practice. His widow, a pharmacist, continued the business after Cole's death in 1884, building another store next door in 1905, which her son—also a pharmacist—eventually ran. (HN.)

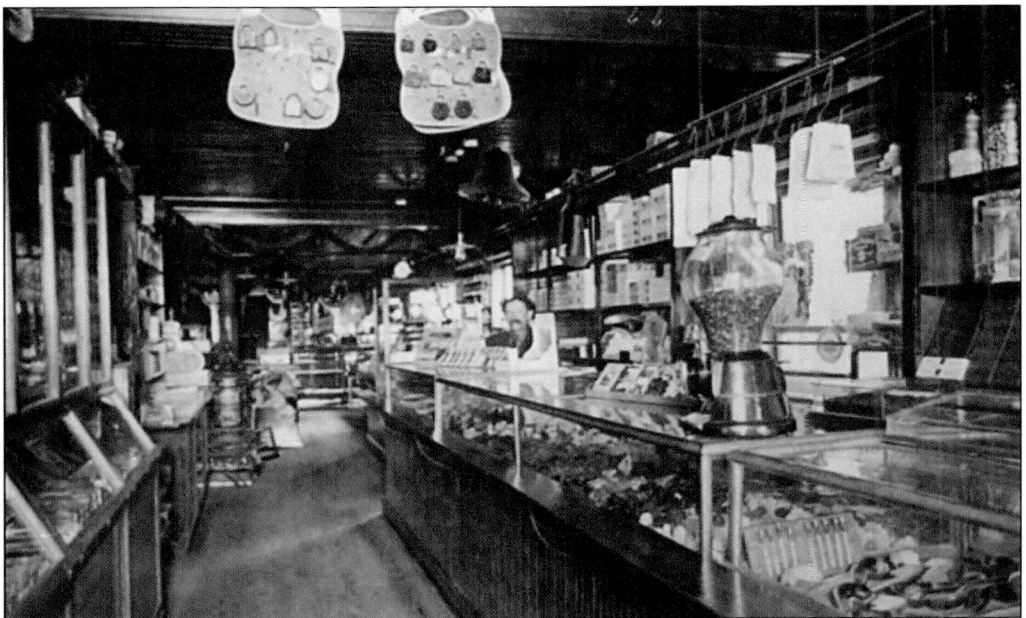

BARDS' STORE c.1920. The Bards sold what was called "notions" at their Pine Plains store in the 1920s. Notions are best described as small useful items both essential and non-essential that might be found in a Woolworths or a ten-cent store. It was the place to go for buttons and thread or inexpensive crockery: a place where a child might find something affordable, within his allowance budget—a most essential store. (LNPHS.)

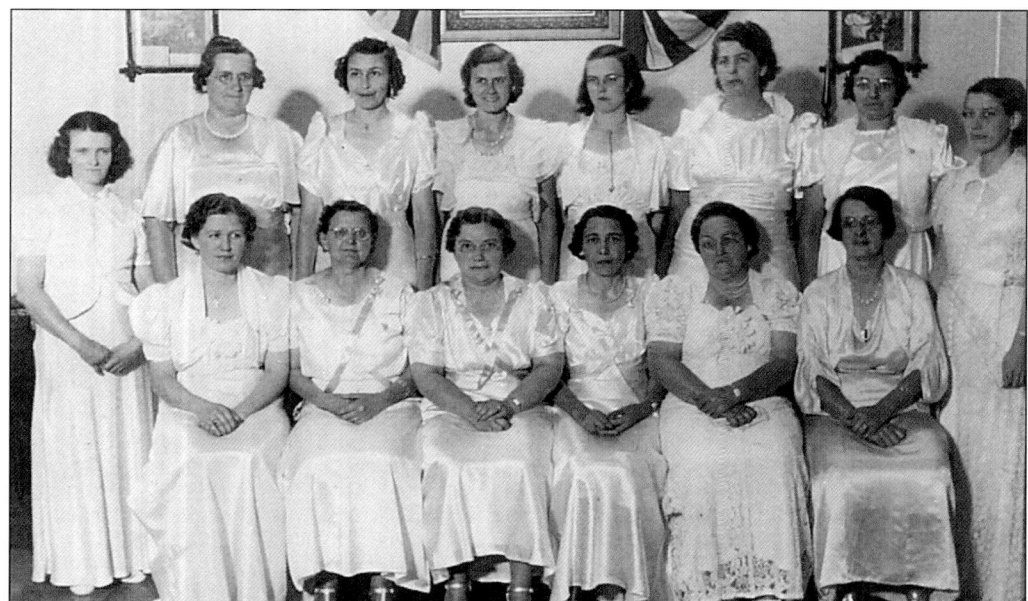

LODGES IN PINE PLAINS. Rebekkahs met in a building (later the town hall) owned by the I.O.O.F. After a meeting c. 1935, Harry Jackson snapped this portrait of the "Degree Team" in gowns and symbols of the order. The women's counterpart of Odd Fellows underwent the same grueling tests as the men, rising to leadership through "Degrees." Free masonry also was here, with a branch from Spencer's Corners Temple Lodge after 1808. Stissing Masonic Lodge, formed in 1866, met at Pine Plains Hotel. (JA/CA.)

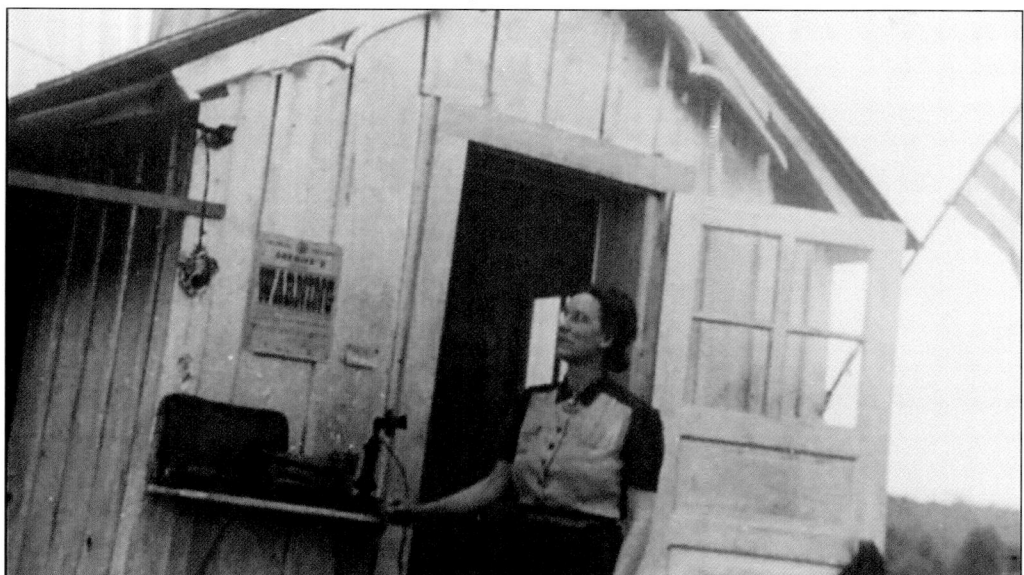

AIRPLANE SPOTTER 1944. A railroad outbuilding served as a lookout post for WW II "airplane spotters." The worldwide war made the threat of bombings, such as those faced in Europe, Asia, and the South Pacific, quite real. Civilian volunteers—mostly housewives—were taught to recognize the outlines of war planes. They spent many lonely hours in remote posts linked by telephone to military reporting posts, scanning the skies for enemy aircraft. (LNPHS.)

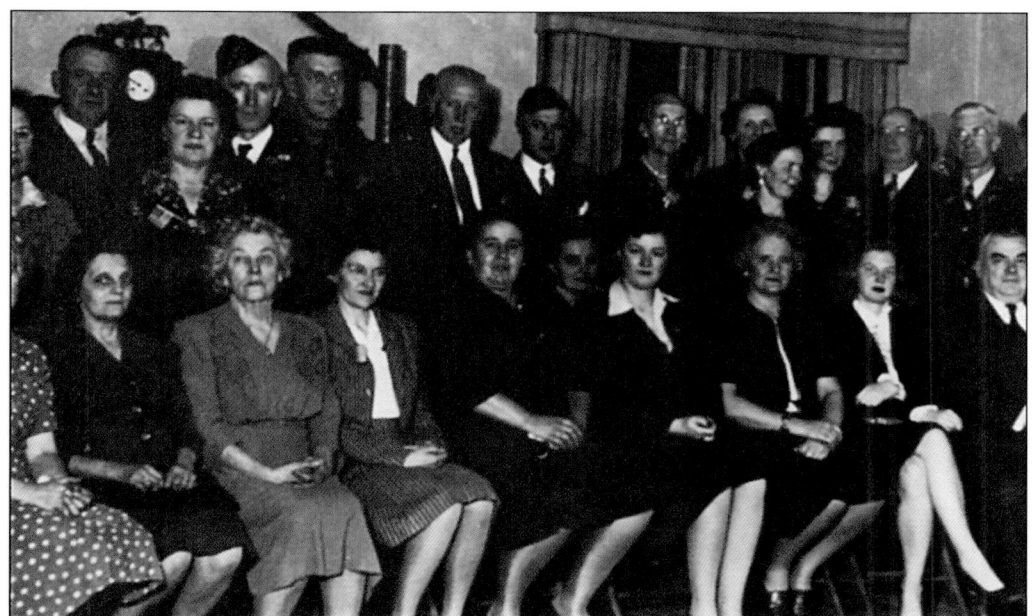

AMERICAN LEGION MORTGAGE BURNING CEREMONY. Patriotism runs high in small towns where veterans' groups find support among neighbors. A place set aside to meet and discuss veterans' issues, conduct fund-raising activities, or just relax is important. In 1929, the local legion unit built on the former site of Barrett's Meat Market and raised funds for the mortgage through carnivals and other fund-raisers. The post opened in 1930 and in 1944, with WW II underway, members took time to celebrate the mortgage burning. (LNPHS.)

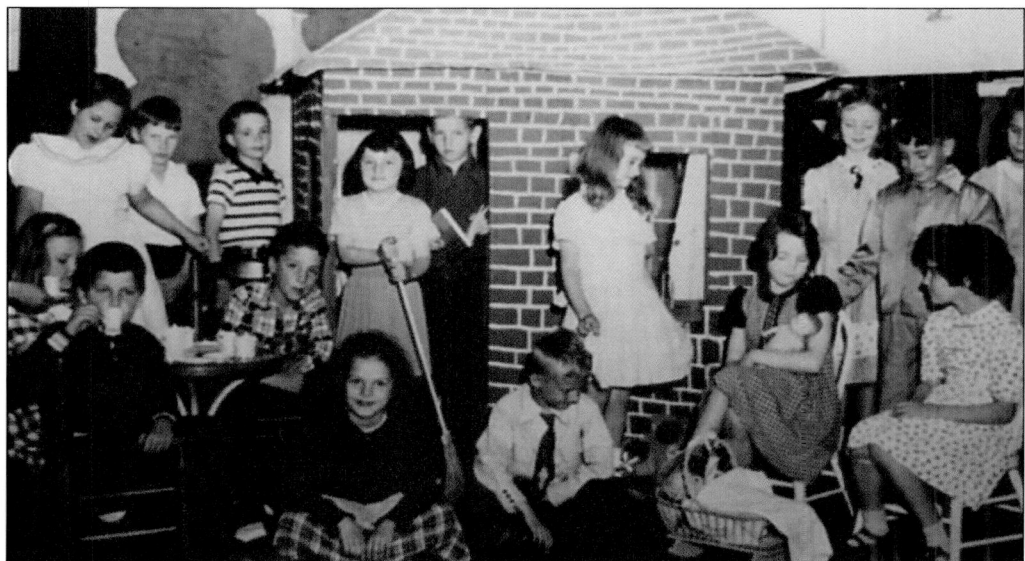

SEYMOUR SMITH THIRD GRADERS 1952. The name Seymour Smith School revives memories of different buildings for different people, but seldom does it elicit unhappy memories. Miss Lulu Kisselback's third graders had a wonderful time back in 1952 with this unit on community and family. They built a house and peopled it with their imaginations. Future lawyer Jon Adams (in the colorful plaid shirt), however, was not too thrilled with the obligatory tea party. (JA/AA.)

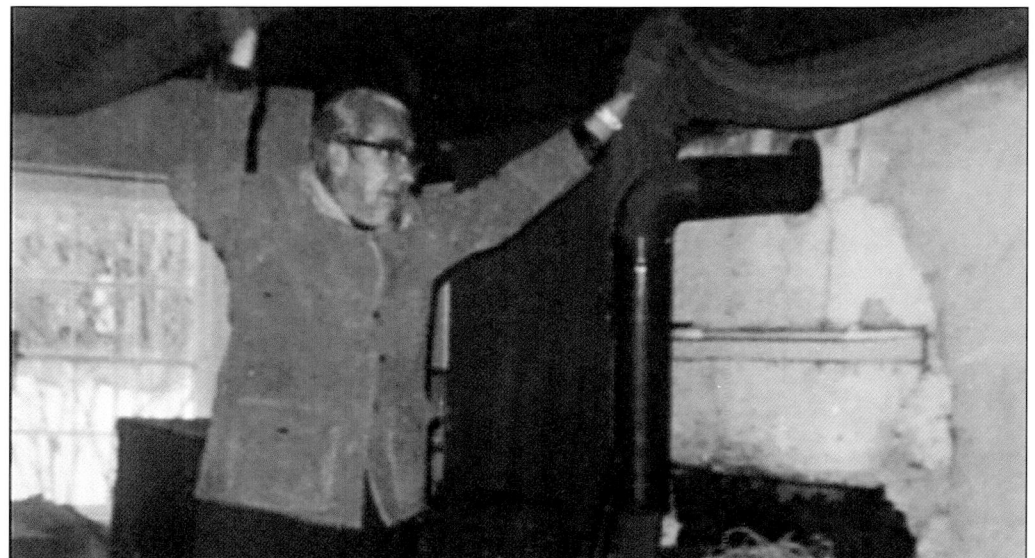

SAVING HARRIS-HUSTED HOUSE. During America's Bicentennial of the American Revolution in 1976, Little Nine Partners Historical Society members took on the challenge of saving the house as a community landmark and meeting place. Frank French, former president of the Society, carefully examined the interior of the structure. Removed from its original site and undergoing architectural restoration, it serves as a venue for local history education. (LNPHS.)

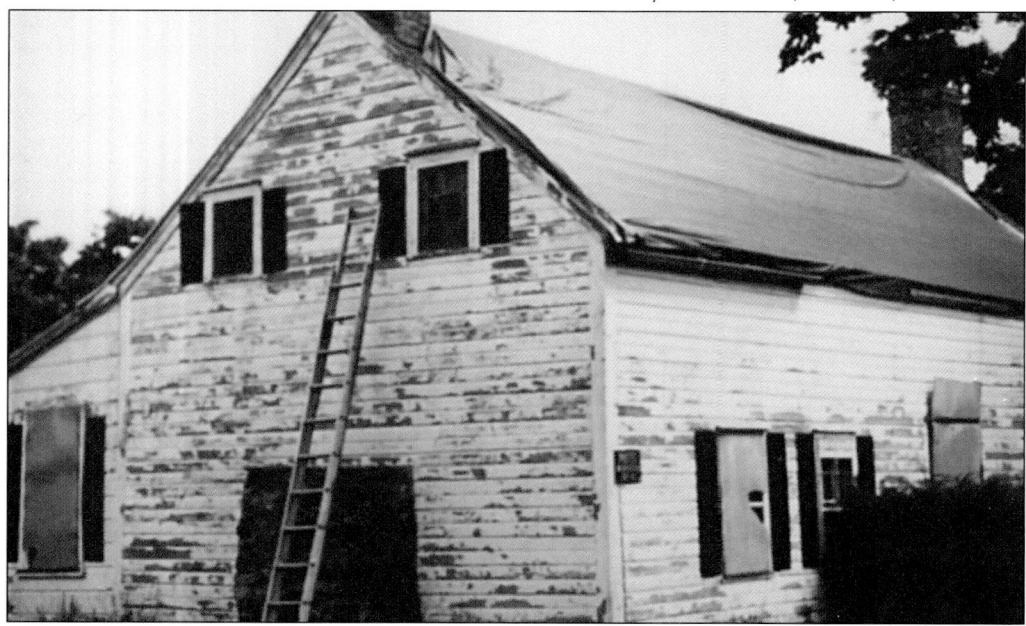

BRUSH HOUSE. Under a shell of 1881 clapboard siding hides a log or block house built during the 18th century when Pine Plains was a frontier trading post in the Little Nine Partners Patent. It may have served as a fort for early settlers. In 1778, it was owned by Lewis Graham. The Brush family, whose name has adhered, was its owner by 1829. In 1998, members of the Little Nine Partners Historical Society began a community effort to save it, raising $60,000 as a down payment. (LNPHS.)

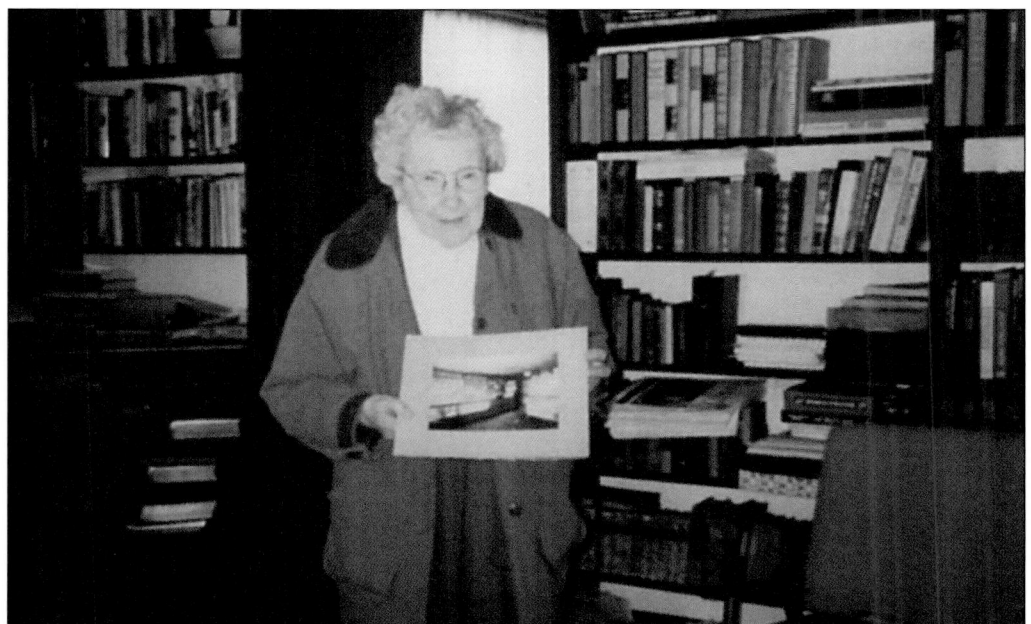

NETTER'S LIVING ROOM. This 1905 home has served well: at one time housing a family and both a pharmacy and the town library. As teacher, librarian, and the town's unofficial memory, Helen Cole Netter has also served. In 1797, residents meeting in Baldwin's Public House (Stissing House) drew up Union Library subscription papers at $2 each to serve the hamlet area. With trustees elected, borrowers rules made, and books purchased, the library opened in 1798. Now moved to the crossroads town park, it celebrates its 200th anniversary in 1998. (JG.)

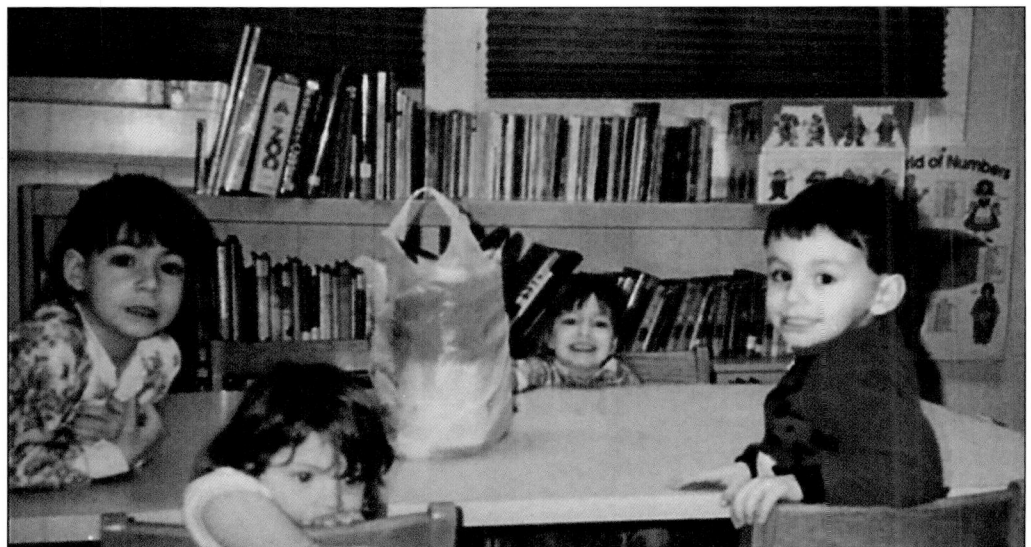

CHILDREN'S THURSDAY MORNING LIBRARY PROGRAM. Libraries these days are information and community education centers linked physically and electronically to whole networks of libraries. Still, the love of reading is what brings most of us into a library for the first time. Pre-schoolers are introduced to the joys of reading and learning at Pine Plains Library Thursday morning story hour. Attire is informal and snacks are the order of the day. (HN.)

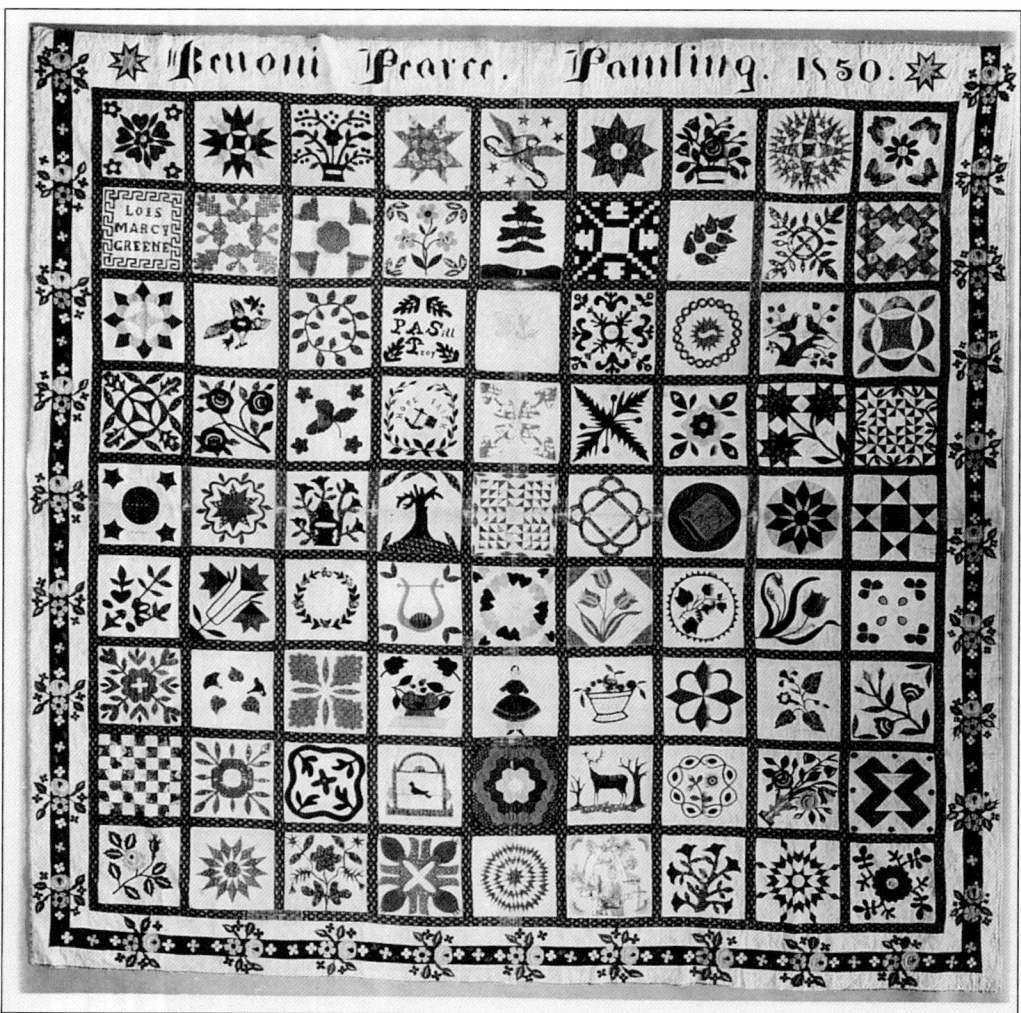

BENONI PEARCE QUILT. One of the finest examples of the art of quilting, the Benoni Pearce quilt completed in 1850 is now at the Smithsonian Institution. It is a visible reminder of the intricate family relationships throughout the Harlem Valley. The women who quilted included Julia, Jane, and Mary Dutcher; Jerusha Burdick; Mrs. Mary Ann Stark Pearce; Mrs. Ruth Smith (probably the mother of Philip H. Smith, author and printer); Anna Birdsall Dodge; Ann M. Burdick; Hannah and Arabella Hoag; Abb(e)y Toffey Dodge (sister of Egbert Toffey); Hannah H.M. Wing; Laura Cook Hurd (wife of William Taber Hurd); Rachel Stark; and Mrs. Mary Dakin, names still familiar in the Harlem Valley. This quilt, created by many hands almost 150 years ago in a small corner of the valley, can be enjoyed today by literally millions. (PH/MH.)

Six

Connections

A glance at a map of the Harlem Valley may suggest a picture puzzle, but a better metaphor is a tapestry with threads seamlessly interwoven into a whole. This last chapter explores these threads that become a single varicolored strand defining the valley as special and distinct yet connected to the wider world.

The hamlets, villages, neighborhoods, and districts that have developed over three hundred years in various parts of the region, have followed many of the same routes to the present, using similar strategies and resources. Geographic elements and human needs have dictated industrial and business patterns. Family decisions, movements, and ties have linked communities. Community institutions and traditions—fire companies, schools, service organizations, and sports teams—have brought and continue to bring residents and newcomers together turning newcomers into natives. Individuals, too, stand out as leaders impelling change.

Transportation and technology have narrowed the distance between the Harlem Valley and the rest of the world. From a time when distance was measured by how far one could walk or ride a horse in a day, and communication was either face to face or not at all, we now live in a world where everyone is potentially our neighbor. How this will affect the beauty and integrity of the Harlem Valley as a region is now in the hands of a new generation on the verge of a new century.

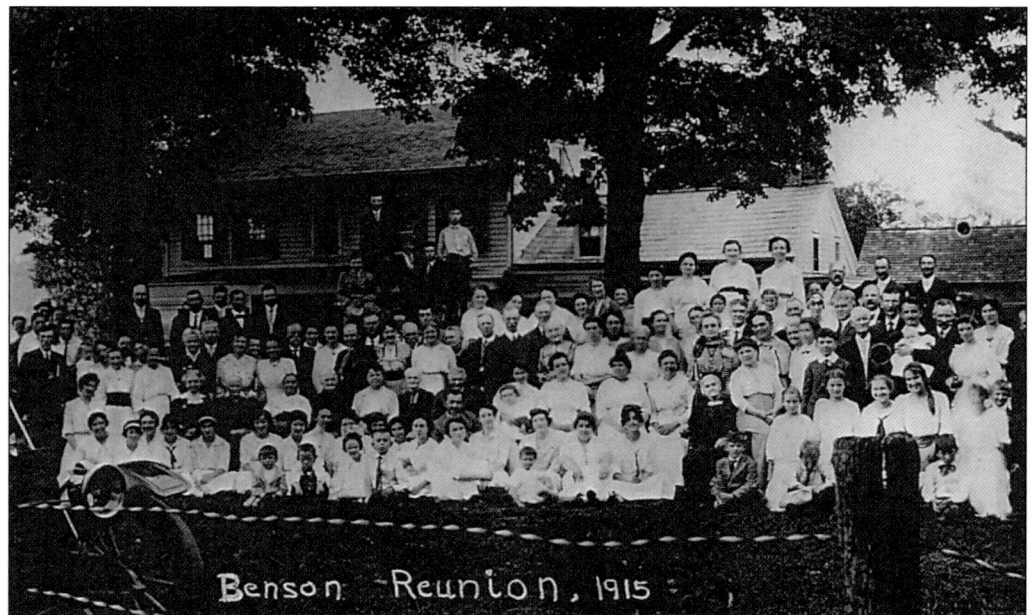

BENSON FAMILY REUNION, 1915. Judge James D. Benson, not yet born at the time of the reunion, provided this photograph of over one hundred members of the Benson family gathered at the Benson homestead located in the area still known as the "Benson Neighborhood," the extreme southeastern part of the town of Amenia. The descendants of Jacob Benson, first of the family to settle in Eastern Dutchess c. 1742, were recognized for the reunion in Arthur T. Benson's formal genealogy. Judge Benson continues to live on the 1742 family homestead today. (JDB.)

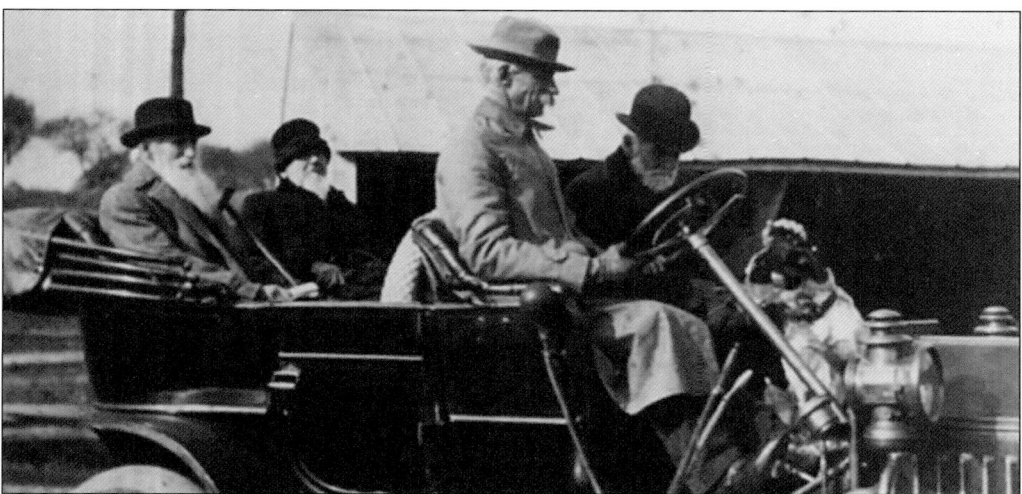

DOVER'S OLDEST VOTERS, BEFORE 1915. When everyone in town is related, elections allow those with strong opinions to disagree privately in voting booth isolation. In an era when the nation hovered on the verge of WW I, women did not have the vote, but nonagenarians did. Lenora Vincent Buck, whose family ties reach back to the 18th century, identifies her grandfather Charles W. Vincent as chauffeur with his father Edwin Vincent up front and neighbors Charles and Elizer Cutler as back-seat drivers. (LB.)

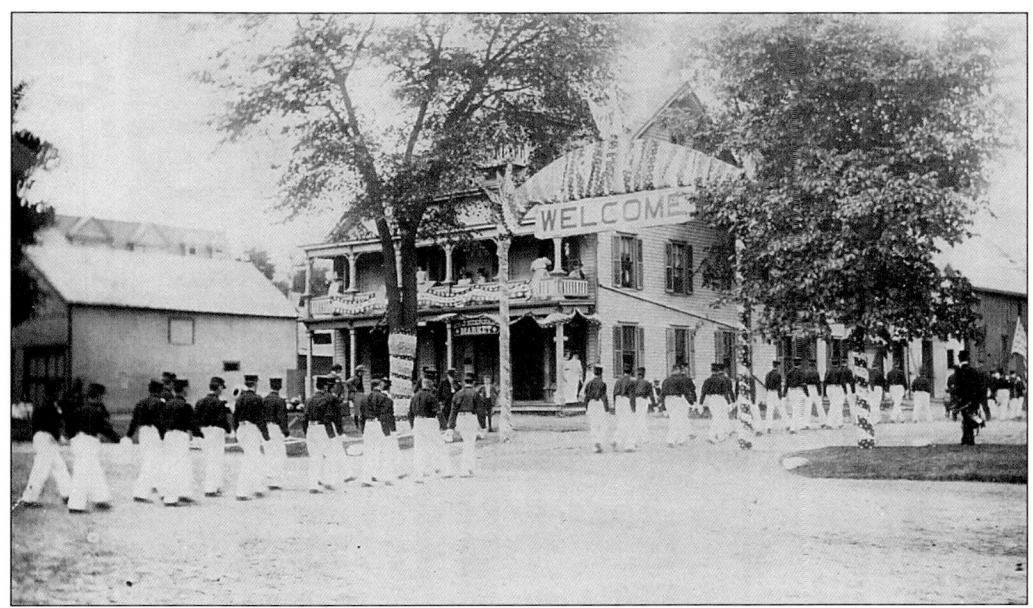

AMENIA FIREMEN AT PAWLING. This photograph, taken in 1900, shows the first annual tournament, held on the second Tuesday in May, of the newly formed Harlem Valley Firemen's Association. This was truly a community celebration. Besides the huge welcome sign, bunting even garlanded the trees. Throughout the valley there has always been cooperation among the fire companies in times of need and friendly rivalry at tournaments. (WJC.)

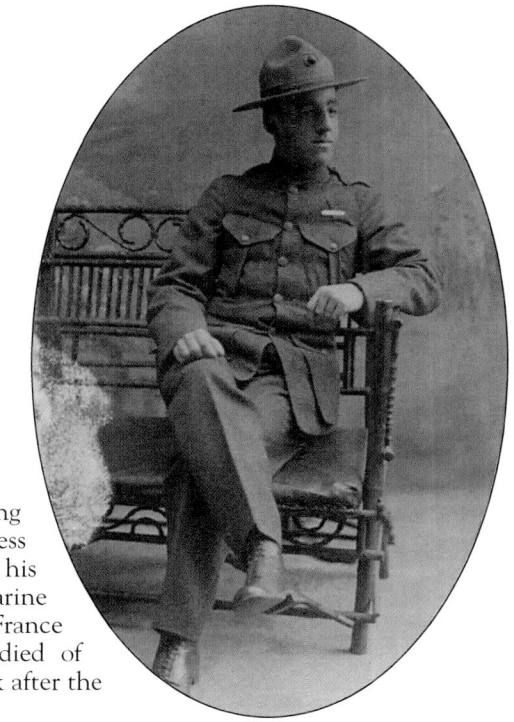

WALTER CAMERON REYNOLDS. This fine young man from Amenia was probably the first Dutchess County man to be killed during WW I. He and his brother Frederick had enlisted in the U.S. Marine Corps in 1917. He died on April 20, 1918, in France during the battle of Seicheprey. Frederick died of influenza on November 18, 1918, just one week after the Armistice. (AM.)

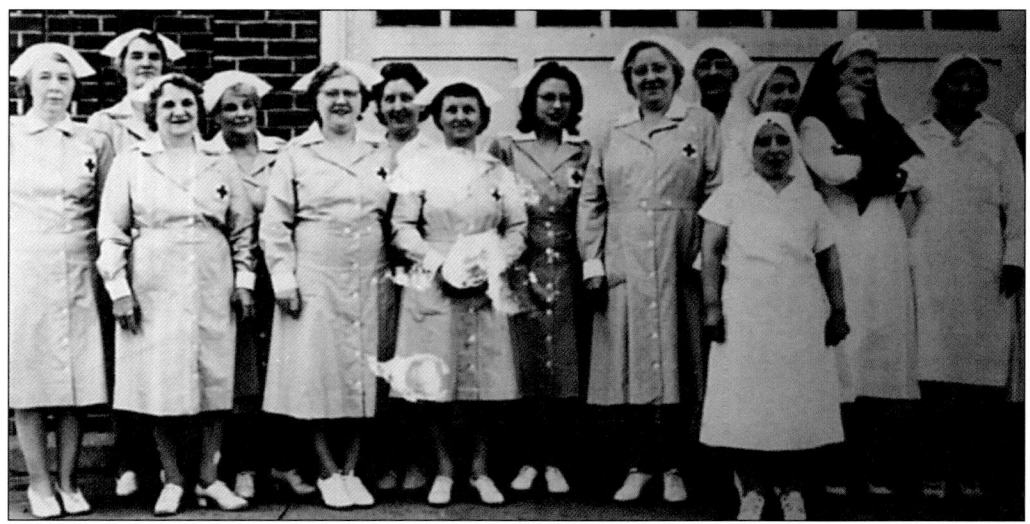

PAWLING RED CROSS GRAY LADIES, MEMORIAL DAY 1944. Just a quarter of a century later, while sons and husbands were at the front lines or working in defense plants during WW II, housewives with children, grandmothers, and other older women became professional volunteers. They did whatever was asked by the Red Cross: rolling bandages, working as aides, or writing letters for wounded vets in hospitals and recuperative centers, and cheerfully doling out donuts and cigarettes. (PH/MH.)

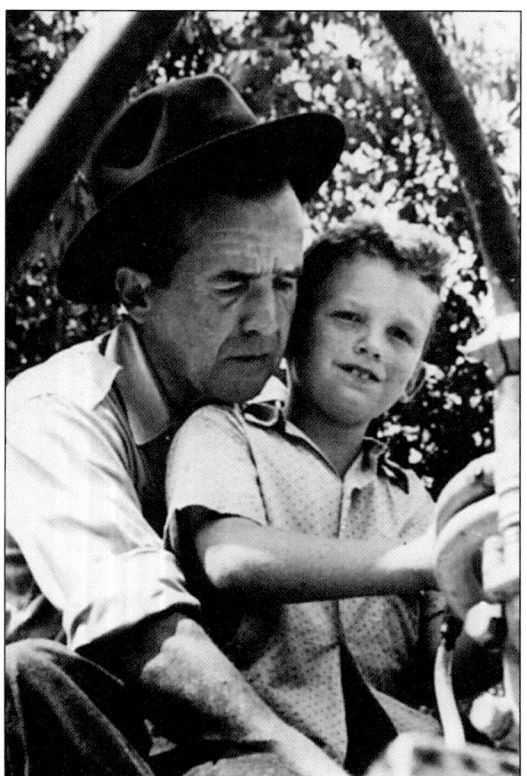

EDWARD R. MURROW WITH HIS SON. Who can forget Edward R. Murrow's wartime radio broadcasts that made the infamy of battle only too real for Americans and his postwar series that set the standard for television news programs? Among those sold on Pawling by Lowell Thomas, Murrow was respected as a good neighbor and honored by a community park on the site of the Burr property adjacent to Coles Mills. Created with support of LIONS Club members, the park was opened in 1966. (PH/MH.)

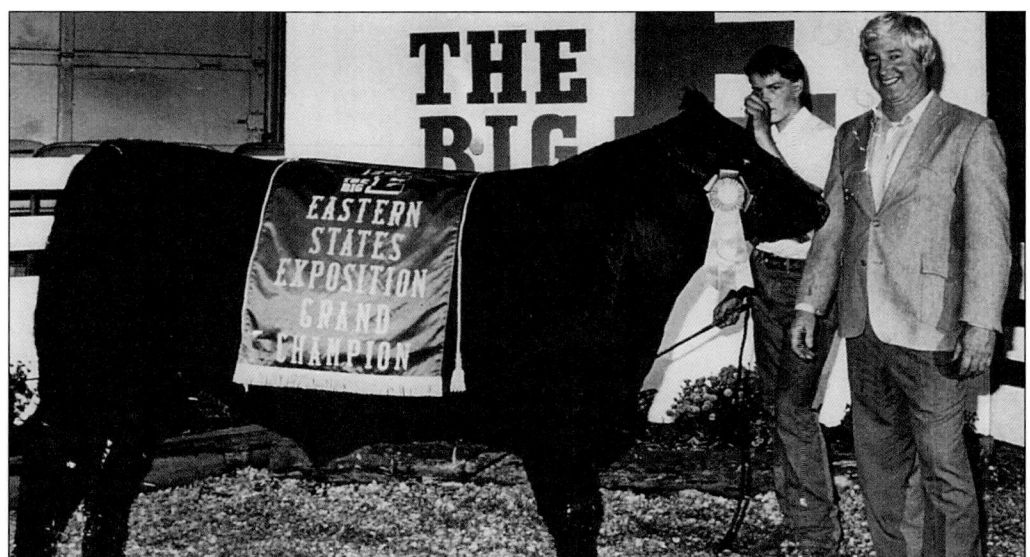

GRAND CHAMPION. Shown here is Blake Mahaffey, Ed and Mary Mahaffey's son, with his steer that became Grand Champion at the Eastern States Exposition in 1989. Like other families in the Harlem Valley, the Mahaffeys live in one community, Amenia, and have their business in another, Pawling. While farming continues to decline as the economic base of the valley, boys like Blake still learn self-reliance and independence caring for their animals, some of which are recognized as champions by outside judges, others only by their proud owners. (EMM.)

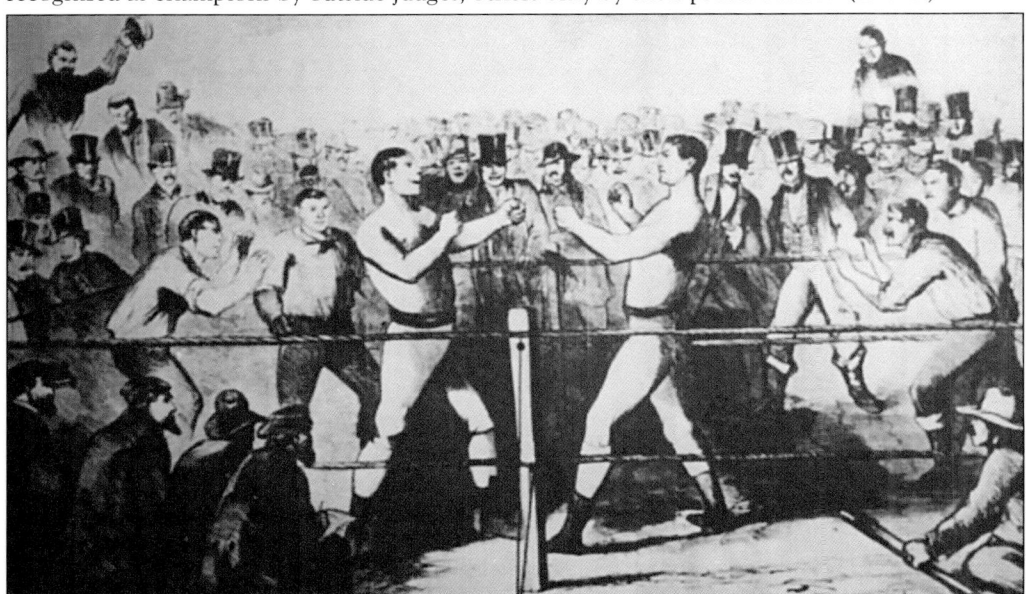

1853 PRIZEFIGHT AT BOSTON CORNERS. The Morrissey-Sullivan prizefight pitted two Irishmen, John Morrissey against "Yankee" Sullivan. At the time the place chosen for the fight, Boston Corners, was without civil authority as neither Massachusetts nor New York claimed jurisdiction. Thousands poured out of the trains to watch the 37 bloody rounds. John Morrissey won and went on to be elected a U.S. representative. "Yankee" Sullivan committed suicide, it is said, while in the hands of a "Vigilance" committee in California. (NEHS.)

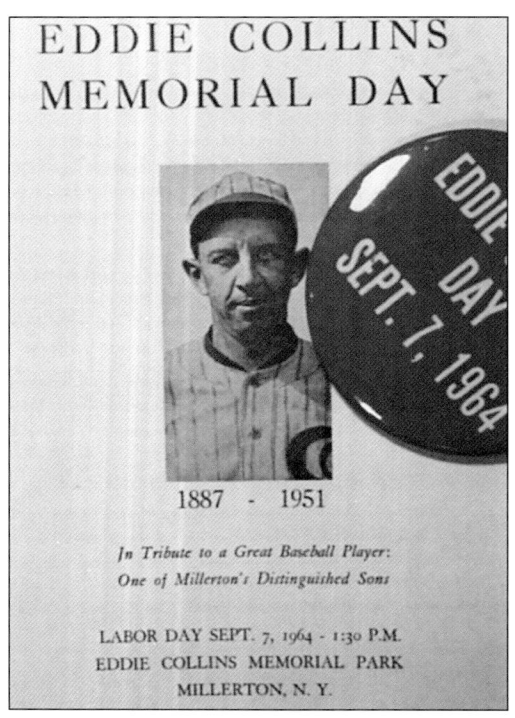

EDDIE COLLINS. The railroad was a major employer of many local residents, including Eddie Collins's father who was a conductor on the Harlem line and later on the Hudson line. Collins, who was inducted into the Baseball Hall of Fame in 1939, played in 2,826 games during his 25-year career, with a lifetime batting average of .333. Millerton residents have remained proud of their baseball great; they dedicated a new park to him in 1964 and proclaimed September 7 as Eddie Collins Day. (NEHS.)

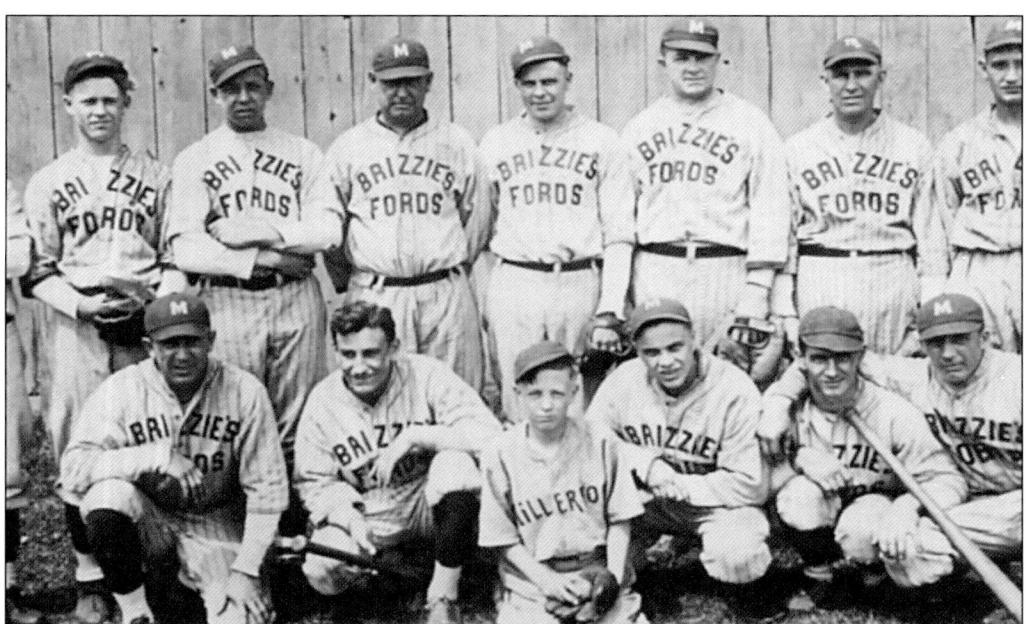

BRIZZIE'S FORDS. Shown in this image is a community baseball team dating from the 1940s. Second from the left (with no hat) in the front row is Al Berger, father of Sandy Berger, a senior member of President Clinton's staff. Sandy was the 1963 valedictorian of Webatuck High School and went on to Cornell while his parents ran a department store where the Oblong bookstore is today. Hard work and caring neighbors have always been part of life in Millerton. (BS.)

PULVERS CORNERS BREEDING FARM. In the past, horses were as indispensable to life in tiny Pulvers Corners and almost everywhere as automobiles are today. They provided basic transportation and were the source of power for many essential daily family and business tasks. Today in Pulvers Corners and all over the Harlem Valley, horses are still important, but now the focus is on riding for pleasure, breeding, polo, and racing. (JG.)

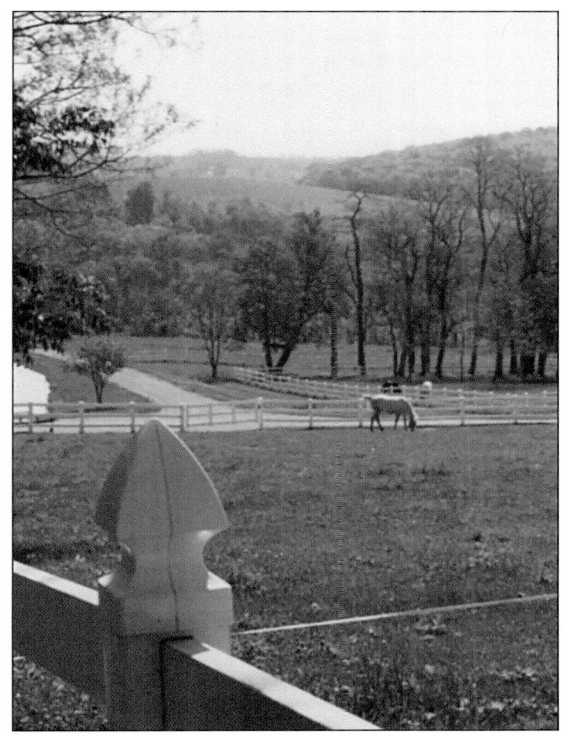

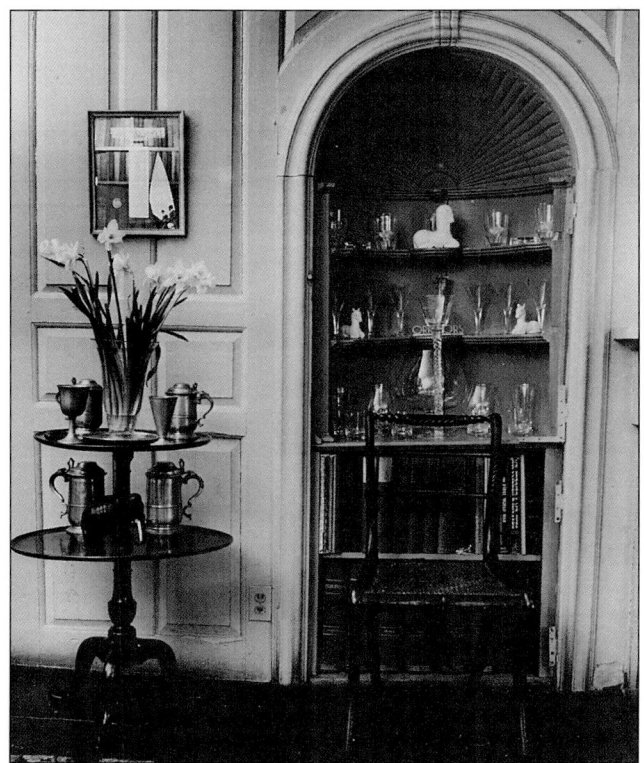

OLD DROVERS INN. A destination for travelers since the 18th century when they arrived by horse, the Old Drovers Inn is graced with this shell cabinet whose twin was acquired by the Metropolitan Museum of Art. In the late 18th and 19th centuries, journeymen carpenters sometimes paid for their winter quarters by doing carpentry and paneling. Drovers became extinct here when cattle took to the rails, glad to avoid newly laid macadam which hurt their feet. (AP.)

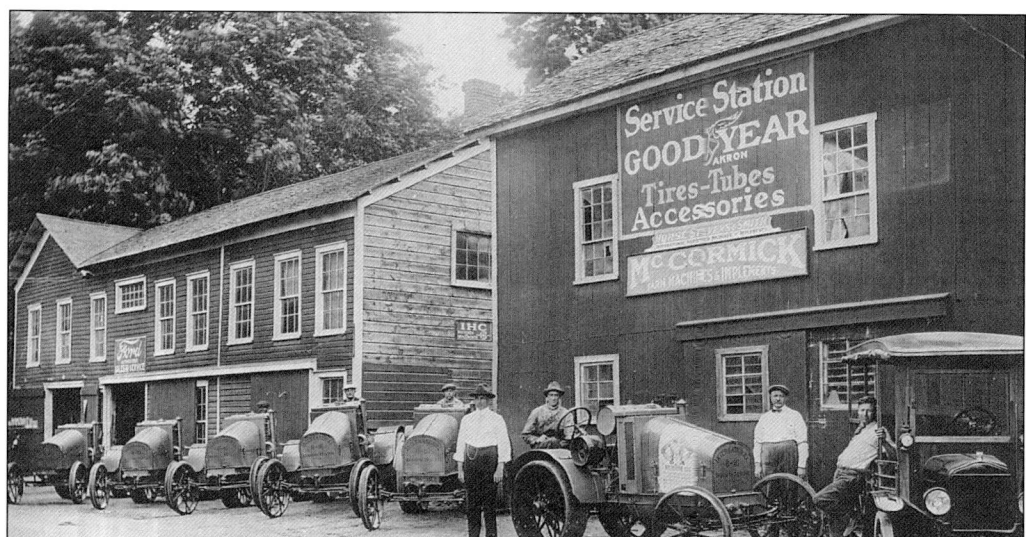

RAILROAD FREIGHT BILLS. These turn-of-the-century bills show the importance of the railroads to the Harlem Valley for the transportation of freight. The railroads also permitted passengers to make connections so they could travel to Poughkeepsie and intermediate stations. They could also get to Albany, Boston, and Vermont by changing trains at Chatham, and to Winsted and Hartford via Millerton. (NEHS.)

MORSE STEVENS AND SMITH CAR DEALER. The change in transportation modes is previewed in this 1917 photograph of a car dealership and service station in Wassaic. The cover of this book is a photograph of Harry Jenkins and the first Ford said to have been sold by the firm. Indicative of the times is the "Uncle Sam Needs You" poster on one of the vehicles. (KH/AHS.)

MILLERTON, NEW YORK, WELCOMES YOU. This early 1930s photograph of Carolyn Hunter Flood from the album of Janet Jenks Burnett is also suggestive of the increasing popularity of the car. The sign seems to have been sponsored by the Harlem Valley Automobile Association, which is touting Millerton as being on the Inside Route to the Berkshires. (JJB.)

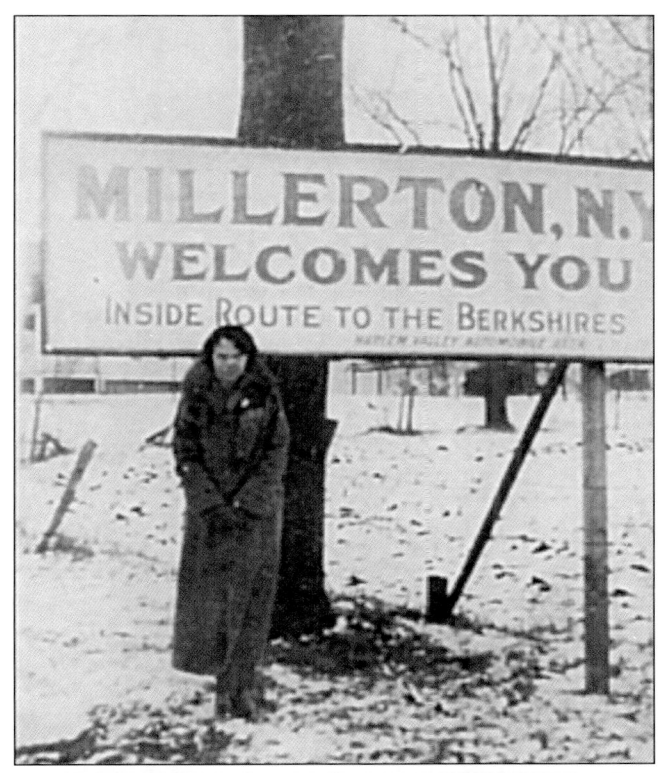

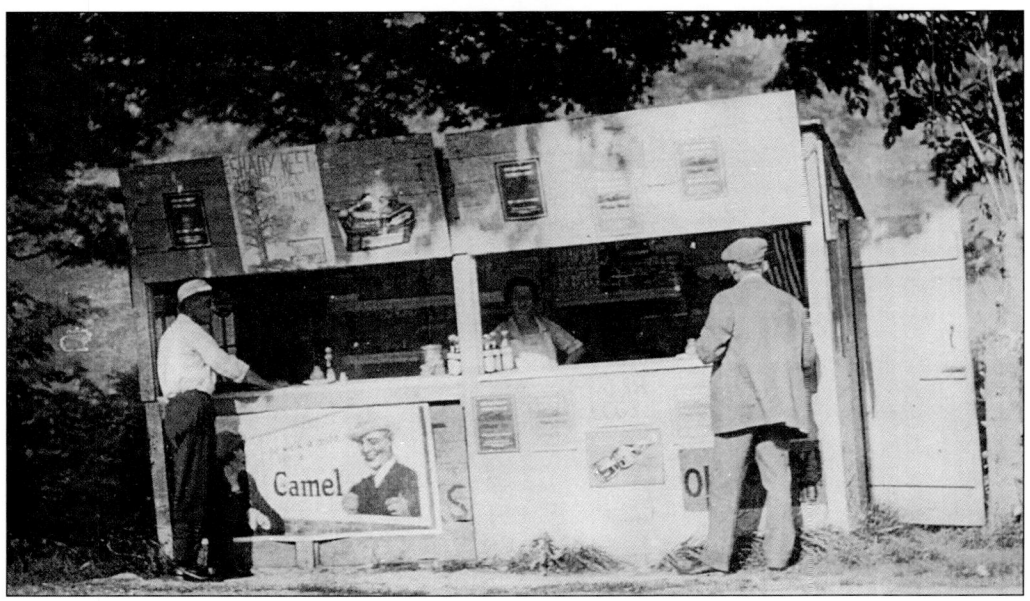

SILVERNAIL ROADSIDE STAND. Another photograph dating from the early 1930s when tourists toured in touring cars shows the Silvernail's family stand at North East Center near today's muffler shop. Pictured are Bernie Silvernail's father, grandfather, and grandmother. Their enterprise was part of a continuing tradition of road stands sprouting on people's lawns to serve visitors attracted to the area by its beauty and historic heritage. (BS.)

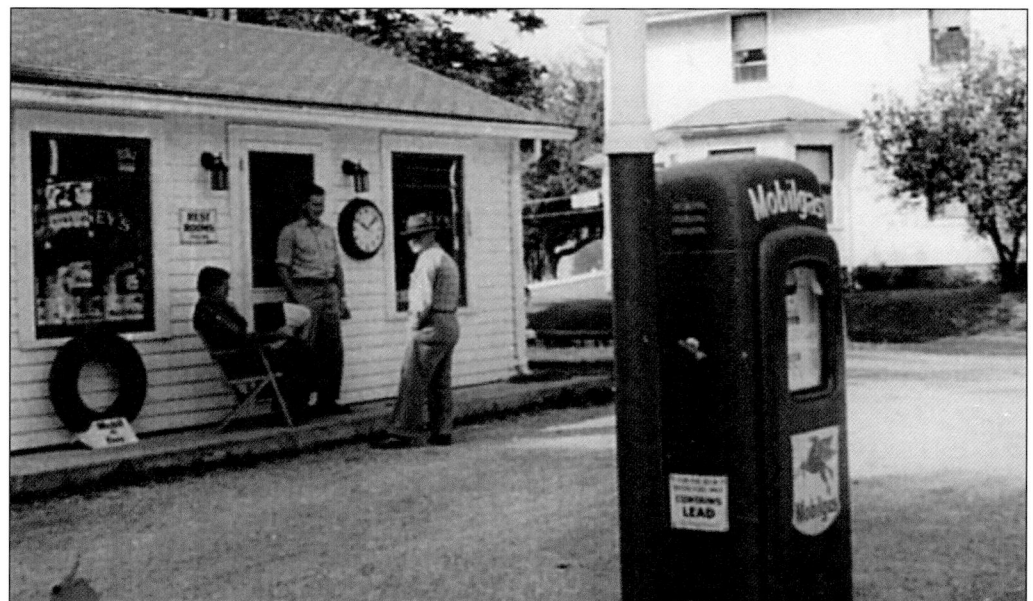

DOWNEY GAS STATION. Cars were fueled for almost 40 years at the Downey gas station, which is now inside the Seagull at Checkerboard Corner, a familiar landmark. Seen here left to right are as follows: Augustine Downey, Clifford Agnew, and George Yakubowski. While the Downey farm remained in the family, the occupations of family members have changed. Ed Downey, Gus's son, currently practices law. (ED.)

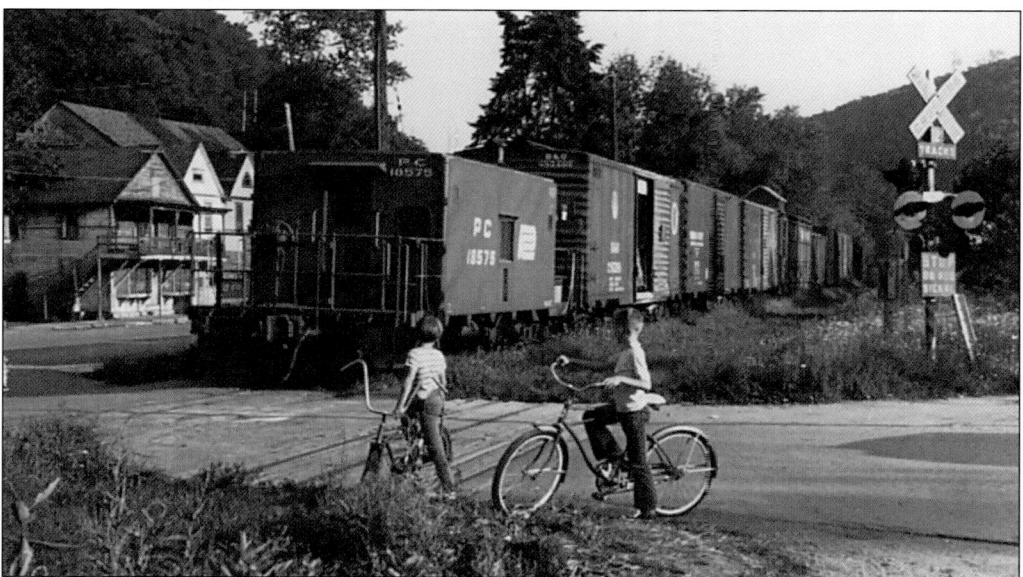

CHILDREN WATCHING A LOCAL FREIGHT TRAIN. Trains continued to fascinate children who came specifically to watch them being switched and to wait for trains to pass through Wassaic, like this one in 1972 en route to the yard in Brewster. At that time, the freight train still ran five or six days a week to Millerton with trips north to Chatham as needed, delivering coal, paper board, animal feed, fertilizer, and building supplies. Note there were no crossing gates, but children learned to obey the signals. (HC.)

PETER HELCK AND HIS WIFE. Peter Helck, who was born in 1893, loved automobiles from childhood and grew up to become one of America's premier artists interested in transportation subjects ranging from antique automobile races to Mack trucks. Also a talented magazine illustrator of everyday life, often using North East residents as models, he lived in the Harlem Valley from 1932 until his death in 1988. His paintings and illustrations document the emergence of the automobile and truck as the dominant forms of passenger and freight transportation. (EA.)

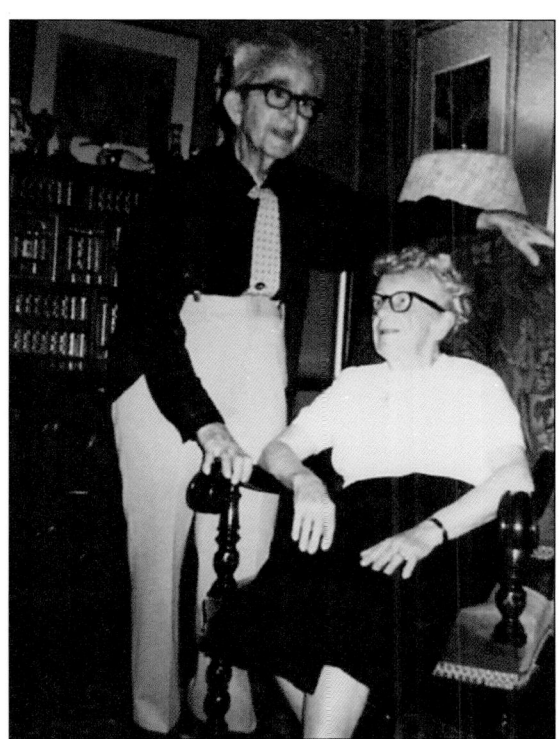

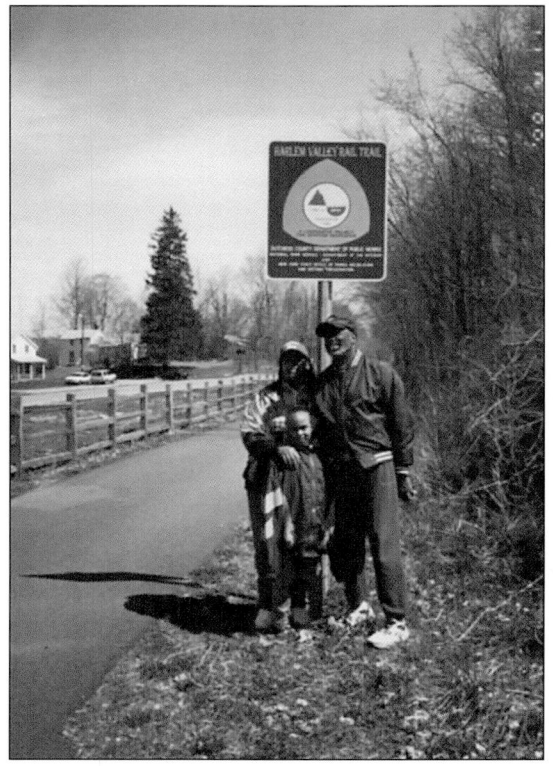

HARLEM VALLEY RAIL TRAIL. These walkers have just finished hiking on the rail trail established along the former railroad bed in the late 1980s. Children, teenagers, and adults enjoy walking, bicycling, and in-line skating on the trail which is now paved from Amenia to Coleman Station (4.5 miles), with the next section north to Millerton (4.0 miles) expected to be completed by August 1998. "Happenings" on the trail such as a "Ride, Roll, and Ramble for the Arts" enhance the attraction of the area for residents and tourists alike. (JG.)

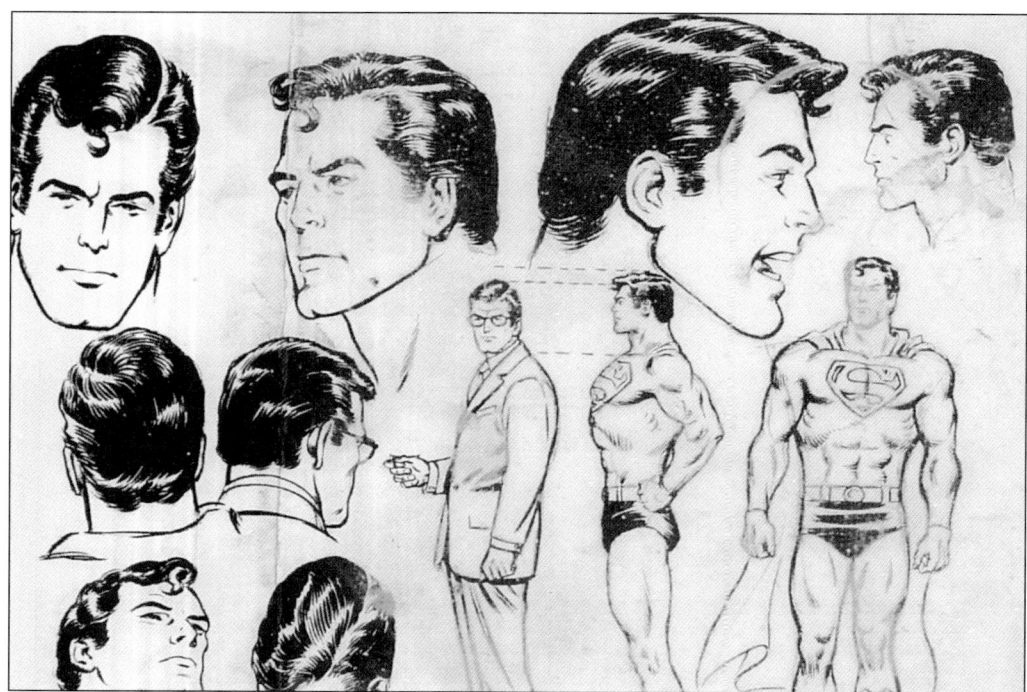

SUPERMAN. Never mind trains, cars, and bicycles, "It's a bird! It's a plane! It's Superman!" Did you ever wonder how "mild-mannered" Clark Kent turned into Superman? This original sketch by John Rosenberger, who drew Superman for a number of years, provides the answer. See how 5'11" Clark Kent grows to 6'2" Superman, a comic book hero who fights for "truth, justice, and the American way." Peggy Rosenberger, John's widow and an artist herself, now lives in Wassaic near the charcoal kilns. (MR.)

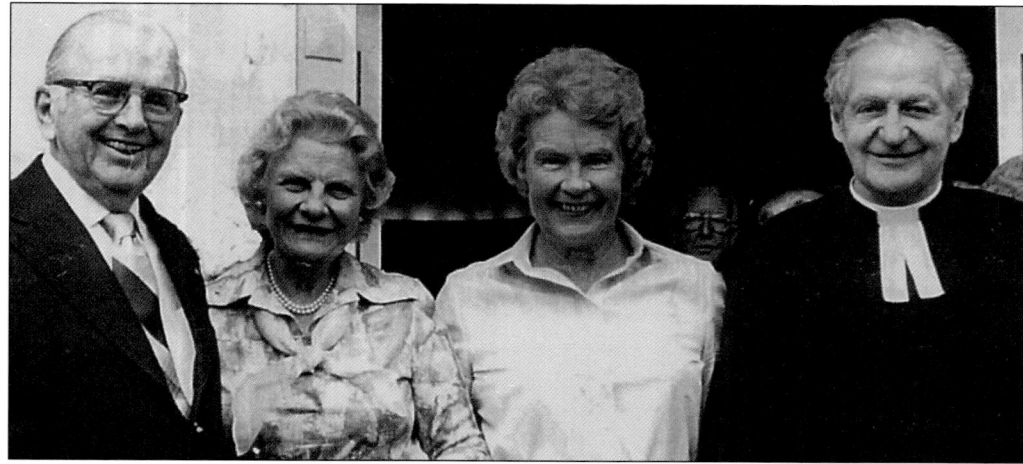

NORMAN VINCENT PEALE. "The Power of Positive Thinking" turned a Presbyterian minister into a world-renowned celebrity. A long-time Pawling resident, Dr. Peale is shown here with Mrs. Peale and Reverend Dr. and Mrs. Powell from Australia. The many awards that Dr. Peale received include the Horatio Alger Award in 1974 and the Eleanor Roosevelt's Val-Kill medal in the 1990s. A small museum at the Peale Center for Christian Living in Pawling documents his life and worldwide influence. (PH/MH.)

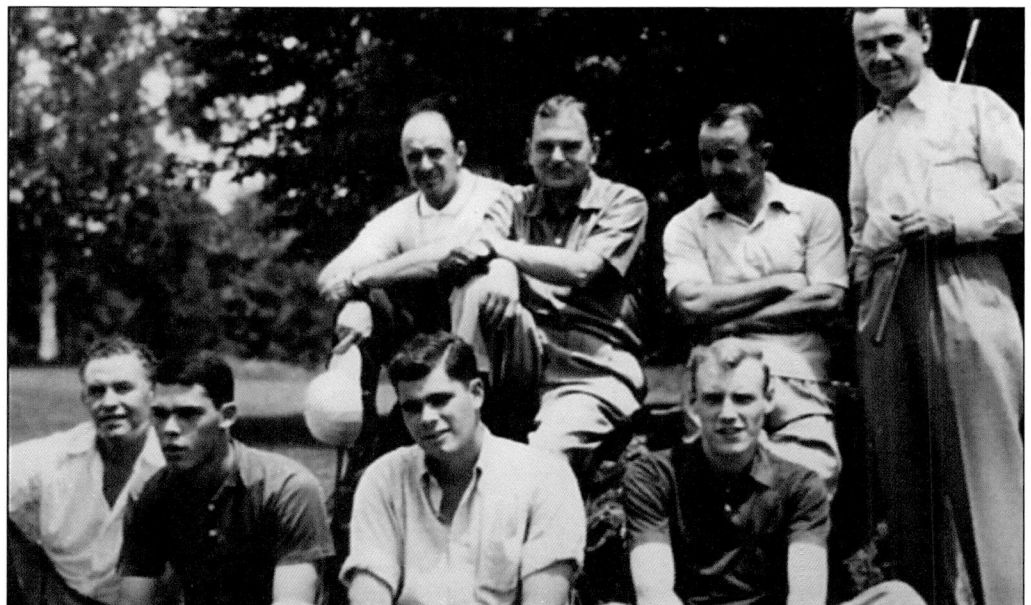

THOMAS E. DEWEY. Thomas E. Dewey is seen relaxing with Lowell Thomas and other golfers, including Sam Snead, Gene Sarazan, Gene Nicks, the Chapman brothers, and Jackie Hogan at the Quaker Hill Hammersley course. Governor Dewey was the Republican candidate for president in 1944, which was the only time both candidates came from the same state and county: Dewey from Pawling and Roosevelt from Hyde Park. Dewey ran once more in 1948 against Harry Truman. He did much better in New York State where he broke records being elected governor. (HSQHP.)

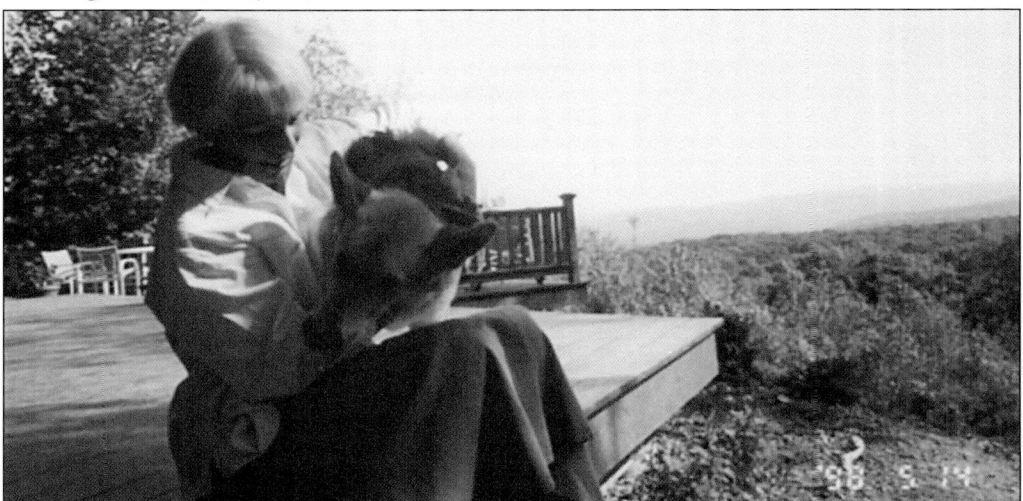

LUCILLE P. PATTISON. A farm girl from western New York, Lucille P. Pattison became a teacher, a political activist, and the first woman in the state to be elected a county executive. Among her accomplishments were the first serious planning efforts for future change in the state institutions. In retirement she has returned to a landscape reminiscent of her childhood: the wooded hills and pastures seen from her home in Pine Plains. She has also continued her efforts to improve race relations. (JG.)

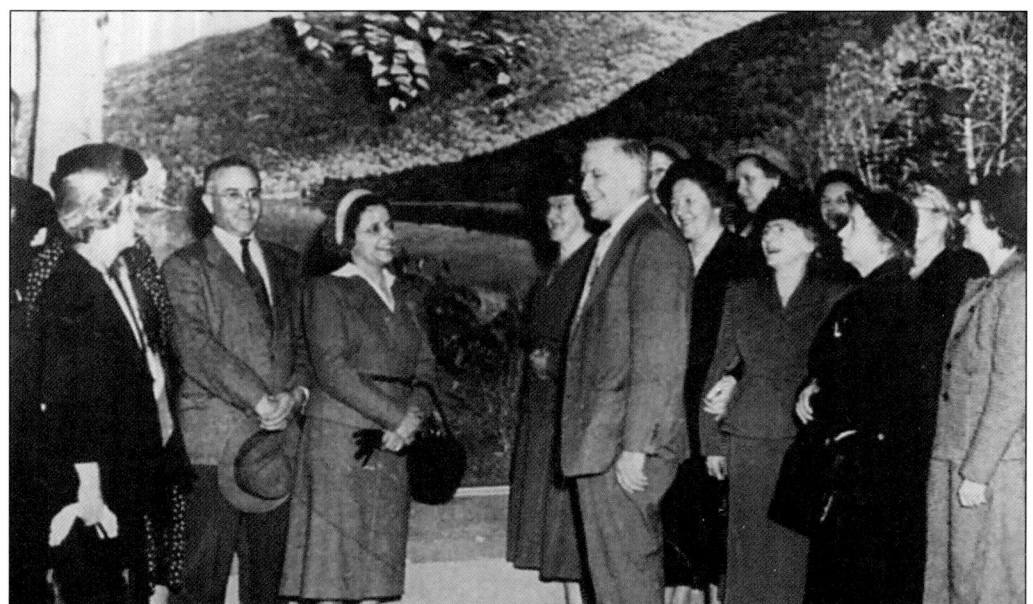

STISSING MOUNTAIN EXHIBIT AT THE AMERICAN MUSEUM OF NATURAL HISTORY. Pictured here are residents of Pine Plains at the dedication of the Felix M. Warburg Memorial Hall in 1951. This exhibit, noted as being that of a familiar landscape "within weekend picnic distance of [New York] city," broke new ground as it attempted to deal with the totality of nature, including the history and effects of human settlement as part of the history of nature. Dr. Harvey Shapiro, head of the anthropology department and summer resident of Pine Plains, was responsible for the mural presenting the role of man. (LNPHS.)

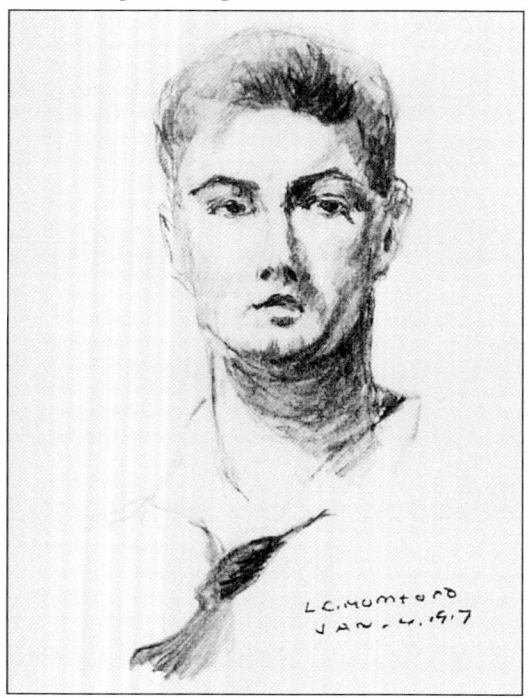

LEWIS MUMFORD. This 1917 self-portrait is of Lewis Mumford, an original proponent of regional planning, whose career spanned the 20th century. His ideal community combined the dynamism and diversity of the city with the enduring values of the village: order, neighborhood stability, and community closeness. His emphasis on direct observation, the importance of organic growth, the transforming power of ideas, and the necessity for human values to guide technology rather than vice versa remain relevant for the next century. (MQ.)

Acknowledgments

AMENIA: Town Historian Kenneth Hoadley (KH/AHS); Town Supervisor Arlene Iuliano; Amenia Fire Company: Andrew S. Murphy (ASM/AFC); Amenia Historical Society (AHS): Ann Linden; Island Green Country Club: Frank Vinchiarello; James D. Benson (JDB), Norman and Adene Benson (NB), Heyward Cohen (HC), Priscilla Herdman (PRH), Kathryn Kane, Allen Merritt (AM), Margaret Quinn (MQ), Marguerite Rosenberger (MR), Muriel Rothstein, Ralph Vinchiarello

DOVER: Town Clerk Caroline Reichenberg (CR); J.H. Ketcham Fire Company: Bridget and Robert Sartori (JFKFC), Old Drovers Inn: Kipper Peacock, Alice Pitcher (AP), Eileen Stanton; Norman and Adene Benson (NB); Lenora Buck (LB), Heyward Cohen (HC), Shelley M. Hunt, Frank Kelly, Allen Merritt (AM), Mary Parker; Richard Polhemus (RP), Wendy Roberts (WR) Town of Dover Historical Society, Nina Williams, Richard Wyman (RW).

NORTH EAST: Town Supervisor David Sherman; Mayor of Millerton Jacob Shoifet; Millerton Village Clerk Beverly Gordon; North East Historical Society (NEHS): Elsie Albig (EA), Diane Thompson; Janet Jenks Burnett (JJB), Heyward Cohen (HC), Edward E. Downey (ED), Josephine Downey, Dick Hermans, the Presbyterian Quilters, Robert C. Quinlan (RQ), Bernard Silvernail (BS), Marian Smith, Philip Terni (PT)

PAWLING: Town Supervisor James Tanner, Town Historian Myrna Hubert (PH/MH); Historical Society of Quaker Hill and Pawling, Inc (HSQHP): Molly McLean, John Daniels; Holiday Hills YMCA Conference Center (YMCA): Judy Ferraro, Gail Orser; William J. Carey (WJC), Ross Daniels, David Gamache, Lou Grogan, Ed and Mary Mahaffey (EMM), Tom Schroth

PINE PLAINS: Little Nine Partners Historical Society (LNPHS): Helen Cole Netter(HN), Betsy Wilmarth(BW); Annon Adams(AA), Carol Adams(CA), Janet Adams (JA), Clyde Chase/Scott Chase (CC/SC), John Duxbury, Betty Schroeder

Adriance Memorial Library (AML): Dorothea Lee, Myra Morales; Dutchess County Legislators: David Kelly, Brad Kendall, Hamilton Meserve, Harry Schroeder; Dutchess County Historical Society (DCHS): Eileen Hayden, Erica Blumenfeld, Stephanie Mauri; Dutchess County Department of Planning and Development (DCDPD): Roger Akeley, Dennis Amone; Dutchess County Tourism Promotion Agency (DCTPA): Karen Woods; Harlem Valley Partnership for Economic Development (HVP): Kathy Schibanoff; Emily Johnson, National Association for the Advancement of Colored People (NAACP), Schaghticoke Tribal Reservation (ST): Paulette Crone-Morange, Donna Hearn, Luciann Levin, Terence Manning; Town of Somers Historian/Somers Historical Society: Florence Horton

A special thanks to Myrna Hubert, Pawling historian, Ken Hoadley and Ann Linden of the Amenia Historical Society, Elsie Albig and Diane Thompson of the North East Historical Society, and Helen Netter and Betsy Wilmarth of the Little Nine Partners Historical Society. We all owe a debt of gratitude to these small historical societies, staffed by volunteers, who are preserving OUR community history. We also appreciate the contribution of the Harlem Valley Partnership for Economic Development. A final word of recognition is due again to our husbands, Bill Ghee and Tom Spence, without whose patience and thoughtfulness, this book could never have been completed.

READING LIST

For more information on the history of the Harlem Valley towns and villages we recommend:

100th Anniversary 1895 1995 Amenia Fire Company. Amenia, NY.

Benton, Charles E. *Troutbeck A Dutchess County Homestead.* Dutchess County Historical Society, Dutchess County, NY Historical Monographs: No. I, 1916.

Dutchess County Historical Society, ed. *Yearbooks 1914-1995.* An index of articles is available at the Society's headquarters at the Clinton House, 549 Main Street, Poughkeepsie, NY 12601.

Eisenhuth, Chester F. *Maltby's Furnace and One Man's Memories and The History of Spencers Corners,* edited ever so slightly by Marian S. Smith. The Northeast Historical Society, 1996

Grogan, Louis V. *The Coming of the New York and Harlem Railroad* Pawling, NY: Louis V. Grogan, 1989.

Hasbrouck, Frank. ed. *The History of Dutchess County, New York.* Poughkeepsie, N.Y.: S.A. Matthieu, 1909.

Hubert, Myrna. *The Village of Pawling Celebrates 100 Years.* Village of Pawling Centennial Committee, 1983.

Huntting, Isaac. *History of Little Nine Partners of North East Precinct and Pine Plains, NY.* Dutchess County:1897.

Jeanneney, John and Mary L. *Dutchess County A Pictorial History.* Norfolk, Virginia Beach: The Donning Company, Publishers, 1983.

Little Nine Partners Historical Society ed. Record, articles and monographs on a variety of subjects.

Miller. Donald L. *Lewis Mumford A Life.* New York: Weidenfelt & Nicolson, 1989.

North East Historical Society ed. Yearbooks, articles and monographs on a variety of subjects.

Poucher, J. Wilson M.D. and Helen Wilkinson Reynolds. *Old Gravestones of Dutchess County,* New York. Poughkeepsie: DCHS, 1998.

Reed, Newton Early History of Amenia with impression of Amenia by Dewey Barry. Amenia, NY: Harlem Valley Times, inc, 4th ed., 1985.

Silvernail, Bernard, compiler. *100 Years Millerton Fire Department 1892-1992.*

Smith, James H. assisted by Hume H. Cale and Wm. R. Roscoe. *History of Dutchess County, NY with Illustrations and Biographical Sketches of Some of its Prominent Men and Pioneers.* Syracuse, NY: D. Mason & Co., 1882.

Smith, Philip H. *General History of Dutchess County from 1609-1876.* Pawling, NY: Published by the author, 1877.

Town of Dover Historical Society, Inc. ed. *A History of Dover Township.* Dover Plains, NY: Town of Dover Historical Society, 1982.

Town of Pawling 200 Years 1788-1988. Pawling: Town of Pawling 200th Anniversary Committee, 1988.

Transformations of an American County Dutchess County, NY 1683-1983. Poughkeepsie, NY: Dutchess County Historical Society on behalf of the DC Tercentenary Advisory Committee, 1986.

Wilson, Warren K. *Quaker Hill A Sociological Study.* Akin Hall Association, 1987.